SMILING SORES

AN AUTOBIOGRAPHY WITH INSPIRATIONAL AND FICTIONAL FLAVOUR

ISH KUMAR GANGANIA

My Parents

Mrs Hukam Kaur &

Master Naveen Chandra

Contents

Preface

Nothing to Screen

Many of my colleagues from the writer's fraternity often asked me to write an autobiography. I asked: What is the need to write an autobiography? I have achieved nothing extraordinary to share as the story of my life? My life has nothing like stardom, and I did not face atrocities to record as FIRs or complaints for the police station; that is an essential feature of Marathi Dalit autobiographies. I couldn't be the one among Hindi Dalit writers who followed the beaten track of sure success in victimhood. I found myself an outsider in the whole episode. Hence, what is the rationale for writing my autobiography?

I stopped them for questioning, but the volley did not let me stay calm. I often thought: Does a person without these merits have no life to reveal? Or does a person like me have nothing worthwhile for others to learn? The situation did not take me to any conclusions. Hence, I prioritised writing a novel, dropping my life story for an appropriate time. One day, I was on a phone call with my close friend Prof. Mukesh Manas; as usual, we discussed literature, women, Dalits, etc. Both of us were frustrated by Dalit autobiographies. In these anxious moments, Manas suddenly blurted —'Why don't you write your autobiography? You have enough experience in life, literature, and the world around you.'

I was spellbound and stopped strolling on the terrace, but he continued, 'What do you say?' He paused to guess my age, which I filled with the words, 'Dear, this October 25, 2021, I will be sixty-five.' He emphasised, saying, 'What are you waiting for? 'Could you write it down?

I upheld his genuineness, saying, 'Yes, but my priority is to write a novel first. I would write my life story later, but it would differ from traditional and Dalit autobiographical patterns; the rest will depend on 'Kis Karvat Oont Baithega', which means the literary circumstances would decide. The phrase caused loud laughter, and Mukesh commented, 'I expect you to write something different, as I find in your stories, poetry, novel, and literary criticism.' It concluded the debate.

The following credit goes to Vidya Bhushan Rawat, a renowned social activist with a massive local and international network. Rawat, too, made a phone call to interview me on Identity, Aajivak, Ambedkarism, Dalit literature, and Dalit autobiographies. While interviewing, he also emphasised writing the story of my life. The incentive of a couple of my friends inspired me to shift the writing of an autobiography to a novel.

As I juggled my job, every step was a learning phase, a journey to unravel the 'how' and shape my prospects, as I had promised Mr Manas. For this purpose, I read dozens of autobiographies and biographies to write about my life and reached a conclusion: We are also an essential part of nature comprising trees and plants, animals, rivers and seas, wild and domestic animals, moon-stars, sun, earth-sky and whatnot. Each gift of nature inspires us to learn vastly. There could be something in my life, too, which may be valuable. My flaws, too, may be material to learn. If not, my family and future generations must know about my life and how I faced the challenges of my life. It may guide them anyhow.

Well, I penned the autobiography within six months. However, the hunt for the appropriate title began earlier but lasted later. The Hindi version of my autobiography is

'Main Aur Mera Girebaan'. For the English version, I opted for **'Smiling Sores'** as it gives me a genuine insight. I write in Hindi, but the rebellion occupying my spirit and mind still compels me to write it in English, too.

I have made my life public where there is nothing to screen. My life is now like a house without windows and doors to welcome the rain, storm or anything else. My life has often been scorchy and stormy, with dark and long nights, but there has always been a soothing and pleasant morning to balm the sores of painful nights. I have lived my mornings to the fullest, not to let the darkness overshadow me. I avoided beaten tracks and explored my own to follow them faithfully. Books, great personalities and the environment have inspired me, but I did not burden them to carry on my back for the future journey. I must compete with none except me, where ample space can cover the irrecoverable.

There are advantages to publicising my privacy to my kin. The rest may have something for sure of their choice. The format I followed is one of my fundamental traits: always keeping myself in an experimental state. I have meticulously looked into the entire episode and found nothing to give up.

Lastly, I am the first person in my family's lineage to enter the writing field. I also wrote my autobiography so future generations can understand our lineage. Here, I am not talking about my records or greatness. I want my family members to faithfully record and underline their life as a prospering legacy for future generations. If they like anything to adopt, they can and stay away from the flaws of my life. I wish them to carry the family legacy and be responsible citizens, take lessons from the past, keep their eyes fixed on the future, live the present most whole, and play a constructive role in society.

My family's genealogy starts from Mr Dhanna in our ancestral village, Rathora, Chhaprauli, Meerut, Uttar Pradesh. I knew our descendants as Dhanna ki Dhad, i.e. Dhanna's army. People called us Heli/Haveli Wale. In the same way, only one family was from Pandits, one from Jats and one from Muslims known for Havelies. Yes, I have heard a lot about Haweli. But three or four times, whenever I visited my village, I saw nothing like that of any Haweli.

Our family tree begins with Mr Dhanna. He had three sons: Mr Badlu, Mr Nagar, and Mr Rambaks. My grandfather, Mr Rodhe Ram, was one of the four children of my great-grandfather Rambaks, namely Mange Ram, Hans Ram and Phool Singh. My grandfather had two children, Mr Naveen Chandra and Baldev Singh. We are six siblings: Chandra Kanta, Ish Kumar, Raj Kumar, Satish Kumar, Raj Kumari, and Naresh Kumar. We are the children of masters Naveen Chandra and Hukam Kaur.

Now, the chain reaches me as my wife, Shashi Bala, and I have two children, Mohit Kumar Gangania and Pooja Gangania. Mohit is married to Preeti Rajaura and blessed with a daughter, Anaisha Gangania. My daughter Pooja is married to Pradeep Kumar Singh, and Kaira Singh and Pransh Singh are their kids. Finally, our family tree of six generations gets its entire shape to let it bloom.

While writing my life story, I regret having no one to give me a second opinion. TP Singh is the only ray of hope left with me, but his health conditions have restricted him between toilets and beds. Small group discussions can take place on the phone, nothing more. My condition is like I am in Iceland, where I have to cook as I can afford.

The start of writing the story was challenging, and the mode didn't shift until the end, but I didn't compromise on the title of my first poetry collection book, which translates to 'never give up'. 'Smiling Sores' is a testament to my commitment to myself and the growth I've experienced through this process. Some of my comments about my fellow friends in my life story may seem prejudiced and malicious, but I do not intend to. Readers' worthy opinions will naturally guide my future perspectives.

Ultimately, I am morally obliged to express my gratitude to **Notion Press,** without which the publication would not have been possible.

Jan, 12, 2025 Ish Kumar Gangania

---OOO---

CHAPTER ONE

Regular Education: A Thorny Spring

I completed my 'Diploma in Basic Training' from Jamia Millia Islamia in 1977 and registered in the Employment Exchange. Since there was no hope of a job, I got admission to B.A. (Pass Course) at Satyawati College (Evening), Timarpur, thinking if I had no government job, I would have gone for private employment and study, which would continue undisturbed in the evening college. Getting a government job would be a boon. I also got a job, but my studies lost their gleam—only five teachers who taught us in the three-year B.A. Degree course is in my memory. Among those who taught Hindi, Dr D.K. Chauhan, Mrs Haldhar (a foreign lady), and Sardar Ji were among those who taught English; apart from these, I am trying to recall everyone's names. I can recall Dr Riyaz Ahmed, Sir, for Political Science. It was a surprise for me, too, that I needed to remember the names of the economics teachers.

After almost 40 years, in July 2021, Dr D.K. Chauhan contacted me for an unusual reason. I was already loyal to him because his village, Tikri Kalan, was about two kilometres from my old town, Kundli, District Sonipat, Haryana. Our D.T.C. bus route was the same up and down to Delhi. But strangely, we have never had time to travel together. After a long time, the teacher and disciple met on the telephone. But I am sorry to say I don't know the whereabouts of my other teachers. The sad state is unmanageable. Hence, it is better to go ahead. I got a six-month job in a middle school in Munda Kheda, District Jhajjar, Haryana. However, the goal of attending college was challenging to chase. Because of the long distance between my job, place of residence and college, the purpose of my studies could have been more varied.

To reach my job destination, I had to walk about one and a half kilometres from my village, Kundli, Haryana, to the Singhu border, from there to Azadpur, from Azadpur to Raja Garden and then from there to the Dhasa border. But this journey did not end there. After this, I had to walk through the fields for an hour from the Dhasa border to my workplace, the middle school. Apart from the walking journey, I completed whatever was, changing three to four D.T.C buses. It used to take three or four hours. In return, reaching the college took about two to three hours. The last class of college probably ended at eight-fifty. I arrived home between ten and eleven. It is worth mentioning that the cremation ground, a Johad, a village pond, some fields on one side and a cold store known as Barf Khana fell on the other side on the way from the Singhu border.

I desperately needed a job because of the family's economic crisis. I could leave neither my job nor college. The college enabled me to get a D.T.C. pass of Rs.12.50 per month, without which such a long journey would have been unmanageable. Because of the lion's share of my earnings, i.e., Rupees three hundred and twenty-two per month would go wasted on transport. The family of eight members couldn't afford such an expense. In such a situation, I spent all seven hours commuting and six hours teaching.

Where would I get the time to sleep and study if both college and my job were to continue? So, it was critical to continue both college and my career. But compromising on a college education was a compulsion. I could go to college for almost as many days as the minimum college attendance required. Hence, the college was no longer a centre of education but a means of furnishing a D.T.C. bus pass facility.

This routine continued for around three months, and I got a new teaching job in Khurampur village, Sonepat, Haryana. I joined it with a new challenge of twelve kilometres of cycling per day. Having completed six months, I had to enter my duty at Ghasauli, near Gannor Sonepat, with a journey by private bus and six kilometres of cycling per day. Finally, I joined a teaching job in Delhi in December 1978. It reduced my fatigue, but I could hardly spare time for studies. Sometimes, I regret it; sometimes, I realize that my professional growth and literary writing, like turtle movements, make it all up. How I managed exam preparation has always been tough enough. Thus, I completed my graduation one challenge after the other and made many compromises with my studies within the stipulated time, but with the title of First Division with Two Body Guards. The sound of this compensation reaches me now through multiple mediums in the form of feedback from my acquaintances, teaching fellow friends, students, and scholars associated with the literary world. My Guru ji, Dr D.K. Chauhan, needs to be mentioned here remarkably.

I wish to return to the point that I can't even remember the names of my teachers. Some friends may consider my third division in graduation as the outcome of my hindrances, or some may take it contrarily. Of course, it can never be attractive to a devoted student. It is worthless to assume how people take it; facts need no revisions. I have been associated with studying and teaching throughout my life. It has always been a part of my life to be determined to respect my teachers. The forthcoming episodes will reveal glimpses of my dedication to my teachers. It encourages me to share one more reason for my poor graduation performance. My shift from the science stream to art meant I needed to familiarise myself with new subjects, except English.

I passed the higher secondary examination in the village of Singhu, Delhi. I had a science stream, and my subjects were English, Chemistry, Physics, Higher Maths, and Engineering and Mechanical Drawing. As far as Hindi is concerned, I passed the Elementary Hindi class 9th in September. On the one hand, all the subjects except English were unfamiliar. The compulsion for being unable to attend regular classes due to the oddity of the job turned to a fit example of the saying-bitter gourd and brought up in the lap of a Neem tree.

It did not limit the educational anomalies to this; they have been integral to my life. As a student of the Higher Secondary School at Singhu, my story is also exciting. This school was situated in such a place that each student had to travel from one to four kilometres on foot or by bicycle. It was about one and a half kilometres from my Kundli house, too, but we attended it even in odd weather. Using a jute sack (Bori) as a raincoat in the rainy season was common. It could save the head and the back and the books we carried.

In this school, the problem was with the teachers. The local teachers were all comfortable, but those who came from outside, i.e. from different parts of Delhi, usually joined in some punishment or the compulsion of a new appointment brought them to this school. They used their energy to relieve the fatigue of commuting. One can easily imagine how much they had left in them to teach. We were taught English by Mr Uttam Singh Chauhan and Mr Tara Chand; they were local and dedicated to their teaching work. That is why I feel proud to be their student even today.

As a working boss of a senior secondary school, I can comment on Mr S.N. Ahuja's teaching us physics. He could derive the formulas of physics by keeping his book open. He also had the quality of simultaneously dating a Hindi teacher, Miss Gupta. It was excellent that they got married during our schooling. Mr Ramnath Gupta taught us chemistry; this was his first posting after his M.Sc. He, too, peeped into the book to balance the equations. But Mr Gupta was easy-going. He could supervise and give instructions, even eating Roti rolls during our practical classes. Mr O.P. Gupta of Maths and SK Munjal of Engineering & Mechanical Drawing managed their jobs well. However, when I look back at the innovative approach that a teacher needs, I find it is missing thoroughly. But they may have their own legitimate and unavoidable compulsions. Therefore, I do not consider it appropriate to put any question mark on the intention and integrity of my teachers.

Significantly, Mr D.C. Gupta, our principal and a resident of our village, Kundli, was utterly dedicated to improving the school and the students. He was physically and mentally inflexible with his dealings. If a student tried to bunk school or run away from school in recess or any period, the principal would run on his Lambretta scooter with a police baton. He gave a brutal thrash in police fashion to bring them back. Another feature of his was that he would sometimes even go around the houses of the students appearing for the board exams at night. If he found someone light off during his visits, he punished them in the morning assemblies. It was a general message to the students not to sleep early. It was an outstanding contribution to the world of education, and I salute it from the heart.

The Principal of Narela School, Mr Hoshiar Singh, was an unmatched example of dedication. He used to convert his day school into a residential school for the board students during the two-month summer holidays. Some of us had the hunger to study. We were quick to cycle five to six kilometres to take advantage of the facility for studies. During this time, Hoshiar Singh Ji used to take the services of trained but unemployed teachers. He gave experience certificates rather than an honorarium. Hoshiar Singh himself used to teach English. The brilliance of his face was visible. I have never seen such a dedicated Principal in my entire lifetime. Whenever his memories haunt me, respect consoles me a lot. I salute Mr Hoshiar Singh for his noble deeds.

In those days, the school conducted pre-board exams before the annual board exams. I had topped myschool's four sections of all three streams, i.e. Arts, Commerce and Science. At this achievement, my principal, D.C. Gupta, summoned me to the office and offered me additional study facilities apart from school. Mr Tara Chand, too, asked me personally for any help. I responded that it was no problem, sir. I will manage on my own. Because of my shyness and ignorance, I need to find out the value of accepting their offers for free. But the final result shocked me, and I was not at the top; Ram Niwas, a art stream student, graced the honour board as the topper.

A particular reason for this was that the centre of the board's examination was in our school, and the mass copying was there. The hidden agenda of the school must have been to win the education department's applause by raising the results. But I remember an anecdote very well. Our English teacher, Mr Tara Chand, was slim but prompt in punishing the students. That's why everyone was afraid of him. He approached me during the maths exam and asked me which questions I couldn't answer. I didn't realize why he was asking all this. I talked about a theorem and one or two other questions. After some time, he appeared with a paper torn from an old book and insisted on taking it. That theorem was printed on this page, which I did not know. I was shirking back from taking it because of fear, and he persisted in giving up. I was afraid that he might thrash me by giving the theorem.

There was an awful experience that I would never forget in life. As a student in class VII, our classroom was noisy one day in the teacher's absence. He came to the class and started thrashing the students; I also became a victim. I was not at fault, so I stared at him angrily. He punished me for this and lifted me in the air, holding my ears. I have never seen such a sight in my lifetime, but the memory of it is still alive in my mind. But when I was in class XI, this fear subsided a lot. Later, I understood him better, and he probably understood me too. I wish to share another strange experience; I was studying on the lawn one day. He was on a visit; he called and spoke a sentence for me to analyze. Though I was afraid, I answered it verbally in a single breath as he asked. He patted me on the back and allowed me to study. Indeed, now, I was a good student in his eyes. Not a rebellious stare at him.

Mr Uttam Singh Chauhan was different; instead of beating, he would pull his students' hair off the side upwards and smile to make the students realize their mistakes. That's why no one would take the punishment otherwise. I was not an exception. It is for sure that I was one of the good students in his eyes. Once, I was standing on the school grounds with my friends, and a public examination occurred; he called me by name and asked, 'Ish, 'apron,' spelt EPRON or APRON? When I told APRON, he said okay, go.

I do not know why he asked, but it feels excellent even today when I recall my teachers, and it energizes me a lot. A long time ago, when I learned about his retirement from one of my colleagues, I went to his house with my family and introduced us all. I gifted him the cap, shawl, and pen, sharing how I remembered him. It was beyond his mind as such discussions between teacher and student at the school level do not occur. He blessed us warmly. The same thing happens when my old students share their experiences with me. Facebook has become an excellent tool for getting knowledge from my students. Student feedback is the best gift for a teacher.

After all, I received the theorem from my teacher, Mr Tara Chand, and recorded it in the answer sheet. I got a distinction in maths, but I still need to understand why he did it. Perhaps he knew my timid nature and that it should not leave me behind in the crowd of courageous copycats. Though it was a wrong precedent, sometimes, such unfair practices have a strong urge for justification.

A similar incident happened around 1990 when I worked at the school in Gokulpur Village as a T.G.T. English. A student named Bhagwati was the class topper in the first and second terminal tests, but a Jat teacher's group wanted to see a Jat student first. Collectively, they made a shower of marks in the annual examination.

The unworthy child took the lead. Being a class teacher, I could not bear the unfairness. Hence, I equalled Bhagwati's marks for the first and second terms. I know record tampering is a crime, but I did it. It is worth mentioning that I have attributed this audacity to my Principal, Mr M.S. Rawat, who allowed me to say, "Son, you can go to any existent."

It is impossible in today's computer age, and one would prefer such a work to do. When the school announced the results, one group member told me about Bhagwati's marks on terminal tests. I argued that whoever you wanted to see as topper, she was. If someone else stands by, it shouldn't be a problem. He had no answer, and the matter took no turn.

Even though I had ensured justice with my principal's support, I still found myself guilty of the act. I am curious to know how my teacher, Mr Tara Chand, felt motivating me to follow what was wrong. Returning to my higher secondary school results, I passed my exam in the good second division. It was also considered a nice one; the first divisions were rare. But today, students above ninety have to face discouragement.

I could not give up the urge to participate in sports during classes IX to XI in this school. We expect science students to avoid games as science students need to work hard. Games are now pre-determined for arts stream students. But my case was different. When the reaping season was over in the village, we used to play Kabaddi and would wrestle there. But volleyball continued throughout the year. The game of country hockey was within our reach. Initially, we used cloth balls and arranged the hockey-shaped wooden sticks. The playground used to be a Gonda, the route the bullock cart used in farms. It stayed packed with dust after the country hockey game.

The credit for fuelling the passion for sports in the school goes to P.E.T. Mr Khajan Singh and N.D.S. Mr Randhir Singh. Both played Volleyball, Wrestling, Kabaddi, Hockey, etc., with the students themselves as part of the team. Besides this, there was a provision for the players to serve the students milk as refreshments after the game. There used to be multi-vitamin tablets in the sports room, which I remember very well. It attracted me to play Kabaddi, Hockey and Volleyball in school. We won the state championship in volleyball. It held its final match at D.P.S., Mathura Road, New Delhi.

Regarding my passion for sports, there used to be a star competition in the school. It combined the long jump, high jump, ball throw and long race. In that combination, too, I won the star contest, and I used to put stars in my school uniform pocket, like a few other students. Remarkably, I saw no such encouragement for sports while working in Delhi for almost forty years.

Even in my education up to class VIII, there are strange voids. When I passed the fifth standard from the primary school in Kundli, Sonipat, Haryana, I was admitted to Singhu School, Delhi, in the sixth standard. The school was in a remote area; I shared it earlier. We could not get a room and a regular teacher in class VI. Yes, I am tempted to share a 'G' nib holder. I learned to write the English alphabet in a four-lined copy. There were inkpots to dip the holder and write. We are having a revolution in the variety of pens today. We used to sit on the Veranda in front of our school's art room. Whether someone came to teach us, the school authority seemed to have no business to worry about. Yes, our art teacher, Mr S. D. Sharma, used to tell stories or chat with us whenever he was free. Somehow, we passed the sixth standard. Meanwhile, the teachers went on strike, and we even passed the seventh standard without giving any examination.

At last, we got a room and regular teachers in class VIII. For the first time in class VIII, I experienced something like a school. I was punctual in my studies both at school and at home. I would go to my maternal uncle's farm with my cousins on holidays to study under the grove trees. It may seem awkward, but the school's negligence did not bother even our parents. It meant parents make a stereotypical comment: 'Master Ji, we need nothing other than the bones of our child, but make the child a human or man by creating a man meant to educate adequately. As I remember, my parents were no exception.

While my younger brother Raj Kumar and I were students in classes VII and VIII, respectively, my father asked us to attend his leather training centre after school. The training centre I am talking about here was a part of the technical education of the Haryana government, and my father was its supervisor. He recruited twenty trainees to this training centre for a year and taught them to make slippers, shoes, leather bags, briefcases, bedding, etc. He was the only authority at the centre with a peon for rendering regular service from the government. The students learned to accord with their abilities. It allocated a new village to my father every year to carry on the process.

Incidentally, in 1971, this centre was shifted to Janti Kalan village, about one and a half kilometres from my school. The same Janti Kalan is popular for Lakhmi Chand's Raganies and songs in Haryana. The intention of giving us this training still needs to be discovered. We followed our father faithfully to walk one and a half kilometres extra after school. Our father would bring us back home on his bicycle in the evening. I don't remember exactly how we met from our studies and homework.

I used calf leather, Rapi, Katarina, and other tools at the centre. I am still unsure if the theory of making sleepers and shoes is still fresh in my mind. I need the certificate for that training, whereas this certificate was to be issued by the father only. I could never raise any questions about getting the training certificate. I can explore only two reasons while writing my autobiography and trying to find out why. The possibilities are as follows: Each of us, brothers, was underage. Two- We used to go there for two hours as part-time learners, and we were not adults for professional training as it was. It is still a mystery to me what motivated my father to take us to his centre without caring about our formal education at school.

This puzzle is beyond any solution, as my father is not alive to answer. Regarding my profession, I am destined to be a teacher, not a leather instructor.

Entering the teaching profession was not planned but a product of determinism. I don't wish it to be misunderstood as luck or a theistic term destiny but as the result of the Buddha's Pratityasamutpada (theory of causation) or the idea of determinism (some actions are not subject to human control) of the Ajivika philosophy.

Having qualified for the Higher Secondary examination and imitating Kishan Lal, a colleague from my locality, I was admitted to B. SC. (Hon) Chemistry in Kirori Mal College, Delhi University. I do not know why he was admitted there. It is silly; I don't know why I followed him. It was like a sheep ploy, and something like this happened without professional guidance. The second stupidity I got into was becoming a second lieutenant after qualifying for the N.D.A. exam. The idea was to solve the family's financial problem, directly killing two birds with one stone.

Without any sensible guidance, I got fed up with N.D.A. preparation. Ultimately, my situation became like 'Na To Khuda Hi Mila Na Visal-e-Sanam, which meant I got both boats drowned. This crisis period is crystal clear to me even now. Our troubles started after my father's retirement in 1972 (when I was studying in ninth standard). It was because of the wrong age entry in his service book, which forced him to retire three years earlier. My father filed a case against it in Chandigarh court. He handed the claim to Ram Kishan Sahrawat, who struggled to find a job in Chandigarh. The education of six children, four brothers and two sisters and feeding couldn't take a break. Hence, the retirement benefits were exhausted, and the families and the court's needs became a big challenge. There was no value in the father's skill in the village. The circumstances prevented him from going to the city at an old age. He could not sit idle. So, my father opened a grocery shop in the town, and it couldn't survive to feed the borrowers for long.

My father, Master Naveen Chandra, and his family saw a visible challenge to survival. It is terrible to recall even now. My mother was uneducated, but people knew her as Masterni. She would help the neighbourhood ladies sew and embroider in leisurely afternoons. She was well-versed even in the most difficult Sindhi embroidery. She used to talk about cooking skills. The crisis compelled my mother, Hukam Kaur, to pick up her scythe to reap the grass. She hails from a farming family, so she had no other option or experience to face the trouble.

Dad and Mom got into aggressive talks and tussles when she talked about picking up the sickle. Weeks later, Dad had to surrender to let my mom be a shearer as there was no way left to escape the crisis. My father understood that hollowing prestige could not fulfil the family's survival needs. Therefore, during this hour of emergency, the first task was to make money by selling buffalo milk. We somehow purchased another buffalo for the same purpose.

My mother engaged rigorously in the battle of economic crisis. The rest of the family, including my father, accepted the mother's leadership without any ifs and buts and hesitation. We turned as if a single unit to face the challenge. 'Energy Saved Means Energy Produced' became a motto of our lives, and we started making money. Mother got up at four in the morning with her hand mill, a Daldi (basket made by the pulp of wet paper) measuring about two to three kilos of grain, as a daily dose for the family of eight members. She used to grind so much wheat in the dark in the morning. In this work of hers, any of our sister-brothers would extend a helping hand to the mother. During this, my younger brother Raju and I used to cut the bundles of Jowar and millet on a manual fodder-cutting machine by wrapping a cloth around the mouth. From time to time, the younger brothers and sisters also did not relinquish their responsibility of cutting the fodder. While cutting dry grass, the dust generated used to darken our nostrils and clothes. It had become an undeniable part of our daily routine. Secondly, to save money, the mother also built a Bunga (enclosure made of wheat plants to store fodder) and Bitoda (section made of wheat plants to keep dry dung cakes) herself with the help of the family.

Buffalo dung and other household garbage were the family's responsibility to heap up at a distance. Similarly, we used to share the obligation of milking buffaloes and Shani (making a mixture of fodder, cake, straw, etc.) I remember very well that we didn't have any division of work, whatever it was. Everything we attended was on the lines of 'Le Tari Ki -De Teri Ki', which meant accomplishing every task with a stormy temperament. The reader may think it is artificial and false they can, but it is true. One more surprising thing to share in this context is that there was nothing like yours and mine in our family, nor did we dare to point fingers at each other's intentions.

As much as the authenticity of the first statement is astonishing, in the same way, it is also a hard fact that we, family members, especially the brothers, do not have any cordial relations among us. Everyone has his horizons, which do not meet as we see the earth and sky meet. Well, it may seem strange that in the hour of crisis, our family had discredited the concept of population explosion–' the more family members, the more the hidden unemployed, as if the burden on the family'. We all had work to do in the family; if not, we would explore it. None was a burden or unemployed. There was no compromise between school and studies at the cost of family affairs.

The family's most significant need was food grains. The story of its fulfilment may seem fantastic to the readers. As mentioned, the fields were only forty or fifty steps away from our settlement. The Jats who owned those fields greatly respected my parents because they had also seen our bright days. They would greet my father first by saying, 'Namaste, Master Ji'. My father would respond later. We decided to reap wheat on Bantai (as one bundle of the wheat crop for reaping twenty-five bundles for the landlord). Mother knew how to reap and tie the bundle of grains with wheat plants as twine. Our father and we could neither chop nor bind wheat, as it was our first experience.

The mother had taught us how to reap and use the bunch of wheat plants as a cord. My mother would address the Zamindars as Kaka (uncle) or Dada (grandfather); we called them Nana, a common hierarchy in the village. She got the information about the farm for next-day harvesting. We four brothers would begin the job there at night and return between eleven and twelve. In the morning, we attended our school comfortably. In the morning, Mother tied the bundle first before reaping to begin. It consumed a lot of time and energy. After school, in the evening, we all piled wheat bundles in the centre of the area. I knew this heap as 'Pahi' in Haryana's language. Later, we learned how to tie the bundle and became skilled harvesters.

This ten to fifteen days of rigorous work enabled the food security of the whole family for six to eight months. We met the rest of the demand with the help of maize, millet, rice and flour imported from Australia at subsidized rates. This food security kept us free from worries as we could eat Roti comfortably with the help of Chutney and onion. We would grow vegetables from our plot, and we had no problem getting Sarson Ka Saag, pumpkin, Tinde, Turai, carrot, and radish from farms free of cost as the standard practice in our village. There was no need to buy vegetables. The use of pulses was beyond our reach as luxuries. Otherwise, Chutney and onion were always our sole privileges. Sometimes, the whole week went without vegetables. I do not deny the exception.

For buffalo fodder, we had to buy hay in addition to the bundles of Jowar and millet. For this, a tent factory across the Delhi-Shimla National Highway at the other end of the village was closed for a long time, and grass kept growing there wildly. Its area was vast. We bought it. The four brothers had to scythe and carry it through the middle of the village. Taking bundles of grass on our heads was a daily routine without hesitation or humiliation. The mother arranged the rest of the grass/hay with her Khurpi, and Daraanti means sickles. We used to assist her while carrying a heavy grass bundle on her head. On holidays, I used to take buffaloes to the fields to graze along with other boys in the neighbourhood. We did this with the same devotion as our studies.

Meanwhile, a scheme to set up a Gobar Gas Plant, which translates as a dung gas plant, with the help of Russia or perhaps Germany, was announced in our village. We took advantage of the opportunity and received a Rs. four thousand grant from the authorities. Our family collectively dug the pit (well) and worked as labourers with the mason to save one thousand and five hundred rupees. We had one more task when we got the facility to cook food with a dung gas plant. Before going to school in the morning, we had to mix buffalo dung with water in the upper tank, and then it went down to the bottom of the well with the help of a big pipe—the used waste outpour into another tank. Having returned from school, we had to empty it with the help of buckets in another plot. It was better manure for a farm. We used some of it in our farming plot and sold the rest for better prices than Kudi, another garbage heap. I would do it faithfully with my brothers; we had become a unit.

Defeating the objective of my N.D.A. and B.Sc. (H) chemistry piled up troubles like a mountain to face with no tools. However, our family did not lose heart. So, I searched for other options and learned that Jamia Millia Islamia Teachers College, Okhla, runs a Diploma of Basic Training programme. Still, the next day was the last date to apply. In those days, the facility to get a photocopy of documents was unavailable, as it is today. All the documents had to be typed with a typewriter. This facility was available at Narela, about three kilometres from our village. Attestation from a gazetted officer was another challenging job. I had no option but to copy all the academic documents and testimonials with a neat hand till nine o'clock. Then, my father and I went to the house of our school Principal, Mr D.C. Gupta, who lived in the village and proved to be a beam in the dark. We got the documents attested. I submitted my application form to Teachers College, Okhla, the next day. The remark of the receptionist, Mr Gulia, is still fresh in my mind: 'Wow! Pathetic means carefree boy; you have saved much money by writing with your hands.' There was success in silence regarding the comment. Any argument could spoil whatever was cooked so laboriously. How could a hungry boy like me take such a risk?

I passed the entrance test and got admission. The work of studies at Jamia College continued unabated. I was almost sure now that I had to become a teacher, not an engineer, because of engineering drawing or something else after passing my B.Sc. (H) in chemistry. During my diploma, I also participated extensively in Kabaddi and Volleyball Inter-Jamia competitions for two consecutive years. I secured the first position in the Wrestling competition with a weight of 53 kg and got a place in the Javelin Throw. I achieved over a dozen certificates in the other inter-house tournaments while completing a professional diploma. I also completed my daily journey from the Singhu border to Okhla, the opposite end of Delhi, with the help of a D.T.C. pass. There used to be rupees one or two as my pocket money, not for spending but for keeping in case of urgent need.

Even my primary education has been uncommon. My father's job allowed him to stay in one village for only oneyear. He had to change his residence and job venue every year to another town. The family travelled with him as a vagabond's cart. As I recall, the caravan of my childhood started in Kharkhoda village in Haryana (now, this village may have turned into a city I never got a chance to return to). The first incident was when I was coming from school. I wore a shirt and half pants with a belt covering both shoulders. I was alone; my school might not have been far from home, so I was coming alone. I forgot my way. I was crying out loud. Houses and people's movements were there, but I could not understand anything. However, a well-built by my father was on the side of the road, and the Chaupal in front of it was nearby. However, I felt as if I was alone in this world. I didn't have the power to think; I remember crying in great panic. My throat was choking in fear.

This panic had such an effect on me that even today, I see a child forgetting the way, or a child coming or going from school, crying bitterly, or a child in desperation to run home before reaching school. It moved me and my childhood fears alive; I empathized with that child. I did not hesitate to register my presence to console the child and ensure that no child felt as scared and insecure as I had in my childhood.

My memories took me to Dighal Beri, a village in Haryana, when I was a first-grade student. Here, we lived in the Kothi of a Colonel Jat by caste. Here, I want to recall my never-forgettable mental block; I must call it a mindless condition. I learned about this state of mental block when I watched Amir Khan's film 'Taare Zameen Par'; I can understand how a child, due to some disease like dyslexia, becomes an object of neglect and hatred in the school, family and surrounding environment.

I was not in a dire situation like Darshil, a child artist from Taare Zameen Par. However, I do not know what would happen to me or my mind if I could not write the 'थ'-'Th' in the Hindi alphabet. I could easily make up other difficult letters of this alphabet, like 'क्ष'-'Ksh', 'त्र'-'Tra' and 'ज्ञ'- 'Gya'. The only problem was with the letter 'थ' of the alphabet. As a result, I fell victim to my father's anger. I remember very well that I got punished with flexible, fine Neem sticks. The fear of my father coming from duty haunted my mother, too. Despite being illiterate, she guided me by making the letter 'थ' in the soil so the son could make it like that. She said, "Your father is about to come, and he will punish you again." I had no option but to plead that I was trying my best to write 'थ'. I do not know how often I have told my mother how to do it; I am making it, but unable to. I can still recall the fear and anxiety on my mother's face for not being able to help me make the letter 'थ'.

I probably finished my second grade in Gannor, Sonepat, and Haryana, but I do not remember anything about this class. When I reckon this phenomenon as a teacher, I realize if there is something like a 'mental block' in a child's mind at a particular point, a teacher, family, or anyone outside should proceed with the assessment based on the overall activities of the child. Later on, the child can understand it easily. That is why I believe we should not torture the child in any way because it can have a lasting negative psychological effect on the child's mind.

The next phase of my memory takes me to the village of Chulkana in Haryana. Here, I passed my third grade. I am trying to remember the classroom here, but I remember only a girl's song, 'Aye Mere Watan Ke Logon...' It was too melodious to explain. The glimpse of the honour she received still showers me when I look into my past. It soothes me a lot.

I also remember the Indo-Pakistan war broke out when we lived in Chulkana, a Haryana village. We did not have newspapers and TV then, but a transistor and a flock of people gathered in the Chaupal near our house. The people were curious to know the news and the current affairs of the war. I distinctly remember Lal Bahadur Shastri's slogan, 'Jai Jawan, Jai Kisan'. I also remember those blackout nights. My father had guided us to dig pits near our house and had soil bags filled. The most important thing I remember is growing vegetables like carrots, radishes, and tomatoes in pots and fasting for one day a week. Each day, my father would analyze and explain the information received through the transistor. It was not only to create awareness among the people but also to prepare them accordingly.

Recollecting the scene of that time, it seems as if we were fighting a war in our homes like the soldiers on the borders. Fasting and growing vegetables in the neighbourhood, digging pits in the place, and keeping sandbags filled was not only a movement, but it also seemed like we were fighting a war for the country. During this, my father also donated some money to the Defence Fund. Whatever the case, even today, I am sorry to say I have never seen the whole country fighting as it had opposed Pakistan under Lal Bahadur Shastriji's leadership. It is also remarkable that we could see the country fighting to meet the food shortage. But today, the scenario and mindset of the rulers and the masses have also changed adversely. We have become selfish and insensitive to our duty to the nation today. The passion for the country has been sheltered, merely luring slogans. I am anxious to find out whether the public or the political leadership is responsible for the terrible loss of the nation.

When I was in the fourth grade, we permanently settled in our house in Kundli, a village on the Singhu border in the district of Sonipat, Haryana. I was fine in my studies but was shy and reserved. Our class teacher, Ms Asha, extended a particular affection to me. One day, when she wrote the names of some boys and girls, I asked her to add my name to the list. She refused, saying no, not you. I was disturbed because this had never happened before. But later, I learned that our teacher was writing the names for the Qawwali competition. Even today, I am an idiot because I do not know anything like singing or dancing. As far as activities on a stage are concerned, I could recover courage after I became a teacher. The world of literature played an essential role in removing the remaining fear and hesitation from me.

I also passed my fifth standard in Kundli village. The episode of my primary education will remain incomplete if I forget to reveal the outbreak of Mr Gupta. He was a fantastic character. While entering the class, he would suddenly repeat a question like, 'Finding the area of a room twelve meters long and eight meters wide.‘ He would scold and punish anyone who asked him to repeat the question. A madam, Yashwanti, came from a village, Katlupur, Haryana. She was smart enough and belonged to the Jat community. I am not in favour of talking about the caste of my teachers, but Ms Yashwanti is an exception. She was adamant. She kept the stick of the Keekar tree to punish the students who failed to answer correctly. She hit hard on the extended palm of the child mercilessly. The scene of her beating still gives an impression of fracture at any stage. Her brutality makes me feel as if it symbolizes her village, Katlupur, a place of slaying.

Regarding my education journey so far, according to the pattern depicted above, my primary duty of getting an education is fulfilled, and the service expedition begins. After all, I took my first board exam in class 5th in Nangal village, about two kilometres from my town, Kundli, and passed it very well. Here, the spring of thorns in the garden of regular education ends. In the contemporary context, it reminds me of a famous slogan, 'Come for learning and go for service,' written in almost every school in India.

---000---

CHAPTER TWO

First Job: A Channel of Challenges

I got my first job as a teacher in a middle school in Munda Kheda, District Jhajjar, Haryana. My appointment was here temporarily for only six months, and its terms and conditions were also unique. There was no provision for any leave other than five casual leaves in six months. The school's head teacher had the right to end the service without prior notice. If I say it in the local language, it was 'Bania's job' where there was no place for the employee's interests and rights. However, there is an anecdote in the Mahabharata about Arjuna. It says Arjuna had to target a fish's eyes rotating on an axis above. He was asked: What do you see, Arjuna? He replied: The fish's eye, the sole target, not the fish or anything else.

In the same way, it didn't matter what facilities were there or what price I had to pay for it. In my case, the fish's eye was merely working to earn money, not to count the cost to pay. The phase of challenges begins with receiving my call letter for an interview. I attended the first interview for the first job of my life in Bahadurgarh, Haryana. It was nothing like an interview; it was a strange crowd of candidates up to middle age. They were twirling and having fun in the office with no hesitation. It was all like a game for them. I had no acquaintances there, nor was anyone of my age. There was no arrangement for the interviewees to sit. I had no choice but to act as the saying -'Do as the Romans do' suggests. I sat on a wall almost three feet high, leaning with a pillared Veranda built in front of the office. People were getting in or out, gossiping and making merry. I was just a silent spectator of the scene. I had embraced my certificate file like a mother holding her sick child to her chest to console.

How was the interview going? It was not soothing to me. But seeing the activities there, I realised I would get no job there. I didn't have any option but to wait for my turn. I couldn't afford to go to the toilet, fearing that if my turn was announced meanwhile, all my work would get spoiled. Eventually, the crowd dispersed, and my waiting time got longer. That's why I had no option but to keep my ear strained and eyes fixed on the door of the interviewers.

It may sound unbelievable, but it is a tangible reality. I was the last candidate to appear for my first interview. I was called inside for an interview. In the name of the interview, the team talked about my educational qualifications. They went through my additional documents with academic certificates. I had NCC, scout, and guide credentials and over a dozen certificates in different sports, which I had gotten at the school-college level. I, too, had my caste certificate.

I also had a state-level championship certificate in volleyball. The interview team also discussed something other than the job perspective. After a few minutes, they said okay and allowed me to go. I returned home overburdened with doubt and despair.

Eventually, I got the job. I found out later that there were only two posts. I occupied one; the other was another teacher who had worked several times for six months. Now, the problem of getting the job was over, but reaching the job venue was more challenging. It was the year 1977. There was a flood in Delhi. By changing three or four buses, I would reach the Dhasa border somehow, but to attend school and work by walking through the ridges of the fields for about an hour was tiresome. Two rivulets had turned into small rivers between the bus stand and the school. I had to take off my clothes and cross. The others, too, were bound to follow the same. On the first day, I crossed these rivers with my underwear, squeezed it in the secluded bushes, put it in my bag, and got dressed again. I joined my job and taught the whole.

Hari Singh Gulia used to be the headteacher of this school. He would wear a kurta-dhoti. His conduct was tremendous, and his voice was typical of Haryanvi and harsh. Although I also spoke Haryanvi because of Gulia Ji's dealings, even his simple instructions that day seemed scary, like an unknown threat. From day two onwards, I put extra underwear in my bag with lunch, which solved one problem. I had to teach English to the middle classes instead of the primary course, and I was comfortable there.

The problem of the two rivers was resolved, but in the meantime, the road between Raja Garden and the Dhasa border broke in two places. I remember one area of this breakdown, Isapur, but now I need to remember the name of the other place. The DTC buses used to run in the same stretch stayed confined between the broken roads. I had to put off my trousers and cross the knee-high water at these two sites. Despite these odds, I never went to school late. Writing all this today seems like a fictional story, but it is one of the bitter experiences of my life.

The routine continued for almost a month. The circumstances took pity on me, and things turned somewhat normal. I have been sharing my experiences from time to time with the latecomers, may it be students or fellow or subordinate teachers. I, too, shared it is willpower and self-discipline that we need to make a part of our personality. It is not always a point of abnormal circumstances. My convoy of memories often takes me back to my past. Still, as far as I can remember, I never felt burdened by these adverse circumstances, nor did I wish for any sympathy by repeating these hardships of my life. I repeated them to inspire my students, teachers and the people around me whenever needed. I've never seen it as a significant milestone; even today, I don't find it a landmark. I, too, never blamed the circumstances in the name of fate.

My compulsions rather than commitments had automatically trimmed these problems. When we used to harvest wheat or cut fodder, we used to carry heavy bundles on our heads through the village, or we would work on a fodder-cutting machine for hours to make the grass, maize, and Jowar (Sorghum)plants eatable for our cattle. Walking for hours and taking off my trousers to cross the water was a lot of work but could always have been better; nothing disappointing. Today, when I look at the delicate approach in my children, I realise that giving too much comfort doesn't let the children learn the practical aspects of life. Although both my children are sensitive and genuinely understand the sounds of sorrow and joy. Still, I find something that does not match the physical and mental toughness that I expect from them. Here, I have no problem standing with Adolf Hitler when he says military training should be compulsory for every citizen of the country. I regret I cannot keep myself blameless regarding my son and daughter.

Because of the above struggle, I could periodically attend my classes at Satyawati Evening College. Attending college meant getting the last bus, which dropped me at the Singhu border after 9.30. Only one bus from the Old Delhi Railway Station to the Lampur border passed through the Singhu border. Its route number, as I remember, was 41. One day, I covered the distance from Azadpur to Alipur by taking connecting buses, and from there, I had to catch bus number 41. The crowd was huge, and I failed to get in. Finally, I hurriedly caught hold of a thick screw visible out of the rear part of the bus. It was probably used to hang an advertisement board, which was not there. I put my feet on the back iron plate used to tie up the two buses with a chain or rope. This may not be the case in today's buses; they have become relatively modern.

The roads were not good, and my foot could have been in the air with the slightest jolt. And I could be in the middle of a busy national highway. If something like that had happened, I might not have been writing my autobiography. My passion for my job and college studies could ruin everything. Nothing like that happened, and when the bus stopped at the next stop, Bakauli, to drop off some passengers, I went inside the bus. I realised the terrible mistake while hanging behind the bus. But nothing could reverse as the shot arrow or bullet never returned to its departure point. But while struggling between life and death on the back of the bus, I resolved never to enter such stupidity. This incident of my coming back from the mouth of death makes my heart beat faster even today.

This incident of my foolishness is not the singular one to return from the mouth of death. Once, I could narrowly avoid such a fatal accident. Our scout and guide team was on a training programme in Ayodhya, U.P. Everyone was bathing in the river Saryu, and I also got down to enjoy the dip. But I did not know how my feet lost hold on the bottom despite all the precautions. I didn't know how to swim and still need to learn. You may call it a coincidence or else. The water went above my nose and mouth, but suddenly, I recovered my foothold. It is still a mystery how I got my life saved.

Let's return to the eccentric tale of my first job at Munda Kheda, Jhajjar. I got three hundred and twenty-two rupees as my first salary. This amount meant a lot to my family and me forty-five years ago. One could buy one kilogram of Desi Ghee for sixteen rupees. It may seem ridiculous to the new generations to use small coins of one, three and five paise. I put the cash in my mother's hand in my father's presence. My mother touched the money on the forehead as if paying thanks to her deity and handed it over to my father. The look on my parents' faces was worth seeing. But I don't remember how I felt. Yes, I remember one thing. I still had only two to four rupees in my pocket apart from the DTC pass. But I dared not spend that little amount. By the way, I could not afford it at the cost of saving time, which was the most significant challenge.

Meanwhile, I got another call letter from District Sonipat. I might have served my first job for hardly two months, but the circumstances favoured me. It was a matter of comfort that I got an assignment in a primary school in Khurampur village, about five kilometres from my town. They appointed teachers in the Education Department of Haryana based on the number of students rather than the number of sections or classes in the school. There used to be an elderly teacher, Roop Ram Sharma, and I was the other. I comfortably taught several courses in a day, as there was not much of an exhausting journey, but bicycling. My bicycle was the sole companion that served me better during my ups and downs. I completed my six-month tenure and retired from service.

Though my job had changed, the other household activities, like reaping wheat crops, cutting fodder for buffaloes, preparing fodder for cattle, milking the buffaloes, etc., went on as before. It was because now we were not eight but nine family members. The ninth member was my cousin Ompal Singh, who was seven to eight years older than me. He had come to our house for better opportunities for a job, for he was unemployed. It was not feasible for him to live in his native place. Staying with us, he used to apply for different posts by filling out application forms. He also completed his B.Ed. professional degree from Jamia University by staying with us.

The financial condition of my cousin's family was deplorable, and it wasn't very helpful to expect any kind of support. Like the other family members, it was the sole responsibility of the family to bear all the expenses collectively. It was appreciable that he stayed thoroughly committed and devoted to the family affairs. He was equally involved in household activities and dedicated to them. Now, we were seven instead of six brothers and sisters.

Bhai Ompal Singh could not get a teacher's job, but the B.Ed. degree helped him fix his engagement with Laxmi, a girl from a well-to-do family in Sonepat. Be it a coincidence or something else, even before his marriage, he got an appointment letter from the Union Bank of India to join the Sangrur branch in Punjab. It was a festive atmosphere for the family. This appointment letter further added to the excitement of marriage in the family. I don't know which hellcat hit our happiness that my grand auntie, who attended the wedding, passed away the night before the marriage.

We had scheduled the marriage procession to reach Sonipat at ten o'clock, but there was a ruinous atmosphere of mourning instead of celebrating pre-marriage activities. My grand uncle refused to take the dead body to Tagore Garden, his Delhi residence. Now, the priority of marriage has shifted to the deceased's funeral. Having the cremation taken place, we decided the scheduled marriage programme must go on as it would be a total loss for both parties. Finally, the marriage procession departed to Sonepat at eleven o'clock. Thankfully, the marriage reached its glory, and the darkness that had entrapped the ceremonial mood vanished. Bhai Ompal Singh's family came with no financial help but two kilos of sugar; it served the needs of the women who visited for Ladies Sangeet.

The brother went to Sangrur after marriage. He visited the house once a month. He would give Rs. two hundred, which he saved from his salary, but take the bus fare from my mother. The mother said cleaning the buffalo dung at home was better than a job without economic support. What's the use of your job? Mother's comment had no change in his routine. Finally, within six months, the brother shifted to his in-laws' neighbourhood in Sonipat. The brother's stay in the in-laws' house exasperated the family. Hence, the chapter of our relationship with Bhai Ompal Singh ended almost. The brother never knew the expense of his marriage, nor did we ever need to tell him. It was beyond my parents' ethics.

Meanwhile, after a long interval, primary teacher vacancies were announced in Delhi. The recruitment process was ongoing, but getting the job was still far away. I had a teaching job for the third time on a six-month basis in a middle school in Ghasauli, a village in Khadar on the Yamuna River, three kilometres from the Gannor bus stand in Haryana. I had to travel by private bus for one hour and cycle three kilometres to get to my workplace. I had to bear an expenditure of Rs.6 per day. My partner, the DTC bus pass, could have been more valuable, but it could have been more helpful. Undoubtedly, it served me faithfully when I had to attend college at Timarpur, Delhi.

There was one more episode of further expenditure with no increase in family income. We fixed the engagement of my elder sister Chandrakanta with Ashok Kumar at Laxmi Nagar, Delhi. In May 1978, the marriage reached its goal as planned. In the first marriage in my family, my Tai Ji, grand aunt, had died in my cousin's marriage, a sole responsibility of my family, and a new ruckus arose during the sister's marriage. A month before the wedding, Mahendra Singh, a son of Mukhtar Singh, my maternal uncle, a distant relative living in our street, went missing. Despite much rigorous searching, the success turned too far to reach.

A few days later, we received information about discovering a dead body in a well in Narela. Is it the body of the missing child Mahendra? We discussed whether someone should go to Narela and see the dead body. There was no thought of Mahendra's death or corpse in anyone's mind. The idea of his being lost had a grander scale. For this, even Mahendra's father did not consider it necessary to see the dead body. Ultimately, they ignored the consensus decision to see or identify the corpse. Over time, Mahendra's disappearance became a matter of grave concern.

The people around had significant sympathy for the parents of the deceased. Even the Sarpanch of the village joined and expressed empathy. This Sarpanch was also our maternal uncle's Zamindar, a big landlord. I know every landless Dalit family had a landlord to serve as his master several years ago. I am not sure about the present scenario. The same Zamindar used to help his tenant when needed. However, under what conditions may be another debatable topic. The Sarpanch sowed the seeds of doubt in the mind of Mahendra's parents and focused all their attention on not going to see the corpse. Later, they alleged that the master, my father, did not let them go to see the dead body. This led to an era of blaming each other and eventually, the needle of blame turned towards my father.

The practice of finding opportunities in disasters is ancient. It is a different matter that our Pradhan Sevak has used this slogan in the second decade of the twenty-first century to serve political interests. The Zamindar looked up to my parents respectfully and was very liberal while reaping wheat in the fields. His attitude had changed somewhat, and the issue was more comprehensive. It related its strings to the Haryana Legislative Assembly elections held a few months ago. During the election, my father took over all the responsibility of campaigning for Aminchand Sahrawat, a lawyer from Sonipat.

In this election, Nafe Singh, the lawyer son-in-law of the village landlord, was also a candidate. Nafe Singh and Aminchand Sahrawat, both lawyers, lost the MLA election. Both were independent candidates. And, as usual, independent candidates get defeated. The Sarpanch took my father's campaign to Aminchand Sahrawat against his son-in-law Nafe Singh. Before this disastrous episode, we didn't know that the Sarpanch had a grudge against my father for his role in the election. He never articulated it.

With Mahendra's demise, the Sarpanch explored the opportunity in the disaster. He wondered why the master didn't let you go to recognise the dead body. The doubt gave air to the little family differences. It did not take long for a rabbit to be a giant.

My maternal uncle Mukhtyare and his elder brother Hukame smoked regularly in our house, sometimes until midnight. They kept on talking and took a nap in between. They stopped visiting our home. Obviously, in response, we, too, ignored them. But this rift turned into face-to-face enmity when my elder sister Chandrakanta's marriage ended.

In the Bhat ceremony, the maternal uncle gives gifts for the marriage of his sister's children. My mother's parents were no longer alive, so our maternal uncle Charan Singh, serving in the Delhi Police, had to perform this ceremony. He also came for the purpose but did not come to our house. He stayed in the home of Hukam Singh and Mukhtar Singh, cousins of my mother and maternal uncle. He imposed a condition: I would avoid the Bhat ceremony if you didn't call these two cousins. My father was adamant about not inviting the brothers Hukame and Mukhtyare because of their biased approach. Hence, my maternal uncle stuck to his word and returned with the gifts he had carried for the Bhat ceremony. Both stuck to their place, and the marriage took place without the Bhat rituals.

Now, in Mukhtyare's mind, two forces were working against us. First, persistent provoking by a sarpanch. Second, both brothers took my father's refusal not to invite them to the marriage as a social stigma and a direct insult. Despite the current development, my maternal uncles, Mukhtayre and Hukame, had brought us to the Kundli village to live with them. They had settled us there; otherwise, we had nothing to do with the town. It was so exasperating that my father did not invite them to the wedding. Our maternal uncle got an FIR lodged at the police station. The Sarpanch's son-in-law Nafe Singh, a professional lawyer, probably helped for the purpose. The FIR had the names of my father and two younger brothers, Raj Kumar and Satish Kumar, as having information about the kidnapper may be the murderer. We still cannot approve the names of our family and the neighbours, as we have never seen the FIR.

It proved to be a reasonable opportunity in a disaster. The police arrested three from our family and two neighbours on the pretext of interrogation. All of them surrendered to the police and faced torture. After this, the series of arrests later engulfed the entire locality. The police got nothing out of it. Finally, they released all as innocent. Instead of treating the case of missing someone, they treated it as a case of murder. This accident became a source of substantial income for the police. We had left three thousand rupees after the sister's marriage. The dreadful calamity consumed it mercilessly.

Now, the village atmosphere was no longer habitable for us. Those who were our sympathisers and relatives were no longer relatives but only enemies. However, with time, we had a little conversation, which was expected as they could not reach their homes other than the street passing our doors. This tragedy left the rest of the family with no interest in the village. I would occasionally repeat not to live in the town. I understood it was for me hanging like a pendulum between my education at Satyawati College and my job at Munda Kheda.

Meanwhile, the recruitment process ended, and I was among the successors. I resigned on 02 December 1978 from the school of Ghasauli, Haryana, to join as a primary teacher in MCD on 04 December 1978. My mother started talking about selling buffalos, plots, and houses where we lived in the neighbourhood. As soon as the news of selling our assets became public, like a fire in the woods, my maternal uncles Hukame and Mukhtyare visited our residence and said, "Bebe (sister), why are you selling the house?"

My mother cried and said, 'Brother, I am selling all my assets because of you. We don't want to be here anymore.' Their eyes also had tears and remorse but were of no use. The situation had crossed its limits. After all, it took two to three months, and no assets belonged to us now as our own. It was good that Sona Devi, the eldest daughter of my maternal uncle Hukame, bought our house. Altogether, eight thousand rupees came in hand. We had to face the challenges of the current displacement with this money. The catastrophic news reached my aunt's son, Ranveer Singh. He had retired from the Navy. He took our family to his house at Khekra. He arranged two rooms for us to live in and one for a buffalo.

My father visited some residential plots, but the matter still needed to materialise. Our relatives wanted us to buy land in Khekra so we could be permanent residents. Niyati may have had something else to approve. I travelled by train to my job on the C block of Yamuna Vihar. Somehow, we spent a year and a half there. During the stay, we learnt that the place was not fit for us as a peace-loving family. The problem of Satyawati College (Evening) remained the same.

My aunt, I mean Ranveer's mother, had three sons. Each one was one step ahead of the other to invite conflict with anybody else. None of my cousins had a government job. Their life was based on cattle to feed and milk them to make money. They didn't mind thinking about a peaceful future. That's why they would quarrel with anyone on the way, on paltry issues, and bother the least with the police and courts. Our DNA didn't match them at all. The crisis with us was about whether to stand by them in the dispute. All brothers and sisters were struggling for their careers. If we got involved in their tussles, we could be part of the vicious cycle of police and courts with no future. The kinship could be in question if we didn't stand with them. To get rid of the situation, speaking the truth was risky. Hence, my mother convinced the aunt's family about the job and the children's education problem. They had little to stop us. As a result, we bought a 200-meter plot in 1980 and shifted to rent nearby. It was another displacement from Khekra in the GDA colony Balram Nagar, Loni, Ghaziabad, UP.

Building a house was challenging as we disbursed the eight thousand rupees we got from selling all the assets in Kundli on the plot purchase. We borrowed money from limited sources we could afford. For this, we hired only one mason on a daily wage, and my youngest brother Naresh accompanied him as a co-mason. The elder sister was already married. She was not with us. We, five sisters and brothers, worked as labourers required for construction work.

The family, who lived in a two-storey house in the village with Pucca floors and roofs and a dung gas facility, was now bound to live like refugees in Balram Nagar. With a loan of Rupees three thousand, we could build boundary walls and two rooms, a kitchen, and a bathroom. It isn't very helpful to say we needed more money to plaster the walls of these rooms to get the ceiling and floor fixed.

It was when two of my brothers were doing an apprenticeship in DTC, and the youngest was studying in class XII. A sister had completed her studies up to class XII. The next issue of discussion in the family was to find a suitable match for the younger sister's marriage. Anyway, our sisters and brothers' regular education continued till class XII. None considered it necessary to study further. I alone did not stand with my siblings and continued the process of my education. I earned graduation and post-graduation degrees in political science, English, and a B.Ed. I passed the Ayurveda Ratna examinations at Allahabad Hindi University.

The commitment to the family's financial condition relied on my monthly salary of five hundred and sixty-seven rupees. There was no alternative to help from the farm; there was no gain from selling milk and green vegetables for free, like in the village. The family worked on stitching the export buttons, but more was needed. At sixty-eight, the father had to bring clothes on the bicycle from Shahdara to return in well-furnished bags after the night's rigorous struggle. Shahdara, Delhi, was about five kilometres away from our residence. It also didn't work in an hour of need. Neither the mother's agriculture nor the father's technical skills proved any support.

Even the careful and miserly expenses exhausted the total income. The loan of rupees three thousand and the interest did not rest like a working wall clock and kept multiplying. It was the appropriate time for the anxiety demon to attack me. I couldn't sleep as the heaping up of loans did not let my stress die down a little. The nights were scary; I often woke up and sat for hours. I would drink water frequently to get rid of this stress. Last, there was only one option left to get out of debt. We had a gold necklace available in the house. We could stop the devil of loans by selling this gold necklace for a while. But the concern about the marriage of the younger sister sitting idle at home was no less than a leprosy itch. Though my sister was younger than the three of us brothers, her marriage was still our top priority.

Finding a suitable groom for a girl's marriage was more challenging than marriage itself. A loan can be a great help in arranging a wedding. But now we don't have any sources to help us find a boy earning his living for our sister. In those days, alternatives like Shaadi.com did not exist as they do today.

These commercial sites work tremendously to solve the marital issue on the pattern, as called in Hindi, Haldi Lage Na Fitakri Aur Rang Bi Aae Chaukha, the translation of which is: It takes neither turmeric nor alum, and the result appears appreciable. I took the opportunity to find a suitable match for my son and daughter. I needed none to run after for any help. But finding such facilities was not possible for my sister.

It is worth mentioning that the ghost of my sister's wedding was still standing on the doorstep of my comfort with a Latth means log like a cruel loan-collecting agent. Getting rid of this log was my next big challenge. Although I was used to getting hit with challenges from childhood, it was still a formidable deal for my comfort. It left me with no way but to keep following rigorous efforts. Yes, I had mastered playing such a Dhaplee, which has become the basic mantra of my life. The process continues even today and helps me solve life's riddles.

SMILING SORES

---OOO---

CHAPTER THREE

Catchy Story of the Sketchy Love

My regular posting in Yamuna Vihar C-4 was from 1980. As I mentioned earlier, I had a strong interest in sports. As a dance lover inherently vibrates to the music tune, so was my case with sports. How could I stay behind when the initiation of students' sports competitions took place in our zone, Shahdara North, Delhi? During that time, Mr Tara Singh was our school inspector (physical). He had a dark complexion, a sharp nose and attractive features. Mr Vedi was a stocky guy but had a robust body. He was passionate about wearing nice clothes and a sensible look, too. He had a good command over musical instruments, especially the flute. His tone in the song also sounded amazingly melodious. He was outspoken and expert in flirting, anyway. His seriousness did not match his personality. He had a solid addiction to non-veg and drinking. If I borrow the words of another senior school inspector (physical), Mr Magan Bihari Sharma, who usually commented in a comic mood that he did not drink daily, but the next day. The case for him with non-veg and drinking was similar.

My participation in sports impressed Mr Vedi, and he started showing particular concern. He gradually obtained personal information about me; I don't know how. The pieces of information included my family background and caste. Based on this, he jokingly said, 'Ish, Tera Tanka To Main He Fit Karaoonga', which means I will lead in getting you married. I loved hearing this dialogue. I said nothing but passed a smile. My school was co-educational, so I would accompany the students as a coach whenever there was a boys' sports competition. I did the same with the girls' sports competition.

While in day-night camps during the holidays, I played a prominent role. I interacted with all the physical teachers so much that I used to stay in the centre and train the students as a coach. As a result, I became well acquainted with male and female teachers as a teacher and coach. My influence in sports developed so much that several teachers considered me (PET) a physical education teacher. Even when I got a promotion to TGT (Trained Graduate Teacher) from MCD, some teachers would ask me about zonal and central sports dates and venues.

Meanwhile, two teachers named Shiromani and Pushpa, newly appointed in the primary school of Bhagwanpur Kheda, participated in the games. Shiromani was a Vishwas Nagar, Shahdara resident, and Pushpa was from New Delhi. Vedi Ji introduced me to them as a primary school teacher like them. He also said that I came from Haryana. Vedi Ji used to invite all of us for lunch during the sports competitions. There used to be some gossip with laughter naturally, irrespective of our designations. We liked and enjoyed the company of the boss at lunch. One day, our SI, Mr Tara Singh Vedi, briefed me that these two teachers belong to your caste. I am trying to figure out what he said to Pushpa and Shiromani about me, but I don't know. There was no way to get to know each other personally because we had never had such a discussion. Vedi Ji belonged to the Valmiki caste. He was also a top-class artist in terms of laughter and instant response. But we were all accompanied like friends and brothers. There was practical socialism because of the adherence to non-veg and drinking. So, no issue of caste identity takes any shape.

When Vedi Ji brought the facts to my knowledge, my curiosity about Shiromani changed. I initiated looking for a future life partner between the two. Shiromani was a bit more attractive and also had playful eyes. During the initial conversation, she smiled among other colleagues and said–"I like the people of Haryana very much." Naturally, such a compliment from a girl can tickle anyone's mind. I was no exception. The same thing happened when I was mad inside. I never needed to know what that was in the people of Haryana that she liked. Shiromani seemed to me a better choice as my life partner than Pushpa.

Shiromani, a girl of whitish complexion, sharp nose, dimples on her cheeks, and slim and relatively tall, made her attractive. While talking, her body language and dancing eyes gave an aura like a rainbow. The words strolling out of her mouth filled them with different colours. The words that came out of Shiromani's mouth - 'I like the people of Haryana very much' would give wings to my expectations. The phrase would often knock at my mind to colour my dreams. My passion leaves no space to ponder how much reliability or genuineness the statement endured. Since the word 'I like the people of Haryana very much' was said, Vedi Ji had an innate right to have fun with me by repeating the phrase. For fun, he often whispered to my ear,' I like the people of Haryana very much.'

One day, Vedi Ji asked me to take the initiative to talk to Pushpa about myself. I could not trust my ears and kept looking at his face to qualify his words or say it was fun. Although Pushpa was fashionable, her lifestyle suggested she came from a well-fed family. I knew her father served in the railways and lived in the railway colony. That's why Pushpa came from New Delhi. But her features didn't match my choice. It did not mean that my features were better. It was a simple point of priority for a specific choice of an individual. Until now, I was curious whether she liked anything in me.

I was from a rural background with a grown beard, simple clothes, and sports shoes, and my hair had nothing to do with any style. Still, it was beyond my comprehension that Vedi Ji brought Pushpa in the middle instead of talking to Shiromani and her family. But one thing indeed struck me: Vedi Ji was interested in Shiromani. It was a distinct point that Vedi Ji was over forty years of age and also the father of three children.I was sure it was not about marriage but about flirting and fun. Why was he doing so? It wasn't calming if he wanted to let me stay away from Shiromani by bringing Pushpa in. I was not in his way; I could not have been.

I don't hesitate to admit that I have been shy and introverted since childhood. But if something upsets me, I often cross the limits of assertiveness. Even though Vedi Ji was our boss, I clearly said–' If there is anything to talk about, it can be about Shiromani, not Pushpa. I also noted that Pushpa may be from an excellent family, but I am uninterested. Since then, Shiromani has not been mentioned, and the matter seems to have ended. He didn't even make fun of me now by saying, 'I like the people of Haryana very much'.

I accept that even today, Shiromani's laughter, adorable smiles in mutual gossip, and food sharing amongst the group were unlike the mirage but seemed a reality that always attracted me to her. However, due to a lack of courage, the words buried in the chest could not take any shape and could not be articulated for months. Yes, one day, my father's health was a bit bad, and for no specific reason, there was a doubt in my mind that he might pass away. The sister's marriage was still pending. Exploring the possibility of my marriage with a working girl before my sister's wedding could be a better help. If I succeeded, there would be two earners instead of one, and the sister's marriage would go easy. Lost in belief, I left the house to meet Shiromani, thinking I would lay open the month-old fantasies buried in my heart in multiple shapes.

It was a rainy day, and I wore a raincoat when I reached Shiromani's school, Bhagwanpur Kheda. On sending the message, instead of inviting me in, she came to the gate and asked why I had gone there. I could not muster the courage to reveal anything, but in a hurry, I could utter that I needed her printed notes of the BA (pass). I, too, offered to return them soon. But in response, I had kept no familiar smile captured in memories. There was no tingle in her voice or gleam in her eyes as part of her personality. I realised from her body language that I had asked for her kidney, and she was thinking of living with one kidney for the rest of her life or something else like that.

Yes. I found almost everything missing that had attracted my attention earlier. From Shiromani's gestures, I concluded that the person who liked the Haryana man was different and used to accompany us during the Games. Eventually, I came back saying, 'Okay, no problem.' Since then, the man from Haryana has never looked back to the paths leading to Shiromani's world.

Even today, I do not hold Shiromani responsible for anything else. It may be my delusions or a misreading or one-sided love, which Vedi Ji had aired to the fire; maybe there was no fire on the other side. It might be my stupidity that I kept on riding on these winds. My last meeting with Shiromani had a negligible effect on me as we had never had any personal intimacy or seriousness like a marriage. That's why there was no sorrow or shock, as we see in such cases these days. Vedi Ji, the scriptwriter of this drama alone, could explain the authenticity of whether this issue of our love was accurate. But he is no longer with us today to unveil the mystery.

Looking back on this episode, I find I had no wisdom or love that may result in marriage. Another side of the coin is that I could not afford the luxury of any risk of love due to family obligations. Although at that age like mine, it may be foolish of youth to be a little deluded, there is no sense in it. To make my position better, I recall these lines from Surdas:

'Where can my heart find infinite happiness?

Like a bird flying from a ship, it always returns to board a vessel.'

Ultimately, I returned to my abode, where I had knitted the lofty dreams. Everything can be explained in the pattern of a saying- Rat Gai, Baat Gai- meaning the issue vanished as time passed. Two more such tales of infatuation are part of my life. On this occasion, I wish to recall them. Sometimes, such memories provide soothing leisure. It feels even better at this juncture to appraise one's follies of youth. Today, I can understand what was wrong with some gestures I had engaged in. It can also significantly help understand and explain the young generation.

These episodes occurred when I lived in Kundli village with my family in very miserable economic conditions; everything was at stake. We had a plot of two and a half hundred yards on the other street from our house. We used to grow almost everything in it: potatoes, tomatoes, onions, garlic, brinjal, okra, radish-carrot, etc. In the same plot, we would also grow sugarcane, buffalo fodder, Jawar, and Bursi/Birsham. Pumpkin and Turai sponge gourds are used to produce only on the thorny boundary of the property. There was no need for a separate place for them to grow. Apart from all this, the tobacco crop was also one of the essential crops because hookah was a big trend among the villagers, and my father was no exception.

We excavated this plot with a spade and irrigated it with the help of a hand pump. After school, we sisters and brothers used to share the responsibility of irrigation at our convenience. Near this plot of ours was the house of a man named Man Singh, and we used to call him Nana, Grandpa and his wife, Nani, Grandma. Their hierarchy regarding relationships in the village was significant, but they were young, so their children were less than ten. They had a sweet nature and loved us very much. I was doing teacher training when he requested me to teach his son, so I also started teaching him. When the month was over, he forcibly gave me twenty rupees and said that taking it would be helpful in my studies. After some ifs and buts with hesitation, I took the money, and this process continued.

His elder brother, Khajan Singh, lived in Mauhana, Haryana, and he used to do business there. He had two daughters. They visited our village during summer vacation every year. His elder daughter Kusum and I interacted during one of their visits. The conversation turned to gossip, which grew into mutual attraction. Before understanding this attraction, I wish to share one episode of my maturity level. It was when I visited Ghanta Ghar, Delhi, outside my village, for the first time. There was the Amba Cinema. I saw the first English film, Oliver Twist, with my friends. Our English teacher had advised us to watch as it was part of our 11th class syllabus.

I planned to watch this film with two experienced Gupta brothers. I excitedly stated we would sit in the front seats to have a lot of fun. They laughed at my ignorance about the cinema hall. I needed to learn the youth culture to deal with the opposite sex, utterly different from the village Ramlila shows. Contrarily, Kusum lived in the town with a theatre. She had enough money to spend on cinema, expensive dresses and cosmetics. I was a rural boy, and such an environment was foreign. The impact of cinema and openness could be seen in the playfulness in her eyes and the charming smile on her face. It was enough to attract a shy young boy like me. When I used the hand pump in my plot and walked in my field, my eyes would follow Kusum's elegance. Our situation was like 'fire broke out on both sides'. During Ramlila's days, we flocked to see Ramlila in another locality and talked a lot on the way to the venue. She would come for a few days to compensate for the emptiness. When she returned home after spending her holidays, the days of their separation were disturbing.

But we also found a way out and started posting. She had no problem getting a letter at home, but it could be problematic in my case. Hence, I used my teacher's college as the post's address. Our letters often contain gossip and code language. For instance, if we had to say 'I love you,' we used the English alphabetic numbers 9-12+15+22+5-25+15+21; for 'sweet kisses,' we used

19+23+5+5+20-11+9+19+19+5+19+19. There was nothing more to say but a little stupidity and childish time to pass.

Once, I anxiously waited for a letter from Kusum, but in vain. When I met her, I showed my displeasure. Kusum assured me of her promptness. Later, I learned that another student in my college had the name I.K. Suri, i.e. Ish Kumar Suri. He was a student-teacher of B.Ed. Mistakenly, he used to take out my letters from the letter box, thinking they were his own. I resolved this mystery when IK Suri revealed that an unfamiliar girl was writing him letters in my presence. He didn't have any idea of such a girl.

We were not restricted to letters but visited each other's houses. And we also had acceptance at both places. At my elder sister's wedding, Kusum's younger sister Kiran stayed at our house like a family member for about fifteen days. These were family ties and, hence, were beyond any restriction. We limited our intimacy to saying I love you and sweet kisses. There was nothing serious like getting married. If it had been, there would have been no social barrier between us matching Gotra, the surname. There was no resemblance between my native village and her present original residence, but in such issues, non-issues matter a lot in causing multiple and irreparable damages.

She used to be my Masi, my mother's sister in the village hierarchy. But she used to address my mother and father as mother-father like me. I used to call her mother a maternal grandmother and her father a maternal grandfather. We were too young for a relationship like marriage. We limited our world to enjoying a bond of attraction. We could satisfy ourselves by writing to each other, "I love you," and sweet kisses were the craze of our youth.

Finally, one day, she married an engineer from a prosperous family in Ludhiana, Punjab. I stayed for three days at her residence to support the marriage arrangement with no emotional turmoil, which may seem strange, but it is a hard fact. She left for her in-laws' house. A few years later, Kusum's younger sister, Kiran, married Kusum's widower brother-in-law. Both of the sisters resettled in Ludhiana. Meanwhile, we were displaced from the village and came to Balram Nagar Loni, Ghaziabad. My relationship with Kusum was confined to the town of Kundli.

A few relationships are more potent than a Fevicol joint, not to end. After all, one day, Kusum and her mother came to our house in Balram Nagar without knowing how. On talking, she revealed that her son had passed away, leaving her upset. Kusum had visited her mother's house to seek relief. Visiting my house was its extension. They spent one night with us and departed the next day. Our relations had turned as if India and Pakistan never united again, but now we have a new bond to a reunion as we have with Nepal. We didn't need any visas again and could move around without a passport. Now, we had a landline facility where we could interact on the phone frequently.

Once, I visited her in-laws' house with family, and we spent several days together. Similarly, we enjoyed ourselves a lot at Kiran's residence in Chandigarh. Meanwhile, the sisters Kusum and Kiran came to our house in Balram Nagar again. Since Kiran had three grown-up stepchildren, I attended their wedding twice with family. Then suddenly, Kiran had a painful demise.

Meanwhile, her residence and phone number changed. The same turn occurred in my life; my house and phone changed. I shifted to another home, a DDA flat. I had learnt almost for sure that we would never meet again. When all the avenues were closed, Facebook became the medium of our mediator to bring us closer.

As usual, one day, I posted my poem on Facebook. Something I realised happening in my mind in the pattern of Shahrukh Khan's film. I got an enthusiastic reaction from a lady stranger to me. I doubted why this unknown lady casually showed such emotion in her response. Curious, I checked her profile and found several snaps of her family; I was convinced I was not wrong. Now, all three of her children and both of ours were married. Once again, the sapling of our relations over fifteen years had dried up and budded new shoots again.

Now, she has a direct relationship with my family. Even today, she candidly shares all the sorrows, joys, and photographs of her family with me, my wife, Shashi Gangania, and our children. It does not mean her husband is unaware of our relationship; he has known it well since the beginning. Once, Kusum told me that her husband was jokingly asking what kind of boy loves his Maasi. But he didn't take it otherwise, and even today, he talks to her about me now and then. Today, the condition is that she comments regularly on every post of my daughter and mine. Today, she is the grandmother of her grandchildren, and the same is true for me. Even today, the spirit of our relationship sometimes breaks to the tune of I love you and sweet kisses.

My children have known her since childhood, and Kusum has been my friend since college. Even now, she is pretty comfortable talking to my children and daughter-in-law. In this age of Facebook and mobile, I am convinced our relationship will stay non-snapped. I have recorded it in my autobiography, and she will hum even after our lives.

The next name in this episode is Reena. Her relationship came into existence interestingly, like an attractive advertisement company offering one free with the purchase of the other. I, too, am a victim of such attraction. Reena was Kusum's close friend, and they studied together. Today, I was not at all sure how Reena had entered my life. I also took Kusum's help to confirm; now, everything is almost transparent.

Once, Kusum accompanied Reena to meet me in my village, Kundli. She used to share whatever was between Kusum and me with her close friend Reena. Just like everyone has someone or the other to celebrate good times or wipe tears in bad times, Reena played precisely the same role in Kusum's life. Kusum might have portrayed a similar picture of mine, she had in her mind. Indeed, Reena was an inheritor of unique beauty. The fair complexion, the tall face, the sharp nose, the big and charming eyes, and the lips meant to aid her smile more than words.

Kusum wore only a Suit-Salvars, but Reena was fond of the ultra-modern dress of that time. Her bell bottom and top used to make her stand in the line of film star Neetu Singh. Her frankness was like a living assertion of her freedom from her family. How could any creature escape from the trap of so many charms of any hunter? She had the facility to watch movies on the cinema screens in her town. So, what if I was a villager? I could also watch Chitrahar from sitting on the ground on the Panchayati TV available in our village. This feature was enough to spark any ash pile.

Suman, Reena, and I gossiped a lot. I relished meeting Reena. The next day, Reena came to my house with Kusum. The streets in the village were unpaved, and so were ours. There was a drain in the middle of the road. It was easy to cross it in a single long step. Kusum and I crossed it and came to the other side, but Reena extended her hand to get the drain crossed. Hesitantly, I raised my hand, and she crossed the drain. My wife Shashi does not show the courage to hold my hand like Reena, even at this stage of age. Although I am comfortable with my wife, the drain that I had helped cross Reena in the presence of my family still exists as a strange and unbelievable river for me, but it is the truth. I have neither the boat of words nor the rudder of logic to cross it.

One day, when Kusum's marriage had taken place, Reena suddenly came to the Fauji Hotel of Sukhvir Singh, a family friend of ours, on the Singhu border. My younger brother often stayed at the same hotel and usually slept there. I served in Munda Kheda then. Having attended college, when I passed by the hotel around 9.30 PM, my brother surprised me with Reena's presence. As I mentioned earlier, there was a long and high-walled cold storage between Lakhmi Pyau and my house on one side and the cremation ground, farm and pond on the other. It was the beginning of winter.

We were two young individuals alone on a deserted path about five hundred meters. It is not like Pythagoras's theorem to understand how courageous a girl who dares to hold my hand to cross the drain in the family company can be in such loneliness. It is not rational to blame Reena alone. We kissed each other intermittently along the way, hugged tightly and nothing more. We covered the ten-minute route in half an hour. I could not decide how admissible it was, but I was inevitably an equal part of it. I accept it with an entire obligation.

We spent the night at our house, and the following day, my sister, Reena, and I went to Narela and enjoyed the drizzle there. I made her sit on the bus to her town in the afternoon. After that, I went to Mauhana twice. It was not in my active memory that I spent a long time at Reena's house. Suman reminded me of it all. Eventually, the matter escalated to the discussion of marriage. Reena's father visited our village, Kundli, and finally interacted with my family and me, accompanying Kusum's uncle. But Kusum's uncle wanted a different tie. He was adamant about not letting anything like this happen. I also learned later that Suman's uncle did not favour our relationship. I suspected Kusum in this episode, not less than a villain.

As is typical, there is no more terrific villain than the advocates of caste and religion against love affairs. In movies, the hero wins, and the villain loses. But with love romances, often the villain wins, virtually in our society. I do not deny the reality of exceptions. No one should. Eventually, the villain won, and the exercise that started regarding our marriage altogether ceased. The failure of my ties with Reena and the process of my unsuccessful affinity reached an abrupt end forever.

I do not have any regrets and hold nobody liable for the failure. I recall precisely when 'It is all for the best' became the slogan of my life. This affinity is not limited to love but is the reality of every activity of my life today. It does not mean my argument to compensate for 'grapes are sour'. The recipe, 'It is all for the best,' I didn't design to make sour grapes sweet. I experiment with it based on past serial evaluations.

I want to follow its genuineness to explain how my wife Shashi Gangania's entrance into my life as the 'Best Option' turned into Angoor Meethe Hona Hai. When I look back to my life on the trial, Shiromani's 'I like the people of Haryana very much' was just a Jumla. We can easily understand this, considering the magic of rhetoric scattered around us today. Mr Tara Singh Vedi can also comprehend the reality of Jumla bringing a teacher named Pushpa into the middle. Because of village ties, Kusum could never be a priority for marriage. As far as Reena is concerned, the reality of her love fails in the shackles of castes. Our castes were different even though they were not separate. This obstacle was not from my side but from the family of ultra-modern Reena.

Later, I was also engaged to a trained drawing teacher from Aligarh, but the future did not approve of it either. Shashi proved to be sweet grapes and continued to serve and earn almost equally to me. She regarded my obligations as her own and never turned back, giving priority to money. Shashi paddled with me to sail across my family and never let me feel alone. She is undoubtedly an equal partner in all the achievements of my life. Shashi Gangania is sweet grapes, and a strawberry is soaked in dedication and harmony.

This rare diamond did not come in the sack of a poor guy like me so quickly. It was as tough as chewing iron gram, but it was soothing. Now, everything went as it should be in an orderly fashion. It was in the manner of first love and then a long struggle to make it a reality. There was neither a chance of rebellion from the family nor a conflict with society. Despite all the barriers, we took no break before our wedding.

Let's bid goodbye to the journey of unsuccessful love and move on to the journey of successful love. During the trip, I met a new villain as a caste for the first time. It changed many colours like a chameleon and challenged me. These challenges have become even more prominent in the present society. Coping with challenges has become a reality of my life today. Fighting this is our collective responsibility, so let me introduce you to this new villain because it is the brutal reality of Indian life.

---oOo---

CHAPTER FOUR

Encounter with the New Villain

Passion for me was not like the luxuries of an affluent parent's son. It was not like getting a job to keep it changing for further perks. It, too, was not like a never-ending cycle of lust. The exercise of my affinity was an issue related to marriage. My priority to mutual interaction was to know my would-be life partner appropriately. My would-be life partner, the other side of the coin, must follow the same to opine me. Finally, the process must materialize on mutual consent and collective wisdom. This was to ensure the stability and satisfaction of the upcoming marital relationship.

The search for my life partner was on to meet my basic needs, but it was challenging to earn. Most of my relatives were educationally backward and lived as kiln workers or farm labourers. They needed to have such links to meet our needs. The family's regular displacement had made us economically marginalised. My younger sister's marriage made it more complicated. The other issue was my inability to chat, flirt, or propose to any girl for marriage. I didn't have any leading initiatives for the girls I discussed earlier, but I never trailed back in the race of mutual gossip.

My staff members and Tara Singh Vedi, our school inspector, were the only hope. Tara Singh Vedi's attitude regarding marriage had also somewhat changed. But he was still determined to 'Tera Tanka To Main He Fit Karaoonga', which meant he would get me married. I realised it when Vedi Ji told me about a newly appointed nursery teacher in a municipal corporation school in Usmanpur, Delhi. This time, Mr Vedi prioritised the family rather than the girl for marriage. One day, he told me I had to see a stage show with him at Mandi House, Delhi. He also revealed that he would introduce me to a girl and her family there. I have also invited them to see you to watch the show.

Comedy shows like 'Kudi Phas Gayi' and 'Chadhi Jawaani Buddhe Noo' were occasionally held in Mandi House. Whether it persists now, I don't know. Sadly, I am trying to remember the name of the show we watched, but I need help placing it. My wife is no better example of the same. We should have known it, as the show had stopped the pursuit of our life partner. Both Vedi Ji and I reached Mandi House on time. The girl and her father also came there. But her father had nothing like the city's influence, and I was told that their residence was Kotla Mubarakpur near Defence Colony, one of the poshest colonies of Delhi. Her father's dark complexion, tall, slender body, nose and features were sharp, but his looks, clothes, hair, etc., could have been better. But the girl had no such problem. She appeared simple to me and provoked some hope in me. But after a few days, I got a message that her family did not find me a suitable match.

The shock of my rejection was louder because of the unrevealed reason. It may be a coincidence or something else that Rajesh Kundalia, wife of one of my acquaintances, Harpal Singh Kundalia, was an assistant teacher in

Usmanpur Vidyalaya. Mr Kundalia had somehow learned that Shashi and I were seeking life partners in each other. Mr Harpal told me that Shashi was telling my wife, "You settled down with such a smart life partner, and you are telling me such a guy who has no match like yours?" Mrs Manorama's husband was also included in these pleasing husbands. Manorama was also an assistant teacher in the same school close to Shashi.

Indeed, Harpal Singh Kundalia was blessed with an attractive personality, but he was also a primary teacher like me. Rajesh and Manorama were older. Shashi used to address them as Didi. Shashi reacted to my rejection in the presence of both. I realised that my refusal was not from her family but from Shashi herself. Shashi is none other than the same girl whom Vedi Ji took me to Mandi House to introduce. The rejection often comes from the family's elders, even if the denial is on the girl's part. With an unemployed girl, such contradictions come from the boy's side.

Such news was bad enough, but insensitivity doesn't make things pleasant. After a few days, Shashi came to my school, Yamuna Vihar, to get her nursery children to participate in the sports competition. We encountered, but there was no conversation. It is fitting to mention Shashi had to walk a long way from her residence to Usmanpur as there were no means of transport. So, she had already applied for a transfer. It was Vedi Ji's enchantment that he got Shashi transferred to my school. Now we were members of the same staff. She would talk with all the staff members but me. It was an awkward situation for me. How she took it was far from known to me. I learned from the staff that Shashi's parents had a meeting to find her life partner in me, but it couldn't succeed.

Shambhu Dayal Verma was also a teacher on the staff. We all would address him as Verma Ji instead of his name. He was from Rajasthan and a bachelor like me but was over thirty-five in age. We often called him 'Bhaya', another title we used because of his Rajasthan origin. The staff members got him married but could not find a way. One of our companions made fun of him, saying wherever you plan to see a girl for marriage, take such guys with more ripped hair to make you look younger and brighter. Otherwise, these guys around you will be villains and not let you get married. He laughed out loud and said, "Okay, I will follow your advice." Mr Verma was humble and simple and did not consider such things vicious.

Despite his simplicity of nature, whenever Mr Verma talked to Shashi, to be honest, it made me a little jealous. Some of my colleagues sometimes talked about meeting Shashi's parents with Mr Verma's marriage proposal. Shashi's family lived in Bhajanpura, Delhi, then. There was no talk of any submission about Verma Ji. It was not even possible because of the wicked caste barriers. I knew it, but I don't understand why I would be upset when anyone's name was linked with Shashi.

Four teachers belonged to the reserved category but had different sub-castes. Mr Jagbir Singh was Valmiki and was our head. Mr Santram was Jatav, and I had Chamar written on my caste certificate. Shambhu Dayal Verma used to come from the Balai caste in Rajasthan. Their caste was backwards regarding education, lifestyle and progressive thoughts. The status of girls' education was shocking in their caste. Early marriage was another threat to his caste. That's why Shambhu Dayal did not get offers from girls studying beyond tenth to twelfth, even in Delhi, the capital of India. Even his younger brothers were married and had children. Hence, his age was in a despotic state.

For the first time, I had an encounter with a demon of caste. It was a remarkable experience for me to share. Once, I went to Shambhu Dayal Verma's village, Ajabpura. It is in the Alwar district. We drank tea at a tea stall on the way, and Mr Verma washed the cups himself. I could not understand why Verma Ji was cleaning the cups. When we went to stay in a Dharamsala at night, the caste was first asked there. There were rooms and clothes available precisely on caste bases. This was my first experience seeing such a caste character. I understood very well why Mr Verma could not break the shackles of caste to marry into any caste he chose. His marriage age was almost over due to the stigma of caste.

Mr Verma's marriage issue was one of the critical issues of everybody's concern and sometimes fun. But every time, the matter got stuck on age and caste. One of the most visible reasons for Verma Ji's overage was his passion for becoming an IAS, but success still needed to be discovered elsewhere. Although Verma was MA and BEd, he also got a job as a primary teacher when he was on the verge of being overage. His argument for not crossing the caste bar was–'If I marry outside my caste, my family will have to face a severe boycott in the village. All prospects for the marriage of my brothers' children, too, have no future.' He was worried about the marriage of his younger brother's kids.

My case was different, and I had no such discrimination regarding caste in my village and school. Without knowing the dire consequences of caste prejudice, we all advised Verma Ji about how to get out of the caste prejudices. When I visited his town, I understood that Mr Verma's stand was just and practical. The caste identity 'Balai' was insufficient in Verma Ji's marriage. Balai, too, had two divisions: Rapiwal and Sutrawal. Verma Ji was also a Sutrawal superior to Rapiwal. Therefore, to fulfil the caste condition, a girl must meet both conditions, being a Balai and Sutrawal. Finally, Verma Ji got married under certain compromises with his primary choice. The girl was only twelfth pass, and Verma Ji's age was almost double.

This separation between Shashi and me did not last long. Mr Santram told Shashi one day, "What do you keep doing alone in your room during lunch break? Accompany us in the recess period." We did not share lunch alone, but gossip was a routine. It also became an appropriate opportunity for conversation between Shashi and me. It also facilitated our chats and helped us develop a bond. It encouraged me to travel with her to the Bhajanpura DTC bus stand, where she would drop her off to reach her residence.

We had made another abode for gossip at the house of a Sharma aunty when she was away making tea. Sharma's family was open-minded, and the other reason for hospitality was that Shashi had their daughter admitted to our school, and she picked her up for school daily and dropped her back after school. She also knew our relationship. Mr Sharma had contacted Shashi's father regarding his part-time electrical work. Whenever Mr Sharma, a man of jolly nature, was at home supported us and encouraged us to go ahead.

A student in my third-grade class had a plaster because of a fracture in her hand. If I had to say something to Shashi, I would write and put the chit in the dressing to go to the Madam. When I recall the episode today, I feel how irresponsible I was. The lust for personal talks had no bounds. It is not me alone when in love; everybody gets entrapped to cross the boundaries of stupidity.

Shashi was the only female teacher in our school, as there were no male teachers to teach the nursery classes. So, the child's mind was clear about whom the message was to be delivered. She followed the same process to respond. After a specific interval, we concluded that we would be life partners. Shashi often discussed marrying me at her house, but her family denied it. The issue was resolved at Shashi's level and punctured at the family level.

Her familiar arguments were: He has neither attractive features nor a superior post. He, too, does not have a substantial economic family background. He has nothing but a primary teacher. He has a grown beard; there might be a cut or significant injury mark behind to hide. We may have proposals from doctors and engineers; why should we think of a primary teacher with no personality and status? Shashi would go silent on such arguments. Contrarily, no Sundays passed when her parents did not visit to find a suitable match for her. But it was one of the most significant traits of her loyalty to the bonding of our relationship that she never missed to share the details.

Shashi would always assure me that she would marry me and no one else, but the circumstances in her house did not allow her to rebel. Her siblings were younger, and she was the only earner in the family. Her father, whom she called Babuji, was a Class Four employee at the Delhi School of Architecture. Apart from the job, he had technical skills to repair radio and electrical issues. He had a bad drinking habit, and some people used to barter his services with alcohol instead of wages. The family had to pay double the price; the first was the loss of money, and the second one was alcohol.

The onus to look after the family pivoted to Shashi's mother. Strangely, she has been a mother of none, as Shashi's siblings call her, Bhabhi. They had imitated it from Shashi's seven uncles. The titles stuck with Shashi's mother like an enduring tag. To meet the needs of a family of eight, the Bhabhi generated funds through bookbinding at home. She had brought the skill as a dowry at the time of marriage. She also would make candles during Diwali. Apart from Shashi, her youngest brother Rajesh and sister Usha also helped her carry out the seasonal affair.

Despite having a government job, Shashi would extend her hand in candle making and bookbinding. There was a massive campaign to save every penny in the house. Shashi dared not buy her clothes from shops but pieces from footpaths in the Friday weekly markets at cheap rates. Stitching, too, was done free at home through her mother. With savings from her salary, she got two additional rooms that the family badly needed. Under such a miserable situation, it was difficult for Shashi to go against the family's wishes to marry me. But she was determined to carry on the battle of love.

It forced Shashi's parents to inquire about my family and native village. One of Shashi's aunts lived in Baraut, near my ancestral village Rathaura and announced this marriage couldn't materialise as there were no Jatavas, but Chamads meant Chamars in that village. We accept girls from that community, not boys. They are of lower caste. Their profession is based on raw leather, which differs from ours. They discussed the issue with other relatives and had a chance to reject me again. Ultimately, Shashi got strict instructions to stay away from me.

I found the ground slipping from under my feet when she shared it. This was the first time I got a threat from the villain of caste. I have always taken a person as a human being, where caste mattered nil in my dealings. It is painful that caste and religion become a pivot of corrupt politics and deciding factors for my country's future. Still, we, as Indians, have become victims of a dog's mentality who is licking his blood, thinking the bone is blooming with it.

Consequently, surname and caste instincts dominate the top brass of Indian minds so wickedly that they set caste colonies in their offices and localities. How can we expect ordinary guys to break the caste slavery? Still, surrendering can never be a logical option. The fact is: There is no difference between Jatav and Chamar. Many Jatav girls from Delhi got married in my village, Kundli. In the town, calling them Jatiya, not Jatav, was customary. There was no bias, as I noted in my case today. It was the first time I learned people call us Chamad to show their superiority. It was torturous to hear. The so-called upper castes did not cause this pain, but the caste victims did. This is how the sociology of caste hierarchy toils to downgrade to pretend to be superior.

At this point, the whole family got into a caste controversy, but freely discussing things was a healthy practice. None was supreme to make decisions alone. The family would have routine talks about one issue or the other. My mother and father often shared their experiences dealing with the caste's demons.

The caste's chats brought back over sixty-year-old latent memories when I was in first grade, while living in Kharkhoda. My father used to be a friend of Dr Radhakrishna. He was a Brahmin by caste. We visited his clinic and house but experienced no prejudice. The snacks enjoyed at his residence still charm my memories.

The next episode takes me to Chulkana, Haryana. My elder sister was in third grade. One day, a dog entered the classroom and took Madam's lunch box away. Madam slapped my sister, saying to her like a Chamari, "Could you not keep the dog away?" The incident annoyed my father, Mr Naveen Chandra. He reached the school the next day to express his protest. But there might have been some eccentricity in Madam's mind about caste. Instead of accepting her mistake, she threatened, saying, "Go, do whatever you want."

How could a born fighter like my father stay silent over such an injustice? His life is filled with struggles. This story concerns my father, who lived and studied in Kumar Ashram, Meerut, UP, during the country's freedom struggle. He was not bothered by the Britishers' fear while putting posters on the walls against them at night.

He dared to return to his motherland, India, from Rawalpindi, Pakistan's territory, while the bloodshed engulfed the masses at the time of partition. My father was now a citizen of free India and not a bonded labour under feudal lords.

He had a job under the Haryana government. People called him Masterji. How could he compromise with such injustice against his innocent daughter? He filed a complaint against the teacher for her misconduct and threat and followed up faithfully.

The cross-examination in the case came into force and took several months. Ultimately, it took a severe threat to Madam's teaching job. She realised she had knocked on the lion's den. There was no way left but to surrender. One day, she came to my father's training centre with her headteacher and apologised, calling my father her brother. My father's being a fighter did not mean the lack of a forgiving soul. He stuck to his principles and never compromised. He forgave the teacher with the assurance that he would not escalate the issue and honour his words.

To state categorically, I did not know about caste controversies when I was young. I may be too young to realise the complexity of castes, or maybe because there was no tussle about caste in my family. But when I look back, I see a clear picture of my childhood. There were castes and localities based on castes. People of different castes lived in their segregated localities. The feeling of caste hierarchy was equally present even among the Dalit castes. But I don't recall any significant or prolonged caste confrontation, though other conflicts were common.

The prejudice between today's Dalit castes is no longer a mystery. Instead, it is an underlying fact that caste conflicts are getting more challenging daily. I find the caste controversies have left no end to reach because it seems we are no longer human beings but castes. The root cause is the politics and religion that have become tools for narrow-minded and wicked guys. They are toying with it at the cost of the nation and humanity. Illiteracy and irrationality of society support it manifold, for our thinking is too unreasonable. No unique space is left for global and humanitarian interests.

I found my parents often fighting against castes. I want to take my convoy of memories to Chulkana again. There used to be three Mohallas of Dalits, one of Valmikis, one of Dhanakas, and the other of weavers, but they were all rooted in caste conflicts to the deep. We had a buffalo. It would give so much milk that it produced one kilo of Ghee daily. It may sound unbelievable even to me now, but it is true. Children or women from all three communities came to our house to get buttermilk. They kept their utensils in a line. My mother used to pour the buttermilk with dignity and had friendly chats.

Youths from all three castes came to my father's leather training centre to learn to make leather products. They were in the habit of gathering in Chaupal in the evening to listen to the news on the radio. The Chaupal was in front of our rented house. My father would explain the issues in easy ways. He, too, was in the habit of smoking kali, a small Hookah. A weaver named Mange Ram is also usually accompanied.

One day, my father and Mange Ram were smoking, and two guys from the Valmiki community came and tried to sit at a distance. My father asked them to come closer. Hesitatingly, they followed. It was not enough; my father turned the pipe of Kali to smoke. It was shocking to them. Simultaneously, they stared at each other or Mange Ram and my father. Ultimately, they might have puffed on their turn twice or thrice; Mange Ram left pretending to have some urgent work. He could not show his prejudice of caste against those fellows in the presence of my father.

My father had his views and did not care about paltry issues that have made Indian society a hell. He was not confined to running the Leather Training Centre as his livelihood. Still, he did not let the campaign against superstitions and hollow beliefs die down. He shared his experiences of caste and its confrontations, where he played a decisive role in settling the issues, especially among Dalit communities. He also shared how he used his Hukkah and community food programmes to bring Valmikis and Chamar communities in Kundli, Haryana, closer. Hence, he was very optimistic about dealing with my marriage to Shashi.

I need to mention one issue related to one such anecdote to Jora, a guy from the Gurjar community of Chulkana. Jora began visiting my father, and it turned into a close friendship. He looked somewhat villainous; our neighbours warned us to avoid Jora as he would steal our buffalo, and we would never know about it. But on the contrary, Jora asked my father to leave our buffalo free from rope and teether. He assured him that if it was lost, my father could take it back without loss.

When our family came to live in Kundli permanently after serving a one-year term at Chulkana. Jora, a fair-complexioned, robust, blue-eyed, with a grown-up, dense moustache, visited our house. I remember he came to our home but did not eat or drink. Mother arranged his dinner and night stay with an elderly Jat guy named Harsu. It didn't become a big issue for either of us. Neither my father invited him nor has my father ever visited his village since our departure. It was Mr Jora's wish to see us so fulfilled. We didn't bother finding any angle of caste prejudice and caused no strain. It concerns my parents' life and that caste segregation is visible but free from bias.

It is our point of view to observe caste issues. If the guys with casteist mentality have certain reservations, I have never believed in letting it disturb my mental peace. I think my father's openness to castes is because of his association with Arya Samaj. Since childhood, he has been associated with Kumar Ashram, Meerut, and UP. It was an excellent centre for Arya Samaj, free from caste business. It would be far from wrong if I concluded that Arya Samaj influenced Haryana. I have nothing to reveal as caste conflicts at the personal and community level.

My readers may find it strange that I have witnessed no such prejudices and atrocities as we encounter in the Dalit autobiographies about UP and Maharashtra. I give credit to Arya Samaj that we could live in the house of a Jat colonel in Dighal Beri, a village in Haryana, where his wife would say to my mother, "If you want to visit your town, Masterni, go free, I will take care of your children." Though it never happened, such issues helped us understand the caste character in Haryana. But today's Haryana has changed for the worse because I have read and experienced the tales of Dulina, Gohana, and many other casteist atrocities; we may call them genocides to a certain extent.

We did not like the caste controversy aired by Shashi's family. Shashi was unaware of such caste intricacies but was not ready to kneel before them. I also felt Shashi's parents intended to avoid marrying their daughter because of their unstable economic conditions. They were attending one option or the other only to feel the pulse of the people to get their daughter married. But I never shared it with Shashi as being imprudent to think so. I openly discussed the issues of caste as a villain in our relationship with Shashi to brainwash her. I found it essential not to get her entrapped in any insecurity in entering the marriage of the so-called different, somewhat lower caste.

I wish to return to my old village, Kundli, Sonepat, Haryana, to observe caste relations with other communities. These relations have helped to shape the cognitive thinking of my family and me. As I see in Dalit autobiographies, it is the only ground that allows me to claim no caste intimidation. Let me refer to the discussion of my family members' relationships with non-fraternal men and women.

A girl named Darshana Sharma was a classmate of my elder sister Chandra Kanta. She and my sister had a solid intimacy, visiting each other's houses and sharing snacks and sometimes food with no bias. The case of Risalo (Jat) was similar. Out of curiosity, she frequently asked when the festival of Ravidas Jayanti would occur. We like the special treat of Poori and potato curry on the day. Two sisters, Gyan and Babli, who were Brahmins by caste, studied with my elder sister. I knew their family as Sahakoliyas because their ancestral village was Sahakol. This family lived by building a house on the farm itself. They often stopped at our house because it was on the way to their home.

My younger brother Raju has been a strange specimen of inter-caste friendship. Sukhbir Singh, Nafe Singh Captain, Shanti, Umed Patwari, and Mohan had different castes. No day passed when the group didn't have gatherings in their houses. They didn't bother to work as a family member. May it be the work of hay haulage by keeping a bundle in our house. They all attended the wedding of my elder sister and cousin Om Pal Singh as family members, not as guests. And followed the activities irrespective of work, big or small. They addressed our mother and father like our siblings did. Eating at each other's house on the same plate was common. Laxmi Srivastava, a friend of my younger brother Satish, came from the Kayastha family of Kanpur. Their intimacy didn't let them stay away even for a month. He was an enduring member, attending all the family functions till our more youthful sister's wedding. Our ties ultimately snapped as his untimely death was because of cancer.

I, too, am not an exception. I also have some instances where caste played no negative role in my village, Kundli. I saw no caste controversy in my town. There was no tussle over caste in the school as well. In this episode, I wish to discuss the non-fraternal comrades associated with me. Once, my classmates Ajay Kumar Sharma and Hoshiar

Singh (Jat) asked me if they could come to my house to accompany me to study? Of course, they came and stayed together for several hours. I used to go to Ajay's house. His father, a sub-inspector in Delhi Police, appreciated our company.

Pandit Jodha Ram and Dulichand of Kundli were very kind, helpful, and authentic. Since Dulichand was in a higher post in the electricity department, he used to call the people of our locality to his house to offer some jobs. He got many people employed; everyone in the village appreciated his generosity. The Banias, the shopkeepers of our town, too, were away from the filth of caste, hatred, and contempt. There was no such tension at all.

While doing my Diploma in Basic Training from Jamia Millia Islamia, Gajraj Singh Dabas (Jat by caste) lived in Rani Kheda, Delhi. Once, he took me to his house, and we spent the night together. His mother served curd and Roti for breakfast. We shared a typical vessel instead of separate utensils. One day, he stayed at my house for several hours and left in the evening. There was no issue of caste in the Teachers' College, nor any discrimination towards Hindu Muslims. Even though it was a Muslim University, everyone lived together the way they pleased. But today's political mentality has made the gap between castes and religions so toxic that it may take centuries to bridge or return to the original.

When I got a job at MCD, Delhi, I started participating in sports that year. During this time, I was closely connected with RD Sharma, Mahendra Singh Dabas, Rajkumar Bharadwaj, Shobha Goud, and Nilofar, who organised the games in Shahdara North. During the games, we shared food as a strong witness of our bonding. We used to visit each other's houses on special occasions. My house at

Balram Nagar was on Raj Kumar Bharadwaj's village route. Like a family member, he often ate, drank, and even slept at my residence when he was late at night. We all were not without Castes and religions. Still, our beliefs never punctured the lifestyles we lived.

Inter-caste friendship and family ties continued in our new home, Balram Nagar, Loni Ghaziabad, UP. Here, Prakash (Gurjar) village Chudiyala, Loni Inter College principal's younger brother, Anand (Gurjar) principal's brother-in-law village Baghu, Baghpat UP, Mahendra (Gurjar) village Agrola, etcetera were such companions who ate at least two or three meals a week with us. The mention of snacks, tea, water, etcetera makes no sense here. I understand it was because of our family's lifestyle and food habits. If I wish to give credit to something else, our family's purview over caste is the idealistic insight that took shape under our upbringing.

Another unique character in my relations is Mr Tara Singh Vedi Valmiki by caste. If any party's menu at my residence had non-vegetarian ingredients, Tara Singh Vedi Ji, our school inspector, had a prominent role. He had a great passion for food and cooking. At least five to six times a month, the occasions took us to Mr Vedi to host the fete. In other chapters, I need to share more about Mr Vedi as a significant player.

In this context, I need to mention another notable episode. RD Sharma, Mahendra Singh Dabas and I appeared as private candidates in the MA Political Science 1st year at MMH College Ghaziabad in nineteen eighty-seven. The night before the exam, we stayed and had dinner at RD Sharma's cousin's house in Ghaziabad. We returned to our respective homes the next day after the exams. During our stay, we were treated like family members with no caste identity. But when I go through Dalit autobiographies, there are many caste controversies, exploitation and oppression at personal and institutional levels.

It does not mean I doubt their credibility. But I am bound to mention that in some autobiographies, the nature of caste prejudice is too much to digest. Well, I am sharing my experiences in the current context. I do not mean to refute anyone. Yes, I intend to compare autobiographies for microanalysis of the social, economic, political, and geographical conditions responsible for paving the way to discourage any caste exploitation and oppression.

A young man like me, who had grown up in a healthy social environment, got hurt by the divisive caste approach of Shashi's family living in the heart of the country's capital. I had no option but to fight against the ugly, prejudiced surroundings. While analysing the episode now, I find Shashi's parents and grandparents innocent. Her grandparents were illiterate and worked as gardeners in the central government. Similarly, two of her eight uncles were clerks, and the rest were class four employees. None was there with an open mind to fight against the divisive caste character. Breaking the shackles of caste through the less privileged strata was challenging.

The command to reach any conclusions about our marriage was in the hands of poorly educated and equipped family members. Shashi's maternal uncle and aunt were engineers and officers in the central government. They were sick of their status mentality. They believed Shashi deserved a doctor, an engineer or a boy of a decent post in any office. They did not like me with the same pay grade job as Shashi. Neither the educated nor the less educated were of any help in our affairs.

Shashi was in a miserable state. She was not afraid of the ghost of caste and its aftermaths. Her dilemma was how to go against her parents. The process of our meetings was still ongoing. No matter how the family members protested. There was a person named Jhanda Singh, a peon in the school where we worked. He had become as if a prophet of the caste in school. He constantly protested our relationship. His most demeaning comment was–'Kya Jatwade Khatm Ho Gae Hain Jo Shashi Is Se Shadi Karegi.' it translates: Has the Jatav community vanished for Shashi to marry the guy from another community?' He also challenged us to see how the marriage would take place.

Jhanda Singh came from Sirauli, Ghaziabad, UP. Our headteacher, Sant Prasad Bansal (Gurjar by caste), came from Bhagaut, UP. Both had caste reservations and had the same route to school. They went back together on their respective bicycles. He provoked Bansal Ji on the way, and Bansal Ji reacted accordingly several times. He had witty rhetoric to say that those who disagreed would be taken to the room of sticks. He used to point to a store near his office, where some sports goods, some bars, etc., were stored.

In this episode, the role of one of our companions, Santram, was astonishing. He came from Makdoom Pur village of UP, a remote area of Ganga. Sant Ram was the first graduate of his town who used to write his caste as Jatav. He never protested like Jhanda Singh. But Sant Ram said nothing openly but had a pet dialogue supporting his opinion that the decision was on hold. It is a different matter; later, he always stayed with me like an elder brother and cooperated extensively on domestic issues.

Once, Mr Bansal Ji said: You confirm your affirmative stand; I will see how Shashi's family disagreed with the marriage. He had shown the bully because of his Gujjar caste. He knew very well that Shashi's family did not dare oppose him. Shashi's house was in Bhajanpura, near the Gurjar-dominated Garhi Mendu village. Gujjars dominated Shashi's native town, Kotla Mubarakpur, too. He had assured me of marriage because of his caste dominance. But our family has never had outside interference in our family. I couldn't use outside influence in our personal affairs. Anyway, I was not even Shambhu Dayal Verma to surrender before the demon of castes.

I remember an anecdote where an attempt was made to make caste a benchmark of my ability behind my back but failed. I was promoted to English lecturer at Sarvodaya Vidyalaya of Timarpur. I joined my duty and returned home. In my absence, one of our colleagues, BN Sharma, lecturer of commerce, commented, "This guy is young enough; he must be from reservation quota. He would spoil the academic status of the school." A teacher from the Dalit community conveyed what Mr BN Sharma had commented. I made no personal comment. But when the staff hosted my reception party and I, my promotion party, I recited two poems, one on each occasion. One was in English, and the other was in Hindi. It was a response to Sharma's allegation against me.

A teacher from Uttarakhand named BN Dimri TGT of Hindi had a worm of Brahmanism to sneak out. He asked me to write an application in English for him. I knew what he intended to do but accomplished the task without resistance. He understood he had taken the foul move of judging me. I was a member of the same club where Mr Dimri volunteered to make tea during the recess break. As a club member, he made us drink tea for fourteen years and cleaned the teapots himself. When I started taking my classes, the students from other sections applied to get transferred to my course. Meanwhile, the responsibility of anchoring school programs was also imposed on me. I served in the school for several years, but no question of caste appeared on my way.

Though I served several years there, I never disclosed anyone who had misjudged me based on my caste. I did not respond to the ill mentality of the guys in the same tone. For giving a model lecture in the presence of the British Council in my school, I was the only choice of my principal to defend the prestige of the school. Working in the same institution, I entered the arena of authorship known as Ambedkarite. Now, the monster of caste rarely comes to me. Despite this, I go to him to challenge and eliminate.

Today, it is a matter of how we deal with the monster of caste. Let us return to where the devil of caste had appeared as a villain in the way of our marriage. Shashi and I had almost eliminated it at any cost. I have nothing to achieve without struggle, and probably shouldn't be. We appreciate what we get with effort. The battle was ongoing, but this struggle seemed inadequate to get the precious pearl of life. Therefore, the fight continued with a new energetic aptitude.

---O0O---

CHAPTER FIVE

The Decisive Strive For Marriage

It was when Shashi's family refused the alignment based on caste hierarchy. My family also felt the gradation of caste as higher or lower was an abuse. It was painful. If the issue was unrelated to marriage, the answer could be in the same tone. My family directed me to stay away from that girl as we did not want to be involved in caste stupidity. Let them know whether they are higher or lower; we do not feel any further dealing with such guys.

Our family's financial condition had deteriorated, but my family was far ahead regarding an ideological and progressive approach. I want to credit my father, who had an education till high school and was a fantastic canvas for dealing with such issues. His association with Arya Samaj was the first plus point that made him open. My father's mobile job was to stay in one village for one year and shift to another for the following year. The mobility of his job had made my father a social reformer and boosted my family's maturity.

It was nothing new for my father as he did not hesitate to clash with society's orthodox and worn-out traditions. Contrarily, Shashi's paternal heritage had less space for education and openness of mind. But it was not the same with the relatives of her maternal lineage. Another orthodox approach was patriarchal superiority, which had no scope for the matriarchal intervention as inferior. It was working against our marriage. Shashi's education and point of view on this matter had no ground as she was a direct party in this episode. Second, she was a girl and younger. Shashi dared not speak or even stand against her father, called Babu Ji, because he did not even think for a second about slapping. Shashi's mother had been the most suffering victim of his wrath. Under these circumstances, there had been no mutual relationship between her family and mine.

We did not share our views with our families earlier. By the way, it left nothing to discuss as the tension had engulfed everything constructive between us. But gradually, the vehicle of our attachment returned to its old track. We started meetings at the university apart from the bus stand. Being a non-collegiate, Shashi had to go to the university to attend classes every Sunday. It was a golden option for us to cry out our pangs. Shashi, too, was more interested in meeting than attending her classes.

The Science Faculty of Delhi University and the deserted area near the State Bank of India were the best options for solitude. We were not alone, but the place remained occupied by young couples. Sometimes, we would sit on the stairs, and occasionally, we would use the solitude appropriately by creating a park, trees, and plants as a shield. It did not mean that our families were ignorant about our activities. They could guess the fire the smoke would leave behind, but they overlooked it. While enquiring directly, I could not avoid telling the truth. Shashi had an excuse for college, but I had no reason. If I had, I could not have availed it for lame excuses. Frequently, if I wanted to avoid telling the truth, I diverted the issue but didn't lie. Such a claim is incredible in the recent lifestyle, but I do not consider it crucial to explain. The situation sometimes turned tense, but our passion took us to old ways, and we did not know how.

Shashi made excuses for her family to meet, but they caught her with no severe effort. There would be scolding in the place; she got other instructions to mend her ways, but in vain on both sides. It is worth mentioning that Kumar Gaurav and Vijeta Pandit's first film, 'Love Story', was released in a cinema hall in Moti Bagh in 1981. How could we escape without making it a part of our love story? Shashi had to make an excuse to visit her bank. This film gave wings to our spirits, and the university get-together continued unabated. Once Babu Ji reached the university wearing Sardar's turban, Shashi saw him but did not tell me. It was his gentility that he did not scare us with his presence and returned home silently. On that day, the whole secret of our meeting was revealed. There was a lot of uproar at Shashi's house that day.

When Shashi's family had rejected me, Mr Vedi's role was almost over, but he had an eye on further development. Vedi Ji occasionally talked with me steadily. He could take no more initiative on the caste controversy as he was a victim of caste as a Valmiki, lower in the caste hierarchy. Our affair gradually evolved into a discussion in the entire Shahdara North Zone of education.

Mrs Ramesh Gupta, school inspector (nursery), would also show her concern as a reporting officer. She intended to get minute details whenever Shashi attended her monthly meeting or whenever Shashi visited the office for any reason. She often consoled her for her support. Mrs

Gupta, as an elderly family member, interacted with me to familiarise herself with the state of affairs. Mrs Gupta and Mr Vedi wanted to ensure the department that there was nothing unethical in our relationship.

Dharam Pal, a Gurjar teacher living in Gadhi Mendu in Shashi's neighbourhood, called her Lali, a daughter of his village. Because of our relationship, he started calling me Lala, masculine of Lali. Mr Dharam Pal often said villainously, 'Aur Lala Kya Haal Hai means, how are you, Lala? ' He just enjoyed our relationship but created no nuisance, though he could. If he wished so, he could spoil it to the unrepairable.

The frequent uproar in Shashi's family enhanced our pain and problems. But it was a disgrace for us to step back, and problems were the only ones to worsen. Our condition had become like the snake mouthed with a shrew neither to swallow nor to spew. The second issue for us was to do our job in Shahdara North. If we planned to get married elsewhere, the news of our relationship could threaten our future married life. Hence, we needed a secure way to go on the beaten track we were following. There were no Sundays for Shashi's parents when they were not out for a suitable match for Shashi, or someone did not visit her house for the purpose.

During such a struggle, Mrs Asha, Shashi's next-door neighbour, called her Bhabhi, sister-in-law, and supported us. Shashi spent her spare time with her for consolation. When we needed to meet, but the restrictions were too strict, she arranged our meeting in Chandni Chowk, one of the most popular markets with a glorious history. When Shashi's birthday fell on Oct. 26, Shashi gave a non-veg party at her residence. I, too, joined it as a staff member and nothing else. Ram Kumar Sharma also joined the party.

He, a Brahmin and staunch RSS devotee, was sincere and quite mature ideologically but had a funny thing about the non-veg parties. He always took advantage of such non-veg parties, which may be pork. He had pet words: ' I would bring Garam Masala, hot spice, and the rest of the arrangement is your responsibility.' The story of this hot spice continues to be a source of much entertainment amongst our friends even today.

Now, the patience regarding the heat of this relationship had left the way. Finally, my father came to our school one day and talked to Shashi and me. We agreed to snap the bond because of Shashi's family's rigid and hostile approach. Being the family's eldest son, my family was in no mood to wait. So, with no heart, I surrendered to my family's desire. I eventually got engaged to a trained drawing teacher from Aligarh. The engagement was accomplished, but the first love was not giving up. The feeling of losing each other made us both rebellious from the inside. Finally, one day, the engagement of our new relationship from Aligarh ended, and we got free to return to the old world again.

The relief that Shashi's family received after my engagement was lost. Shashi told her family, "Okay, I agree with what you say, but if I do not marry him, I will marry none." This was a big challenge for Shashi's family, but they kept finding a suitable match for Shashi's marriage. Meanwhile, my post at Yamuna Vihar school was surplus. I got a posting for the morning shift at Gokul Puri School, which is just a road between our workplaces. The working hours and the bus stand were the same, so the meeting continued.

One day, I saw a boy standing with Shashi at the bus stand. He worked in Canara Bank and lived in Anand

Parvat. Shashi's parents had sent him to see her. It was a strange coincidence that I found the fellow from Jamia Teachers College, my old acquaintance. I asked him how he was there. He told me he met this Madam, pointing to Shash,i as their parents had been in dialogue for their relationship. I told him we were already in a relationship and planning to get married. I acted as a villain. Shashi asked me several times, 'What did you tell him?' I always said, "Nothing but you and I are engaged in?" Indeed, he was better than me in appearance and earned more. Shashi may have liked it, too.

The tension became a permanent living feature in Shashi's house. It adversely affected Shashi's health because of regular discord; she even missed her routine food. Shashi's mother made a notable comment to discourage her: "Ish Kumar has five brothers and a sister, and all are unmarried. You will die earning money for their marriage. Still, I do not have any problem; your babu Ji does not stand with me." Contrarily, her father would say: 'I have no problem, but your Bhabhi (mother) disagrees. What should I do?' Both would try their best to win Shashi's trust, but the result did not console us.

It was their strategy to get us to surrender our claim. Shashi had turned into a pendulum to swing between yes and no. Being a Tick-Tock among two families and friends often bothered me. Despite all sincere and concrete efforts and stands, my maturity was at stake, like Shashi and her family. I had no option left but the grain between the two grinding stones of a mill. My attitude has never been so casual as it was in that situation.

My maturity was questioned without a firm decision in the episode, though I was in whole spirit and spine since the beginning. None can agree about clapping with a single hand. Well, the dilemma was not letting me relax a little. After being fed up with the embarrassing situation, I found a solution. It was to get her in writing that she was pregnant, so she couldn't even think of shifting her sole stand. However, the fact was far from reality, and there was no question of blackmailing at all. It worked brilliantly and helped us get rid of the pendulum-like situation.

It was the time the harmony in the family got thrashed. Even her siblings developed an adverse chain like her parents, but Beena, the younger sister. All three younger brothers seemed to have no business but to follow their parents. Usha, the youngest one, was reactive like her parents. Only one middle sister, Beena, was in the middle order among the three sisters and occasionally stood against her family's solidarity to support Shashi. As I mentioned, Asha, the next-door neighbour, had the heart to openly stand against Shashi's parents. Shashi passed her enough time at Asha's residence to dilute her sorrow-stricken soul.

The Non-stop stress-causing environment of the family seriously affected her health as she couldn't have her diet appropriately. She often fell ill and had turned no better than a skeleton. It had shaken me, but Shashi did not lose courage despite the multiple miserable menace. During all this unrest, Shashi's visit to my house on my nephew Amit's birthday relieved me. My family showered her with a lot of love. She was impressed by how my family greeted her. She was now well-versed in my family and our ways of life. The same impression my family members had because she was down to earth. Another reason that enriched the bonding was that she had a good experience dealing with the financial crisis that both families were going through. It was an explicit feature of her body language and dealings.

My colleague Savitri, a Gokul Puri school nursery teacher, contacted me during this time. She and Shashi were already familiar, holding the same post and department. They used to go together to attend monthly meetings of nursery teachers. Savitri, too, was a bachelor and had no caste barriers like Shashi. She, too, showed interest in me. Savitri was from Rajasthan and used to come from Bidanpura, Karol Bagh, Delhi. Her body was robust and had manly features. She was outstandingly cheerful and of a jolly nature. Her dressing sense was impressive.

Her gestures, body language and engaging conversation showed something more than mere attraction in me. It lured me, too; I showed no sign of letting her know my inclination to her emotions as I was already in relation with Shashi Bala. I gave my arrest when there was a teachers' strike in the year nineteen eighty-two. That day, she had brought me non-veg to see me off to a noble cause. I closely observed her heavy heart and the void in her eyes as a farewell, as if I was going away for a long time, which she couldn't bear at ease. I also found precise changes in the natural complexion of her face. I felt it closely but revealed nothing.

I had briefed her about the affairs Shashi and I were engaged in. Despite knowing our relationship would materialise in marriage, she continued her concern. Even one day, she told me, 'I wish your relationship to end happily; somehow, if not, share it without hesitation. It was undoubtedly a marriage proposal; I could understand it reasonably. In response, I smiled at her honest and genuine approach but had no way but to divert the issue. If Shashi and I had been free from any previous engagement, I would have honoured her sentiments faithfully. She was not free from her passion for me when her marriage was close to someone else who was very well-known to me through her day-to-day gossip. Well, I have nothing to comment on but to call it a relationship that was not destined.

Meanwhile, Shashi's sister-in-law Asha advised her to observe sixteen consecutive fasts on Mondays in honour of Lord Shiva as a widespread belief for any marriage to materialise. Shashi carried them out with complete sincerity. During this long process, the decision of Shashi's parents changed to favour us, and Shashi gives sole credit to these fasts and Lord Shiva. She claims she had observed a fast for sixteen Fridays to please the Goddess Santoshi Maa. It is common practice to credit any deities rather than the individuals' rigorous struggle as the natural source of victory. I find it the primary source of individual neglect, which the preachings around us keep ensuring merely puppets in the hands of fate and the Gods beyond numbers. Let's return to the core issue.

The role of these fasts in bringing our love story to its happy ending is beyond my grasp. But it was inevitable that the graph of Shashi's hope rose remarkably because of blind fasting beliefs. The opportunities remained the same. After all, one day, the scene changed because Shashi's babu Ji lost patience with us. He called his close and influential relatives, including Shashi's maternal uncle Chetan, Om Prakash Dagar, and Mausa Jag Ram; they were all elite in Shashi's affinity.

The debates went on like a court. Shashi was as if under interrogation. They asked if I had any of her offensive photographs or any letters that scared her, and I would reveal them. The answer was 'no', but tears from the eyes fixed on the ground had no bounds. The intelligence and reputed positions in their respective office needed support to find a solution. They had nothing left but to beat their heads without finding appropriate answers. After all, they went away after eating a feast, a standard feature of their visit to Shashi's house.

However, they had no logic and weight in their arguments. They did not even have an idea that being a teacher is not enough for the entitlement of a doctor or engineer for a marriage. The status of Shashi's family and ideological level did not match what a doctor or engineer aspires to. But everyone may dream, and dreams pave the way for reality. That's why I did not have any sense raising questions about Shashi's family dreaming too high. However, goals that are too big cause pain when broken. After all, Shashi's family encountered their reality and dropped the idea of getting a doctor or engineer son-in-law.

After all, one day, they said 'yes' to our engagement, and provided my younger brother, Raj Kumar, we called him Raju at home, would marry Beena, Shashi's younger sister. No doubt, she was straightforward. Her looks were ordinary, and her mind was below average. Hence, she could study to reach the 10th standard somehow. Contrarily, my brother was sharp and intelligent enough to serve in the DTC workshop as a regular employee. He, too, had dreams about his life partner. Later, he fulfilled his dream of marrying a Christian girl.

The issue of our love marriage differed from a contemporary business strategy to buy one and get one free. It was a question of our ethical standing as well. How could I sacrifice my younger brother's interests to fulfil mine? After all, I bluntly rejected this unfair proposal. Had this condition stayed the only option for our marriage to materialise, I could have given up on my love. Still, I could not even think of any such bargain in the relationship. Shashi was not selfish and did not support this bargain, as she believed pious relations like marriage must have no space for such an ugly thought.

Shashi's family might have realised the vulgarity of the deal, but we finally got 'yes' to our relationship. Troubles do not come alone but in bunches. This proverb justified it as Shashi had put some monthly sharing in local committees and borrowed advances against her deposits for family affairs like construction work. She had to pay the lion's share of her earnings. To solve this problem, her parents offered Shashi the option of paying the outstanding instalments from her salary while living with her in-laws.

We were okay with this proposal as the issue was not to get an earning member in the family but to honour the first love affair. Money has never been my priority for the relations I love and prefer. After all, in rage, Babu Ji, Shashi's father, called a baba, an elderly middleman of Garhi Mendu village, and asked him to conduct the preparations for our engagement, the Sagai ceremony.

The arrangement ceremony was simple: They gave me three hundred fifty-one rupees, honoured other family members possibly with notes of Rs. five and eleven, etc., some clothes, and a basket of fruits. We had passed a stage in the marriage process but regularly feared that new rumblings might make our dreams merely dreams. Thankfully, there was no such fuss to spoil our deep desires. Our marriage took place, and as the condition of paying all the loans by Shashi was concerned, her parents did not let us pay anything. They cleared the loans on their own.

Finally, it was the day of June 14, 1982, which was fixed for our marriage; we had struggled a lot for two years. The goal was no less challenging than it often had been. Before the stipulated time of the wedding, a storm was in its full orgy, with the rain to multiply its fury. It uprooted even the giant trees to occupy the road to Bhajanpura, and the streets had turned into pools of dirty water. It encouraged Shashi's Babuji to comment, 'Look, even God is shedding tears because of the wrong decision of your marriage.' He seemed consoled for what he had done for a long time, not to get us to succeed.

Shashi had no option but to remain shocked as the excitement of the marriage was already missing from the faces of the family. She did not want to invite any trouble, making any of her reactions. The consequences of opening her mouth could take the caravan where it had stepped in. Hence, there was no scope for thinking of ways other than accomplishing the marriage ceremony.

Because of a natural mishap, the photographer couldn't reach the spot for photography. The tents that were set up in the house's courtyard got uprooted. Since Vedi Ji wore white trousers, he passed through the water and, for months afterwards, narrated the story of his pants. Somehow, the procession reached Shashi's sister-in-law's house. It had enough space to accommodate the caravan, Barat. During this, there is a ritual of taking the Barat. The ornaments, clothes, and other items brought from the bridegroom's family as gifts were handed over to the Panchayat, which included the bride's elderly relatives.

The process was simple, but a new ruckus arose other than nature's fury. The luggage had only one sari; the rest were left at the house because of the rain and storm. Then what could be the other scenario than the family members raising the sky on their heads? The main dispute was that it was the first marriage in Shashi's family of two grandfathers and eight uncles. They emphasised that only one sari was for our teacher-daughter, the bride. Such a blunder was unbearable for Shashi's grandfather. That is why Shashi's grandfather threw that sari and made offensive remarks in the presence of older adult guys on both sides.

My father kept control with self-restraint. He did not react to their lines. He habitually extinguished the fire with water rather than fire. His experience handling several issues brilliantly entangled in the village kept him calm. He sent someone and arranged the rest of the saris from home, hardly three kilometres from the bride's residence. He did not take any of such matters on his mind.

Things got better at the community Panchayat level, but it took a lot of time to digest in Shashi's house. On hearing about one sari for the bride, a teacher by profession, Shashi's Babu Ji, got so angry that she went inside the house, gave two consecutive slaps to the bride and said, 'Look! We are getting too much insult collectively among the relatives and the settlement because of you.' However, all the family members condemned this brutal reaction of slapping the bride. But he did what he had to. His anger did not subside, and he went out somewhere in displeasure, leaving the marriage activities.

It was not enough to dismay us; while Jai Mala, the garland ceremony, was to occur, the power went out. Candles were the only help to perform the ceremony. Naturally, it was an occasion for making fun; Babuji's slap and absence of light turned it into a formality. Thankfully, our photographer was already absent because of the rain and storm, or it would have captured the remains of the deep melancholy of the environment in the photographs tokeep the wounds unhealed.

Babu Ji was slightly different, never bothered by the outcomes of the actions he occasionally got into. It was another shock for the family that he stayed away even during the ceremony of Kanyadan, which the bride's father solely performed. Some people visited all the locations to ensure his presence and his role in accomplishing, but in vain. Ultimately, the family had no option but to bring Shashi's eldest uncle, Sohan Pal, forward for the Kanyadan ceremony. On a lighter note, I would like to know whether any of my readers have passed through such a situation where a bride got slapped during her marriage rituals or ever seen a father disappear from the marriage. It seems to me just a nightmare now; I am bound to recall it to share with my readers.

Please let me know if anyone has any knowledge of such an experience. I am interested in learning what forces a father to take such an extreme step against his daughter, who did not have a second thought other than the family's brighter future. Is she preferring to marry a guy she loves and feels would never be a hurdle in her freedom of thought and support to her family? If such a cruel reaction from a father has social approval, every person who loves should be ready to face such accidents.

Another side of the coin is that a girl committed to the family and endured the agony still could not stay away without preventing the Laddoos from splashing in the rain while sitting in the bride's costume. Often, I pass through the cruelty of society, who act no less than gangsters against the couple who prefer the choice of their love, ignoring a prejudiced mentality of caste and creed. It often takes me to my past love and marriage struggles. It reminds me that much has stayed the same in the feudal mentality, even in the twenty-first century, where one has to pay some cost to get one's love. Some prices are too high for the couples, and they fail and leave the world.

Our marriage episode taught us the lively experience of the famous saying: 'Misfortunes never come singly but in groups.' I can replace misfortunes with troubles as I don't believe in the philosophy of fortunes. So, we won over the one, and a new problem awaited us to encounter us. The rain and storm rooted up the pavilion set for our wedding. Thankfully, some people held it firmly, and the custom Pheres, taking seven rounds of the pious fire, got completed somehow.

I had concealed one more fact at our marriage, but it seems incredibly relevant to share. My Jai mala got broken when we sat after the Pheres ritual. But I didn't let anyone realise it. I just fixed it secretly. Had this secret been revealed, they would have added one more lousy omen to our marriage's list. Shashi would have been the victim of the additional humiliation.

Even today, if people had come to know about it, my family, too, could have been trapped in the trap of a bad omen. The text of the comments could no longer be a mystery. But I have known since the beginning about such worthless superstitions. If I had shared the episode with my wife, she could have been under certain insecurities and ill-conceived notions. I am making it public now, where there is no room for it to turn into a bad omen because we have passed the stages of life of an ill omen.

We got married, but her family's anger was still not subdued. Because of their antagonism, the family did not give us the sofa set that Shashi's aunt had gifted at our wedding. A wardrobe was available in the house for the marriage, which got lost because of the family's anger. Yes, we got a cycle gifted to us by Shashi's uncle, which was of great help to us for years in fulfilling our transport needs.

We are the backbone of arranging eight marriages in my family on our own. We did not let any business for dowry occupy any space in the marriage process. It was everybody's privilege to manage the way one desires. I am sharing the episode of the gifts regarding our marriage only to reveal that the gift presented by relatives and friends cannot reach the deserving hand. It is a punishment to the couple marrying for their love and choice. It sounds awkward to see and hear.

This is how our struggle attained the goal of marriage as a witness of our genuine love. Our house had four rooms, two of which were newly constructed and did not have doors. Though we were both earners, we couldn't even dream of going out for a honeymoon trip. After all, we, the poor guys, celebrated our honeymoon in a room without doors, which we called our drawing room. No matter how many storms come into our lives, our family lives continue with the same passion.

In this episode, one of the most remarkable and witty comments came from the orthodox corner, from Shashi's grandfather, at the time of farewell: "This is the first time a girl from our community is entering a different community. My child, remember that no action of yours must defame our family and community name." Having lived over forty years of married life, I find it the most beautiful gift that reminds us how we should lead our life, discouraging the caste mentality. In this way, we defeated the caste demon within the Dalit society and laid the foundation for preventing caste discrimination. The result is that in Shashi's and my family, there is no space for caste discrimination and religious disparity.

---oOo---

CHAPTER SIX

An Event That Made Me An Author

My life is a blend of many coincidences. My access to the writing area is also a strange co-occurrence. The credit goes to Mr. S.D. Tyagi lives in my vicinity. He is a very active and committed volunteer in RSS. One day, he came to my house and left a leaflet protesting conversion. The leaflet contained a Hindi quotation referring to Gandhi Ji. An overview of the content is: 'If Christians, instead of purely humanitarian work and serving the poor by medical aid, education, etc., get involved in conversion, I will ask them to leave because the religion of every nation is equally superior to the religion of any other nation. Surely, the religions of India are enough for the people here. We do not need religious conversion." (Gandhi, Vol 45 p. 339)

It was true to life for me to be uneasy after passing through Gandhi Ji's comment. Several questions agitated me regarding this leaflet. I realised Gandhi Ji knew that the living conditions of the poor were terrible. He also knew well the poor social and economic conditions of the Dalits and tribal communities responsible for their inferior education and health conditions. But Gandhi Ji was not worried about the community's beastly social environment that was responsible for the religious conversion. He, too, was more bothered about rectifying these threatening circumstances?

Gandhi Ji seemed comfortable prioritising the religion and its worthless practices rather than the life of Dalits and tribes. It was merely a green pasture for most of the hypocrites engaged in the politics of religion to flourish at the cost of the ignorant masses from the lower strata. My quarry was that our constitution advocated the nation's secular character, which is what the national religion Gandhi Ji talked about. The question kept pinching me whether Gandhi Ji's hidden agenda was to keep upholding Hinduism as the nation's religion under the disguise of secularism. He asked the British or missionaries to avoid conversion and, if not, quit the country. No matter whether the conditions of the Dalit tribal get worse without missionaries' support.

The idea was unfolding in me to conclude that Gandhi Ji's love was simply an eyewash that had nothing to do with reality. Is Gandhi Ji's adoption of skimpy clothes a part of Gandhi Ji's strategy to be a Mahatma? If not, what stopped him from paying any cost for the upliftment of the poor? He should also have realised that the person or society lacks education and usually lacks sufficient food to survive. He shouldn't have ignored the innocent guys with malnutrition and multiple diseases that make their lives miserable, ultimately the prey to untimely death. Does religion make any sense for those who have their lives at stake and uncertainty? I wondered why Gandhiji prioritised faith at the cost of the poor's hunger, education, and health.

If an enormous mass of poor guys would survive no more, what pickle of religion would Gandhiji wish to make for? It seemed Gandhiji, too, was a follower of the beaten track, which laypeople do. They mean for the religion, not the faith, for the people to emancipate them morally and face the challenges in life. The business of politics or the politics of the business of religion has nothing to do with the life of the masses. Nothing matters if morality and ethics have become foreign to politics and faith today. But I was concerned about Gandhi Ji then, a person known as the father of the nation whose comment did not leave me a trace of sleep that night. I could also see Gandhi's thinking pygmy at the country's level. Why could he not understand that a country's foremost condition of progress depends on the quality of education and health? If we consider it in terms of India, religion has nothing to do with this. What the faith advocates is different; it safeguards the superiority of a specific class ruling over the society. Dalits and tribes are bound to pay a heavy price for thousands of years. I was enraged and helpless in dealing with the critical situation I got entangled in.

I must not, but I learned that Gandhi Ji was no less a fundamentalist who kept religion on the top, then the country, and then the citizens. Whether or not the citizens can stand on their feet, faith must enjoy the supreme status. The questions that had provoked me about the leaflet got me agitated overnight. It is because religion's advocates have given legitimacy to wicked practices in the name of religion. Hence, mob lynching or other daily acts of hooliganism have become standard features of our day-to-day lives. Terrorist activities like 'Love Jihad' and 'Ghar Wapsi' have also become a mirror of society and country.

Before I could overcome the pain Gandhiji's statement provoked, Swamiji appeared before me. Swamiji means Swami Vivekananda. His presence seemed to me no less torturous than a monster. It may not be enough for RSS to have Gandhiji in the leaflet; they quoted Swami Vivekananda as Brahmastra: 'If a member of the Hindu society converts, not only does the number of the society decline but an enemy of the Hindu society grows.' The thought added petrol to the fire the RSS leaflet had set in sharing Gandhiji's views on religion rather than the involvement of Christian missionaries in education, health, and, ultimately, the conversion.

I found the conversion of Dalits, the victims of Hinduism, a helpful option to take revenge on the enemy. Vivekananda considered us enemies only because he did not like our education, health, and betterment. Keeping us weak strengthened Vivekananda and others like him, as the process was reciprocal. The practice has been for thousands of years to keep the Dalit in slave-like conditions. Suddenly, I remembered his World Conference of Religions in Chicago, USA. In this gathering, he addressed the world representatives as brothers and sisters, and as claimed, there was a lot of applause. A question struck abruptly: when people of all religions in the world conference were brothers and sisters to Swami ji, how did the converted people in India become the enemies of Hinduism, the faith he practised and preached broadly and faithfully?

The logic made me conclude double standards are in the blood of staunch Hindus and the advocates of Hinduism. On the one hand, this so-called faithful breed of Hinduism treats Dalits and Adivasis as lower than an animal. Conversely, suppose any local or foreign missionaries work for their education, health, social and overall upliftment. In that case, they conspire to maintain the status quo of Dalit-Adivasis as a religion. Hence, the so-called sages, sannyasis, Mahatmas, Swamis, Acharyas, Dharmacharyas,

Shankaracharyas, Bapus, Mahants, etc., pretend to be the friends of the oppressed classes, but are merely eye wash, even today, a well-rehearsed hypocrisy of ethics. Throughout the night, it trapped me in the maze of these Mahatmas, Swamies and RSS, and I woke up in the morning with a strange restlessness.

It was Sunday, but the peace of mind was missing. Eventually, I could not abide by it for long, so I reached one of my friends, Mr Jai Prakash Kardam's house, living in the neighbouring DDA flat. I knew him as a writer. I knew him well because my wife, Shashi Gangania, and his wife, Tara Kardam, worked in a school in Amar Colony headed by MCD, Delhi. Both were excellent friends. Because of this, once or twice, Kardam Ji visited my previous house with his wife in Balram Nagar, Ghaziabad, U.P. Such meetings helped us become well acquainted even for mutually comfortable discussions. It was a plus point of the forum in neighbouring DDA flats on Loni Road.

As I recall, it was 1999. It was the first time Kardam Ji was editing a journal named Dalit Varshiki, a Dalit Annul journal. I visited his house and told him, 'Look, what are these RSS people plotting?'. I poured out everything that was boiling in me after receiving the leaflet. He shook his neck in affirmation and kept registering his consent. But he did not lose his temper till I explained. Finally, his calm reaction came, 'Write whatever you feel on this issue. I will see what I can do with it.'

I said, 'Okay, I will.'

Though I had written nothing before this commitment. I had yet to comprehend how to write on such an independent subject. Yes, I would write poems and essays for the students to read or recite in school programmes organised on different occasions.

Regarding writing something other than the school agendas, I recall writing some love letters without the spirit of love to Kusum. I am reminded of another exciting anecdote regarding writing. When Shashi and my hopes of engagement got lost, I got engaged to Mr Shankar Lal's daughter. He was an employee in the Aligarh lock factory. It may sound awkward that I don't remember the girl's name now.

It was 1981 when I was working as a primary teacher in MCD, Delhi. Because of some reason, this engagement could not reach the goal of marriage. I wrote several letters to Mr Shankar Lal to get the wedding proposal cancelled. It was difficult for a father to bear the pain of such a negation. Mr Shankar Lal was not an exception. He used satirical language in one letter during correspondence: 'Looking at the notes, you should be a writer, but alas! You remained a primary teacher.'

Mr Shankar Lal took my post as a primary teacher, a poorly equipped professional. The other side of the coin is that if I had not refused to marry his daughter, my being a primary teacher would be an elegance. He might not have given this response to depress me, but I was not disappointed and took it as a compliment. Today, while I am talking about this issue, Mr Shankar Lal, though he was a mechanic in a lock factory with little education, was worthy of judging me as a writer, which I couldn't claim on my own. But I was not at all a writer. Even in my response to the leaflet, I did not see myself as a future writer. Such a thought did not emerge in my mind. On the contrary, being an author of someone was a big deal for me, which I wasn't even in my dreams. From this point of view, Mr Kardam was an outstanding, rather towering personality for me.

As Mr Kardam suggested, I recorded my reaction to religious conversion the same night and rejected Gandhi Ji's and Swami Vivekananda's arguments state-forwardly. Not only this, but I also discussed the issue as a conspiracy of RSS quoting the two renowned personalities. The next day, I appeared before Mr Kardam with my write-up. Having read it, he said, 'You have written an excellent piece of an article. Your language is also excellent.' he also assured me, 'I will print it in my Dalit Varshiki.' Eventually, my first write-up became a part of the first annual Dalit journal under the editorship of Dr Jai Prakash Kardam. It was when I got consoled by putting my point of view that naturally was contrary to Mr Gandhi, Vivekananda and the RSS, the persistent advocates of Hinduism.

Dr Kardam repeated his words of distinction and reassurance, and his enthusiastic body language moved me. Even then, Dr Kardam's praiseworthy statements were confined to the article and nothing else. I want to share another issue: The first proof of my response covered four magazine pages. Dr Kardam asked me to proof it. I said, 'Do it independently; what better proof I can have than you.'

Today, when I recall not reading proofs, I realise how ignorant I was. I learned the importance of proofreading my write-ups while working under Dr Tej Singh as a subeditor in Apeksha, a quarterly journal for literary criticism. It was an agreement that the composer, Mr Awadhesh, would provide two drafts of the magazine. But depending on my affinities, I would take three and sometimes even four drafts of my write-ups. My write-ups were often extended by up to 25 to 30 percent because of these proofreadings.

I enjoyed reading my article, 'Conversions and Dalits, ' published in Dalit Varshiki, Dr Kardam's annual journal.

Even today, whenever I go through my first article, I wonder if I had written this article with no plan and understanding of writing skills, but brilliantly. The journey of the article on conversion did not end up getting published in Dalit Varshiki. Later, Dr Kardam included this article in his book, which was specially planned for views on conversion. Out of the thirteen write-ups compiled in it, one is mine with the changed title: ' Conversion: Society and Hindu Manas'. He gave the title of my article to the book: 'Conversions and Dalits.' It is a matter of pride for me, and credit goes to Dr Kardam.

I was a lecturer in English, now, not a primary teacher, and had joined the community of writers. I realised what I didn't know about myself, Mr Shankar Lal from Aligarh had announced twenty years ago. It was a satire to humiliate me as a primary teacher. Should I call it his far-sightedness, frustration or something else? It turned me into a boon, not a curse.

With the article's publication, I was attracted to Dr Kardam not as the husband of his wife's friend Shashi but as a lover of writing. I also got the author's copy and read it several times. It would be a mistake if I didn't mention the journal Dalit Varshiki was based on Dr Ambedkar's philosophy. In this episode, one more surprising point is that till 1999, I knew nothing about Dr Ambedkar. I read my article first and then reviewed others published in the journal. While passing through it, I read about Dr Ambedkar for the first time. I admit this was my first time reading about Dr Ambedkar. It would be better to credit Dr Kardam for introducing me to Dr Ambedkar.

I often hear from my literary friends that they had heard about Dr Ambedkar at a very early age or read about him during school. Such statements give me an inferiority complex even today. Why couldn't I read him earlier? The question forced me to look at my past to find something to console the loss. This is not because we could not look outside the world where Dr Ambedkar put everything at stake. I confess it must be my backwardness.

Because of the turmoil of these questions, I face strange confusion in finding the reasons today. Reflecting on my father's life, I see him submitting to too many social activities. But even today, nothing in my memory leads me to Dr Ambedkar's thoughts and philosophy. I noted that our house's main walls displayed calendars like Netaji Subhash, Bhagat Singh, Nehru, Gandhi, Bhim, Arjun, Karni-Bharni, etc. I don't remember any picture of Dr Bhim Rao Ambedkar among them. It bothers me to think If my father was unaware of Babasaheb's Struggle. If not, why? If yes, why do I not remember any of the conversations about him? Whatever it has been, it makes me uneasy, but I didn't surrender.

Chasing the reason, I came across the Arya Samaj that left no space for Dr Ambedkar's thoughts. My father, too, was under the influence of Arya Samaj since childhood because he was a student at Kumar Ashram, Meerut, Uttar Pradesh, an institution famous for Arya Samaj's practices. The area where I lived in Haryana had Arya Samaj deep-rooted in its practice and preachings. So, there were rare caste clashes. Dr Ambedkar's movement primarily had its roots in eradicating caste prejudices responsible for inequality and anarchy in society to hamper the peace and progress of the substantial section of society. Hence, no caste prejudice means Dr Ambedkar did not influence Haryana. It would be a blunder if we confine Dr Ambedkar to caste alone; his canvas of thoughts, whether local or global, brilliantly attracts the world community. Another reason for the time when I learned about Dr Ambedkar might be my family, which was struggling for livelihood badly and left no space to study additional books other than the syllabus. I was only an ox of a crusher during that time.

Naturally, it was an appropriate time for me to enter the world of authors as my children had entered the self-study mode, and I owned a house. I have also completed my master's in English and Political Science and earned my professional degree, B. Ed. I have already mentioned other additional qualifications. Overall, this time was suitable for diverse study and writing on social issues, the need of the hour as a responsible citizen. Having gotten my first article published in Dr Kardam's Dalit Varshiki (Annual), the passion has not let me rest to date.

Kardam Ji's school of thought was and still is a school for Dalit literature. So, I read only what Dr Kardam's school syllabus contained. This school trained me to look at everything around me through the lens of caste, which I had never taken like that before. My passion opened the doors to composing poetry as an addiction. So, most of the leisurely hours were spent weaving the fabric of poetry. My nights turned as if synonymous with restlessness. Hence, no night passed without a notebook and pencil close to my pillow. Whatever caused turmoil under the semiconscious state would become a rough pen portrait of my poetry. I couldn't afford the dreams or thoughts to go wasted for nothing without coming into a poetic frame. Rarely, if I failed to do so, it annoyed me. I, too, could not afford annoyance; that is why paper and pen became the sole companions of my pillow and sleep.

I would present whatever I wrote before Dr Kardam when he returned from the office. I was so keen, somewhat selfish, to get feedback on my writings from Dr Kardam that I would not mind a little of his personal life and comfort. I realised the bitter truth when Dr Kardam commented in front of our familiar friend: 'When I come here in the office, Satya Prakash brings his writings, and when I go home, I found Gangania and his wife waiting for me. This affects my writing, and I cannot write anything new.' Dr Kardam's remark was logical and justified. It shook me badly, and I realised my passion for literature made me too blind to see Dr Kardam's helplessness. I feel guilty for the disturbance I caused in Dr Kardam's life because of the blindness of my passion for literature.

Meanwhile, my first poetry collection, 'Har Nahin Manoonga' was ready for further review. I fixed a Sunday with Dr Tej Singh, Rajni Tilak, and Jai Prakash Kardam to complete at my residence. We accomplished the job of eating Pakodas and other snacks with tea. The pattern was that I read each verse, and everyone listened carefully and critically to comment. This friend circle made certain amendments to the lyrics faithfully wherever necessary. Then, a second assessment round took place to refine the content. It turned out like a mini workshop. I sincerely thank my colleagues for their spare time and valuable suggestions. Eventually, my first collection of poems, ' Haar Nahi Manoonga', was published in collaboration with Dr Kardam.

With Dr Kardam's incredible support, we launched the poetry collection 'Haar Nahi Manoonga' on 05. 11. 2000 in the Constitutional Club, Delhi, in a splendid hall. It is a matter of pride for me that in this program, national level personalities, Kamleshwar, Dr Maheep Singh, editor of Sanchetna, Dr Tej Singh, Balbir Madhopuri, editor of a Punjabi edition of Yojna Patrika, Mohandas Nemishray, Rajni Tilak, Jai Prakash Lilwan, Writers like Surajpal

Chauhan etc took part with enthusiasm. The hall had other literature lovers, family members, and acquaintances. I am confident that I have released no book to date, as well as the release of my first collection of poetry. Indeed, this launch was a memorable release in every respect.

I also feel remorse for causing a disturbance during Dr Kardam's leisurely hours, which his family deserved more than anybody else. In the preface of my book ' Haar Nahi Manoonga', I have already confessed the blunder that took place unintentionally, and I have the burden of it even today. Another notable fact I feel necessary to share is since the publication of my first book in 2000, Dr Kardam and I lived as good neighbours till 2020 and shared each other's sorrows and joys equally for twenty years; about two dozen of my books are available in the market. I never took advantage of Dr Kardam for my literary upliftment or growth. Now that he has shifted to Dwarka, there is no question for my past mistakes to chase him anymore. On a light note, our future is free from any undue disturbance for each other.

I am grateful to Dr Kardam for allowing me to participate in Dalit Varshiki, which paved the way to becoming an author. In this episode of giving credit, I would sincerely thank my neighbour, Mr Tyagi, and the RSS. If I had not received that leaflet, I would not have gone to Dr Kardam, nor would I have become an author.

Apart from the above ifs and buts associated with my being an author, I would like to term it as the result of Niyati, which is determinism. It has no business with fatalism. Wherever I talk about Niyati, it is mandatory to keep clarifying that determinism is not fatalism as it has direct roots in theism. It is just determinism, so certain things are beyond the individual's reach, but keeping connected to the individual's life is essential. Being an author is a clear example to illustrate my belief.

---OOO---

CHAPTER SEVEN

Love For Legacy And Loyalty

Legacy and loyalty have no set of mathematics. They can make a person responsible and open the giant doors to struggle. I have always had multiple doors opened to harbor my love. I don't understand when these commitments crossed my personal and family boundaries to become a permanent part of my personality. Before I talk about the incidents of devotion to duties in my life, I need to know their sources and where the gush gets in? This search led me to reflect on how my parents lived through their activities, and I found that they inherited a love for legacy and commitment in me. However, we are four brothers and two sisters. I want to avoid getting caught up in scrutinising what amount they inherited. They have choices of their own to live with no resemblance to mine.

My mother's name is Hukam Kaur. I do not know how 'Kaur' became the last name. Generally, it indicates the common identity of Sikh ladies. My mother was my maternal grandparents, Hriday Ram and Balwanti Devi's second child among five siblings. They lived in Khekra, Meerut, Uttar Pradesh. They had no land to cultivate but were associated with multiple agricultural activities as labourers. My mother generally shared her experiences harvesting sugarcane, where her parents engaged primarily. At night, she obliged my maternal grandfather to mill sugarcane from the crusher. She often said, ' Bapu, you are exhausted enough; go to sleep for a while. I will wake you up after midnight.' She replaced him with his manly job and jealously offered her services like a dedicated boy. Her sole intention was to free him from any embarrassment of a son's support. Hence, she didn't wake him as she often promised. Sometimes, he woke up bothered and bound for a fatherly scold for not waking him up earlier. But my mother had a set reply to ensure more and more comfort as a daughter was no longer inferior to a son.

When there was no sugarcane season, she worked in the field throughout the day or took several rounds to carry cattle fodder on her head from the farm to the house. She also actively participated in activities like preparing buffalo fodder and milking buffaloes. When my maternal uncle was not born, my mother would say to my maternal grandfather – 'Bapu, nothing to worry about; you don't have a son. I am your son. Whatever a son can do, I will do it brilliantly. So, nothing to worry about. I will see everything.' It was not that her other three sisters were insincere; they supported family affairs nicely, like a boy. But my mother had a dominance to cover up the absence of a son in the family.

Consequently, she managed to do what a son is expected to do, such as massaging a father's waist while bathing, preparing Hookah and filling Chillum, etc., which are essential even today for village life as a daily routine.

My mother had to pass through the same village life in Kundli as she had lived in Khekra after my father's retirement when we had no other scope for our living. The time stretch was from the year 1973- 1974 to the year 1980.

My mother worked more vigorously during this period than any male farmer or labourer. She carried the family out of the troubles when the family had no way to escape the ocean of problems. I have already discussed the issue in detail in a previous chapter. Yes, an episode needs to have space here. My uncle's son Om Pal Singh came to our house from our ancestor's village, Rathora. He was a graduate but needed a job. It was remarkable when it came to keeping him in our home during the economic crisis and helping him as a family member; my mother did not object. She took all his obligations, considering him her seventh child. He got his B.Ed. Degree and lived with us to get a job. Before getting a job, there were offers for his marriage, and finally, he got married in Sonepat, Haryana. She bore all the liabilities faithfully like a mother; whatever expenses were incurred in marriage, the family stood firmly by the commitment while facing terrible financial conditions.

My father, Mr Naveen Chandra, has been a classic example of tackling such critical issues since childhood, which was the pivot of the episode. He had lost his mother, I mean our grandmother, in his childhood. My grandfather, Mr Rodhe Ram, as my father shared with us during emotional moments, was not sincere enough in my father's upbringing. I am still determining how my father went to Kumar Ashram, Meerut, in childhood and stayed there. It was the time of freedom struggle in India; he would tell us that he passed posters on walls at night and carried out some sporadic activities. I need to find out from where and how he took training in making slippers, shoes, office bags, briefcases, and bedding. But based on this skill, he and my uncle, Shri Buddhadev Arya, worked in a briefcase-making factory in Delhi. They lived in a hut in Nehru Kutiya, Delhi. My mother told us that after working all day, they dug out stones from the ground at night. They had made two huts using a heap of stones.

The people from Dalit communities in our paternal village, Rathora, and the neighbouring villages own no cultivation land and no source of income other than landless labourers or could be seasonal Killen workers. So, unemployed guys from those towns visited my father for jobs and support. He would wholeheartedly keep a separate hut for such frequent visitors. He managed his family affairs in a single shed. It was not limited to their shelter, but their feeding and other essential financial support needed for travelling to interviews, etc., were met by compromising the family's needs. In return for the selfless service, my father asked them to take an oath: 'Having got a job, you shall help at least one candidate get a job or become self-dependent.'

Though his economic resources were limited, my father managed by minimising family expenses. The family followed a simple diet and lifestyle. The question didn't strike my mind while he was alive; perhaps he was influenced by Mr Gandhi, so he wore a Khadi dhoti-kurta or Pyjama.

When my father got a job in the Haryana Government, he left for his destination. He handed over his hut to my distant maternal grandfather, Mr Hari Singh, to live in as he had no abode in Delhi. He also had come to Delhi in search of work. After some time, the settlement at Nehru Kutiya was vacated, and each occupant was allotted a plot of eighty yards in Tagore Garden, Delhi, for the replacement. But my father left all that for my maternal grandfather, who got a plot. Several of our relatives and my mother insisted my father get his rights to the property, but the father did not budge. Although my maternal grandfather initially said the property was ours, my father was made of a different clay to tell where he would go with the children. He knew he couldn't afford a new apartment as a class four employee. My father never asserted his authority over the property.

My father's generosity was not confined to such a singular example. When my father was at his government job, it was typical for one after the other to keep visiting our house to seek monetary help. My father was unfamiliar with 'Denial', and the family often had to compromise on simple expenses. Some relatives visited asking for a new loan without paying the previous one. Some did not even return the money because they couldn't. In such a situation, I often saw my father arguing with my mother on such issues, but in vain.

It was my father's generosity. He dug a well at his own expense, facing the Chaupal on a roadside in Kharkhoda, Haryana. He also got an iron bucket tied with an iron chain for the public. It was one of the easy ways for the passersby and the people of the settlement to fulfil their water needs. He took this step, knowing his tenure in Kharkhoda was only one year.

When we permanently settled in Kundli, He formed a thrift and credit society locally to solve the monetary issues and traditional loans. This paved the way for freedom from the exploitation of moneylenders. Primarily the guys from Chamar and Valmiki communities were the sole beneficiaries of the endeavour. A Valmiki family in the village was too poor to repay the loan and had two daughters on the verge of marriage age. My father arranged a non-refundable loan based on consensus to solve the issue. Once, my father stood surety against a big loan to some guys from neighbouring Narela, Delhi, but they failed to pay the debt. Honouring his words, my father gave his buffalo to the moneylender.

Similarly, there is another big story about the same village, Kundli. My father bought twenty bighas of land for farming in the town in the early years of his service. The maintenance of agriculture was unmanageable when my father got transferred from Kundli. Some conspiracies, like grabbing our land, came to light. My father's peaceful flavour of life had no space for any controversies. That's why he sold that land to the Sarpanch family of the village just at throw-away prices. However, the trading needed the appropriate authorisation of the land. It was not taken care of by either party. When my father returned to reside in Kundli permanently, some prominent villagers approached him to let him know that the ownership still rested in his favour. They tried to lure him to get it back legally with their direct intervention, but in vain. It was extreme when one day, the new village sarpanch, probably named Chhotu Ram, I need to remember correctly, approached our house in Balram Nagar, UP. He had brought some papers prepared and said, 'Master Ji, just sign these papers and nothing else to do. He offered a hefty amount for the signature.

The land was now a costly industrial area of Kundli, at a prime location. My father flatly refused, saying, 'Chowdhary Sahib, it is the question of my words I honour desperately at any cost. No price can tempt me to compromise. Sorry, I can't help you.' At last, Choudhary Sahib had to return empty-handed, somewhat disappointed. It proved the final attempt to test my father's firmness to the principles he had set for him.

It is worth mentioning that it was an episode that took place around 1980 when we suffered a terrible debt of three thousand and had no way to settle it. We were five siblings, including one sister, all unmarried. My father's skills for making money had turned worthless. Primarily, I was the sole breadwinner of a family of seven members. One day, a neighbourhood property dealer, Mr Gupta, approached our house and asked humbly, 'Master ji, what do you do all day long at home. Come to my office. Oversee the work of tea and water and maintain the office. It will help you make some money and be a good time pass. I need some help.' My father preferred making tea, washing filthy utensils, and faithfully obeying Mr Gupta but rejected the corrupt trade of crores against his principles.

My father worked as a tea maker and caretaker in a property dealer's office, which pinched the family. Still, he had no option for the family in a do, or dying situation. It was soothing that Mr. Gupta never treated him as a servant but as an older adult worthy of respect. Whatever it was, my father did it passionately. Meanwhile, Mr Gupta renovated his office; he gave extra articles like iron beams, wooden sticks, and stones in negligible pieces. My wife and I had no option but to honeymoon in a room made of this material without doors. Now, it is used as a drawing room in Balram Nagar.

It is the bitter truth of my family. Another bitter one is that my country's vast crowd, rather than the upper strata, is available today with an invisible tag for sale. It is painful to see our constitutional institutions without a backbone. Their episodes remind me of Rajesh Khanna's film 'Aaj Ka MLA Ram Avatar'. In this film, Rajesh Khanna has files of each MLA containing everything in black and white of their life to control their malicious activities. He forces them to work in the public interest rather than satisfy his selfish goals.

Contemporary rulers also follow Rajesh Khanna's film. But here, the situation looks a bit different. The regime gets the leaders and the bureaucracy to do whatever the boss desires, whether or not it satisfies the public's needs. It may be another issue, but something broad black is crystal clear at the bottom. Righteousness is inaccessible, while fraudulence is convenient. It is a matter of an individual's preference to stand with or go against.

Let me come to the legacy of loyalty, an integral part of my life. In 1977, when I was about twenty, I temporarily got my first job in Haryana. My monthly income was Rs. 322 to hand it over to my mother. There was a strange trend in our life: expenses emerged first, then income. It came into existence with my cousin Om Pal's marriage, and within a year, my elder sister also got married. This expenditure was met by my salary savings, a loan from a thrift and credit society and the return of funds paid at the time of marriages in the neighbourhood as a Shagun (gift) for years.

At 22, the responsibility of two marriages had made me as profound and calm as an elderly family member, as if I were the father of my sisters and brothers, not a youth. My father's pension was of little help. The legacy of commitment and taking responsibility automatically rested on my shoulders, as my parents had inherited it at an early age.

When we left the village Kundli in 1980, my first responsibility was to ensure a roof overhead. We got Rs. 8000 by selling what we had of our own for the family. Since Dec. 1978, I have had a permanent job in Delhi with a monthly salary of Rs. 567. We needed more left by purchasing a plot in Balram Nagar, UP. We hired a mason on daily wages and did the labour all together. Taking the lead in carrying out the obligations did not mean I had a special status in the family as a Chaudhary. I was the one among us in the family but always prioritised my parents' sole desires.

My marriage to Shashi Bala was the third one in Balram Nagar, Loni, Ghaziabad, UP, in June 1982. Two of my brothers were doing apprenticeships in the DTC workshop and got a nominal stipend. The best part of this marriage was her joining the legacy I inherited as an equal partner. She never shirked back to date to let us go victorious. Shortly after our wedding, my younger brother Raj Kumar left the house and went somewhere unannounced and returned, embracing Christianity.

Now, it was another big assignment for my younger sister Raj Kumari's marriage that squarely engaged both of us, husband and wife. We both owned memberships in Nagrik Sahakari Bank and Vishnu Co-Operative Thrift and Credit Society, which proved to be one of our life's best sources of getting loans as lifelines to satisfy our financial needs. One of our distant relatives helped us find a suitable match for my sister. The boy was then educated in Geography and worked in the post office. For me, his job, educational qualifications and general appearance, resembling us, were enough to go ahead. Whether or not the boy had a house and another basic requirement essential for a comfortable married life was immaterial to me. I discussed the issue with my parents to seek their consent. Ultimately, the whole family agreed to proceed, and gradually, one ritual after another reached the appropriate goal. Finally, the marriage took place graciously, and they lived happily married. My brother-in-law Ramesh Chand Javeria is retired from the post of income tax officer and is committed to furthering literature with the title Vidrohi 'a Rebel'.

It took a year or two for us to pay off the loans. After this, another separate accommodation was built for my younger brother Satish Kumar, considering his marriage and the privacy the couple needs after marriage. This could be possible with the financial support of the finance society and the bank. The thrift and credit society and the bank had the facility to borrow another loan by paying at least three-fourths of the existing loans, and the remaining debt was added to the new loans. The exact process of arranging funds for accommodation and my youngest brother's marriage was chosen. It consumed the prime youth of our life as husband and wife. But we had and still have great relief, having four brothers and two sisters, including my cousin Ompal Singh and my eldest sister Chandra Kanta, who were faithfully married. My younger brother Raj Kumar had been married to Christian customs independently without any information or involvement of the family. The family learned of his marriage when he visited home with his wife to get her introduced. I feel delighted to have a legacy of sweet and sour experiences of my journey while I passed through the different marriage episodes.

While busy with my joint family affairs, Hem Raj Gupta, a friend from my village and colleague at Jamia Teachers College, often remarked on my exhausting and selfless involvement in my family– 'Master Kyun Bawala Ho Raha Hai. Koi Bahan-Bhai Kisi Ka Nahi Hota. Sab Matlab Ki Duniya Hai' meant, 'Why are you getting mad in family affairs. No brother or sister is akin to anybody else. The world is of vested interests.' I never got discouraged by what he opined about brothers and sisters and the world. His concern for me was based on his family value system, but my thinking was contrary. My value system never lets me think that 'I' am someone special or doing something incredible. Looking back on the past and living in the present, one thought dominates me: I am no one else to do anything as something outstanding. I always took it as a normal course and followed it with no idea of any credit. The circumstances take me on like a natural flow of river water in a rhythmic way in solace. I knew we were a joint family, a single unit, and we had to stand together like we had been a unit since childhood under our parents. It sometimes disturbs me to think that most of my sisters and brothers have grown up wise and too grown up, and they do not seem even to think of family togetherness in childhood and youth. But I have no longing to grow up like that. I cannot afford to be deprived of my remaining obligations to be a family. I want to possess whatever is left in the name of the family, my parents' legacy.

Now, all three brothers were self-dependent and had families. The parental property in two hundred yards in Balaram Nagar was divided into four parts. I handed over my share to my elder sister because her financial condition was insufficient. Even today, she lives in the same house with her family. I shifted to the MIG (DDA) flat East of Loni Road, Delhi-93.

Shifting here, we need to share what the most challenging job was like. My wife had a transport problem reaching her serving place. Her patience gave way one day, and she insisted on not staying in Balram Nagar. When the issue of purchasing the flat became a severe concern, my younger brother-in-law, Manbir Singh, informed us about an apartment in his precinct. I talked about my financial inability. Still, he insisted, saying, 'Dare to manage a little; Rest we will see somehow. We are not far from you.' After thirty years of a relationship, he is still more intimate than a brother. I am proud to have a younger brother in Manbir Singh, not a brother-in-law. He is always like a troubleshooter in the hour of our needs.

There was a question of having 2.5 lakhs, and my pocket was empty. I talked to Hem Raj Gupta, who had discouraged me from spending money on a joint family, saying—'Dude, I want to buy a flat.' He asked me the cost. I told him flatly. He further asked, 'How much do you expect from me?' I said, 'Total.' Instantly, he consented to his support in buying the property.

In 1993, 2.5 lakh was a giant amount for me. My friend's assurance encouraged me, and I zealously explored other sources within my reach. My wife Shashi and I withdrew an advance from our GPF and arranged debt from Nagrik Sahakari Bank and Vishnu Co-Operative Society. Manbir Singh supported me as promised. Ultimately, I needed only twenty thousand rupees from Hem Raj Gupta. I have no words other than that if Hem Raj Gupta had not assured me of the capital, I couldn't have dared to buy the property.

Paying the debt was a mammoth challenge, and savings from our salary couldn't meet it. We needed to explore ways of making money rather than minimising expenses. Being a teacher, I knew that compromising my children's education was a blunder at the cost of buying property, but I had to. I enrolled my son and daughter in a government school for one year, but soon, I rectified it by enrolling them in Green Field School, one of the best in our vicinity.

To deal with the financial crisis, a teacher has no worthy option other than giving private tuition. Since I was an English teacher with ample scope, I only cared about rigorous working hours, ignoring adverse effects on my health. I was up at 5:30 AM to work until 8:30 PM. The routine continued more or less from 1993 to 1998.

It was to meet critical financial needs, not as a lust for money. Life was no longer routine, but I didn't compromise on teaching students, my job and my sole responsibility. I knew some of my friends who were loyal to tutoring and visited the school to rest without concern for the morality of being teachers.

Despite having such a rigorous workload, it is remarkable that I did my post-graduation in English as a private student in 1994-95 from Himachal University. It needed some extra time for preparation, which was unaffordable. It was when the students' exams drew nearer and required more attention from me on both fronts. It was a test of my devotion to duty and my morality. I couldn't be selfish and betray what I had earned with loyalty to duty, my parents' legacy. How I resolved it demands detailed discussion in the next chapter to deal with miracle-like events that are just like regular and enthusiastic in my life.

It doesn't mean that my legacy of owning obligations is confined to my family alone; it has been an essential part of my life, but the pattern is slightly different. While serving as a primary school teacher, I contributed equally to sports. As mentioned earlier, I was an integral part of the team our sports bosses selected for the residential camp of students for special coaching to participate at the central level during the Dussehra holidays. While working in Yamuna Vihar B-block, one day during the regional competition, my headmaster, Sukh Lal Sharma, asked a fellow sportsperson, Devendra Sharma, who won the Kabaddi championship. Devendra Sharma said arrogantly, Ghonda North, his school, and who else would win?

The students of Ghonda North school used to win in games like Throw-Bal, Kabaddi, Kho-Kho, etc., because they were rough and tough as they were from a rural environment. Our urban background students could not match their height, stamina, etc. That day, I committed to myself to challenge Devendra Sharma's ego. Since I was posted on the evening shift, I had a tuning session with the headmistress of the shift school. Hence, I would reach the first shift in the morning around 10:30 and coach my kids in different games. When the next regional competition occurred, we beat Ghonda North in Kabaddi, Throw Ball, Teni Quiet and Kho-Kho; they had a monopoly. The school's honour board comprised sports students and me as a coach this year. There was no extra remuneration for such work other than feeling proud.

In 1988, I got promoted to TGT (English) in a school in Gokul Pur village. This school was operated in DDA Park with no building but hedged with Eucalyptus trees all around, and some shady trees and shrubs were also there. Many Khalifa-type teachers from Gokul Puri School were deputed here in this school to harass them. The school began around 10.30 AM and closed at 12.30 PM, roughly for two hours daily. I want to name it a unique and unbelievable school worldwide. In the name of physical resources, the school had two large polythene sheets, two rugs/large carpets, and an iron box to keep school records, such as teachers' and students' attendance, and other registers used for different purposes. Wooden blackboard, chalk, etc., necessary for initial school running were kept in a store-type room of the village headman, based on a personal and mutual understanding between the teachers and the headman. In the morning, whatever was necessary was brought to the park. There was no furniture, and teachers used polythene under each carpet, one for the office and the other for the staff members. The teacher in charge also used to sit on either of these two rugs. The student brought whatever they could afford for their seating. When the school hours were over, all the belongings were returned to the head's house.

In the morning, this park used to be the open toilet of some people in the village. People often visited the park to defecate while the school was occupied with boys and girls students, teachers, and engaged in teaching activities. In summer, the classes were held under trees and in winter, under the open sky in the sun. Twenty minutes were set for each subject per day, considering the total duration of two hours of school.

Along with me, a teacher named Kishan Swaroop also joined the school on promotion. We had never seen or even thought of such a ridiculous show in the name of education and school. While the senior Khalifa-type teachers enjoyed the show, we were severely scared of the drama, thinking about what would happen if any officer visited the scene as we were unaware of the officers and the new department. It was the beginning of serving our probation period.

We planned to come half an hour earlier to commence the school's morning assembly and executed it faithfully with the help of some students available there. I conducted the morning assembly as I was well equipped with the pattern because I had the additional charge of a physical teacher in the MCD school. I stretched the task from twenty minutes to thirty so the other teachers and students could join their classes directly. When the Rest came, they were surprised. They were a little surprised but didn't have words to oppose it. We kept this routine for three days. Then, we followed a pattern of preparing the schedule by ten minutes for some days, and within a short span of one month, the school started running almost full-time. Now, the late-coming routing also had a remarkable change, but our in-charge, Devaki Nandan Sharma, would often arrive late and say he was late in buttering God rather than offering prayer.

Gradually, the issue got settled due to the installation of tents and tin boundaries from Lallu Lal & Sons. Later, the department made arrangements for old desks from the neighbouring school. Under the open sky, with no furniture and appropriate resources, the school turned into a tented school. Since the students in this school came from rural environments, extra hard work was required. To help the students, I bought a hand-held cyclostyle machine. It was kept in a small wooden box. At my expense, I would purchase stencil paper with round holes on both sides and carbon in the middle and help the students write their paragraphs and applications in simple language. Today, I agree that it was inappropriate from the psychological point of view of teaching. However, I adopted this approach to simplify the language and have an easy understanding of the language. Though it consumed a lot of time at the cost of my family, it remained one of my priorities to comfort me.

Also, I took extra classes for the students of class X while the board exams drew near and during the Dussehra holidays. Students from other neighbouring schools could avail of the facility with a free conscience. Some local students studying in Shahdara attended my classes. This period of extra courses has always been a part of my life. As a lecturer (English), other teachers also needed to take additional courses for board students. Apart from class XII, I often continued taking regular special classes for class XI to ensure a better foundation for the next board class.

When I served as vice principal and later HOS, head of school, I dealt with about 3,000 students and 125 teaching and non-teaching staff as the post of Principal, one Vice-Principal, and one DDO was vacant, so I alone was accountable for attending all the responsibilities, I would regularly reach my office at around 10:30. Whatever correspondence, reports, RTIs and other reply-related to multiple areas, I would get all done before stipulated office time 12:30. I didn't compromise with the school's academic environment. I taught all the board classes at least once a week regularly to remain in touch with their overall performances. I supervised most of the teaching classes by their respective teachers sitting in the classrooms to ensure a better teaching-learning environment. It was mandatory to send online reports, but most of my worthy colleagues did the job sitting in their offices.

I did not let money occupy space other than serving my fundamental needs. When I got promoted to Lecturer (English) in 1998, my loan for the flat was almost paid off. Since then, I have not charged any money for my teaching. On the other hand, I taught my neighbourhood kids as charity during the holidays. After a few years, I bore all the expenses of my elder sister's daughter, Bhanji, like a father on the same lines I had gone through for my daughter, Pooja. Debts remained a part of my life. About four to five years before my retirement, I got rid of my debts. Otherwise, the loan stayed with me in one form or the other throughout my life.

While working as an English lecturer at Sarvodaya Vidyalaya Timarpur, our librarian, Urmil Handa, whom I treated as an elder sister, became surplus. As a single parent, she had never-ending family issues to face. She was about fifty books short, and Mr Kanna needed to cooperate in settling the case. I could see her in trouble, so I asked her to register all the books due in my name to resolve the issue later.

She got a discharging order with the remark nothing was pending. But she was such a self-pride woman, not to get the favour of her brother. Her prayers remain a priceless treasure for my family. She often mentioned that we were not born from the same mother but were like siblings. May it be because of our previous births. Fifteen to twenty years have passed staying away, but the intimacy is still intact. I, too, have such a fair bond with my students as well. But standing with anybody else who needs support gives me the impression that I am helping myself. Such self-help energises me to go on.

I don't believe in showing off the little charity I engage in. I love the line of a saying- 'If your right hand is helping someone, your left hand should not know of it'. Today, when I see people giving even a bag of flour to people in need, they get it photographed and share it on different social media platforms for cheap publicity. But my wife is outside the frame of the right or left hand and knows everything black and white. The Facebook platform is full of needy guys, but when someone's voice appeals to me, I listen to it to answer.

I am sharing a dilemma regarding the legacy of owning the Obligation. I am in the habit of revealing everything to my life partner. Once, a friend of mine fell seriously ill. I sent him an amount in two instalments for only the receiving hands, but I had no idea how to get it back. Yes, I would have received it if the friend insisted.

It is sad to share that my friends couldn't recover and left us missing them painfully. But his kin later informed me: 'Several of our familiar friends helped the deceased, but I was the one who refused to receive back the money, and the Rest asked for the money they had contributed instantly after the permanent departure of my friend from the world. When his kin insisted on returning it, I replied: 'I could get it back from my friend, but not from you, who is uncomfortable without his help. Please keep the amount with you as the last perk from my departed friend.' My wife was listening to the chat on speaker and said: 'Need not be benevolent; why don't you take the money back while the one is insisting.' I told her: 'It was the help to a friend without having an idea of getting it back. That's why I feel very awkward about taking it back. Taking it back would be like deceiving myself. If you say take it back, it will hurt me. You may be fine at your place, but think a little bit from my point of view.' Ultimately, we agreed not to talk over the issue again.

In this context, it is necessary to share one more episode. I have an old hairdresser in Balram Nagar. I visited him for cutting only two or four times a year while living in the MIG Flats, Delhi. He told the sad news of his son's marriage and death within a week. He talked about his treatment expenses and debts. I had empathy for him. I told him: 'If you feel worthy of help, let me know. A few days later, he called and demanded twenty-five thousand rupees. I went to his shop and gave him the money. I declared to the family that there was little hope of the return of the money, but let's see what happens. But he was gentle enough to return twenty-three thousand after two years.

Sorry to mention the ungainly episodes above. My portrait would be incomplete without it all. Sometimes, I had to overcome a slight dilemma in obeying my heart, but I am proud of my life partner for supporting me on issues she was uneasy with. Had I not gotten such a commitment from my wife, my life would not have been so soothing and enthusiastic. Some friends may call it my stupidity, but I call it a part of the inbuilt system. I have no control over it.

As a legacy of my loyalty, one of my favourite tasks has been teaching students from my primary school to class XII for forty years, which was never a part of any syllabus. As a teacher, it is my sole asset. I have always contemplated contemporary issues of society and human life. I correlated my thoughts with the subject content to encourage my students to form general opinions about society and humanity. While doing so, I put my opinion open-ended on each issue with appropriate logic. But I never imposed my beliefs and ideology anyhow. Even today, following it faithfully as an author is part of my personality rather than a responsibility to me. I title my literary activities Samay Se Samvad, which means 'discourse/dialogue with time'. I will discuss this topic in detail while dealing with my role as an author.

CHAPTER EIGHT

In-Service Journey for Education

My regular education begins with class first and ends with higher secondary to pursue my professional diploma in basic training from Jamia Millia Islamia. My in-service educational journey has been based on the economics demand and supply principle. The first demand was to graduate; I graduated from Satyavati College (Evening) of Delhi University in 1980. In 1982, I moved to Gokul Puri from Yamuna Vihar C-4 school in surplus capacity and met Mr Mohan Lal Sharma here. His advice to run a clinic after retirement from my job sparked a new goal in me. I needed a two-year Ayurved Ratna course from Hindi Sahitya Sammelan, Allahabad Hindi University.

He described this course AGMS as equivalent to the Ayurvedic medical degree BAMS. His company worked, and I took this exam in Khekra, Uttar Pradesh. In 1983-84, I qualified it. The mark sheets for both years are still available to me even today. But I never registered for it nor showed interest in getting a degree or certificate. I am entirely devoted to writing; I do not see any future in using it now.

The subsequent demand was an SAV certificate equivalent to a bachelor's degree in education. The education department of the Delhi Administration provides it on an experience basis for eligibility for the TGT post, which I obtained in 1987. This was a significant step in my career, allowing me to progress in education. I continued passionately discharging my additional obligations to sports and family affairs, which I never saw as a burden. It disappoints me that most individuals stop studying after securing a job. However, money has never been my passion; it has always been a tool to satisfy basic needs.

When I look at the lives of my sisters and brothers, I see a different pattern. They seemed content with their education and did not pursue further studies. I, on the other hand, was the exception in the family. I chose to seek more, to strive for better. This quest for personal growth through education and experiences is a journey I continue to follow with passion and dedication.

Earlier, it was aimed at professional growth. Later, the goal shifted to multiple scholarly evolutions, keeping society at the centre. Free and logical thinking, the spirit of writing, forces me to change my beliefs, ideological literary stands, and literary fraternity. I plan to deal with my scholarly activities in another chapter to explain why and how the shifts in my study pattern and writing skills occurred. I return to my in-service education episodes.

Studying for an M.A. in Political Science was far from my plan. It has a distinct story. Two of my friends, Mr RD Sharma and Mr Mahendra Singh Dabas, both physical education teachers working in MCD, said one day, 'We want to do an M.A. in political science; would you like to join us?' I also said - 'Good deeds need no permission.'

They provided the company and solved the problem of my migration to Meerut University. Three of us appeared in the M.A.'s first year, but their failure greatly surprised me. My efforts favoured me, and I completed my M.A previous and final in 1988-89 on my first attempt. I take it as a gift from these two friends of mine as I had joined it simply for their company. Their support and encouragement were instrumental in my academic success, and I am grateful for their friendship.

This issue for the company was for good, so standing with it is a matter of pride. However, I have had instances where there has been nothing like pride, but I stood for the company. Srinagar episode is a hallmark. Once, a friend, Harpal Singh Kundalia and I went to Srinagar on a Scouts & Guides tour. An Air Force Jawan was also with us on this tour. I don't know how our intimacy occurred. One evening, we enjoyed a ride in a Shikara in Dal Lake. The Air Force jawan took out a half of whiskey and offered it to Harpal Kundalia. He took two direct sips and then puffed a cigarette. There were no snacks. When asked, I couldn't deny it and followed for the company's sake. No matter if we took cold drinks after the ride to neutralise the side effects of direct drinking, it may or may not be.

Let's come to the point in focus; with the help of my SAV certificate, I got promoted to the post of TGT (English) in 1988. The next step in my promotion was to take me to PGT. While holding the position of TGT, there was a provision to apply for the post of PGT and even to get appointed a principal directly after specific teaching experience and qualifications. Some of my juniors appointed TGT applied for the same occasionally, but I couldn't. They would ask me to apply respectfully. The suggestion put me in an embarrassing situation as I did not have essential qualifications other than experience. I needed a B.Ed. degree and a particular percentage of marks I didn't have. I could have if I could be a regular student and free from other liabilities. I knew it was because of my family's economic conditions. I realised my professional journey was destined to go on step by step, not directly. My future has nothing to do with fate; I term it determinism. I gladly accepted it for what it was.

Whatever I achieved in challenging, rather odd circumstances has always been a source of comfort for me. I know privileged students acquire educational and professional qualifications riding on their parents' shoulders. Hence, I am an exception in this matter. It is not like I am the only exception; there can be many better exceptions than me. I am relieved that after completing higher secondary and getting a diploma in basic training, I did not put any burden on my parents about my education. The journey was difficult, and I faced numerous challenges, from balancing work and study to financial constraints. But I strived, and these challenges strengthened my resolve to succeed.

Looking back on my life at twenty, I find myself capable of understanding how to run a family, even in odd circumstances. After 1977, the family's needs were solely mine to meet. This journey, though challenging, has been deeply fulfilling. The fulfilment automatically became integral to my life and would never end.

Based on the SAV certificate, one could be a lecturer (PGT), but more was needed for the vice principal and principal positions. It was B.Ed., the degree required for regular classes, and there is no provision for private candidates. Earlier, there was no facility for an in-service B.Ed. Program. I needed a way to afford a B.Ed., but the degree required to go on leave without pay. If one has good intentions, the whole universe gets involved in helping him achieve the noble goal. My life is full of such coincidences. To support my belief, a friend of mine, Mr Om Prakash, suddenly visited my school and told me he was doing a B.Ed. under a summer course.

It was like getting a quail landing in the hands of a blind man. The condition of a friend of mine, Kishan Swarup, was also similar. Both of us decided to get a B.Ed. degree in the summer course. More than mere determination was needed to reach the goal. The first requirement was to pass an entrance test. We obtained written permission from our principal madam to appear for this test and secured the prescribed merit. The second problem was that Jain Degree College Baraut, Uttar Pradesh, was about 30 km from our school. The class started at 1:30 PM and ended at 5:30 PM.

The school timings were from 7.30 to 12.40. Attending college and serving full-time school hours was impossible. All our efforts would have been in vain if our Principal, Mrs Urmil Sharma, had not given us written permission to leave the school half an hour earlier. She got our last two teaching periods vacated, directing the timetable in charge. Now we used to go even a little earlier than half an hour. It was a plus point that the bus stand was about a hundred steps away from the school. Undoubtedly, our principal, madam, had taken a significant risk. I will always be grateful to my principal, madam, for her noble deed. Had she not helped us, I would not have achieved my B. Ed. degree, and I would have needed to be promoted to Vice-Principal.

I followed my principal madam when I became the vice principal and, like her, the HOS of my school. Vikas Antil, a teacher subordinate to me, was attending IAS coaching. I provided him with a similar facility in writing. During the

PCS examination, I supported Sumit Gupta and MK Pathak by adopting a liberal attitude to solve the issues related to holidays and other facilities. All three could not reach their goals, but Ashish Pandey qualified for UP PCS because of the similar cooperation. Today, he is working in Meerut. Such facilities were unconditionally available not only to the teachers but also to the students and other staff of the school.

Let us return to B.Ed. The challenge of getting a B.Ed. degree continued after passing the test and making the school environment conducive. The Baraut's B.Ed. degree college students used to come from rural areas. Baraut is that area of western Uttar Pradesh known for its arrogance and, in a sense, for its absurdity. The language and body language seem to prove it at every step. I feel it necessary to give an example of the hallmark. Mohan Lal Gupta was a professor in this college. One day, after the college was over, he was going through the market towards the bus stand, and my colleague Mr Kishan Swarup and I were also following him. A bunch of students from our college would shout at intervals behind - 'Oye Mohan Lal, Mohan Lal Oye.' Mr Mohan Lal looked back several times, but the misbehaviour continued. My native village, Rathora, is also a part of this belt. But I never lived in my village, so it could not affect me. I think it is a caste-specific character. The rest of the castes probably do not behave like this.

There was always a strange fear of any absurdity before joining the college. When we went to attend our class for the first time, the banging started from the gate itself. The future teachers of the country were climbing up the desks and jumping like sheep to reach the front benches. The innocent guys were looking at this sight, standing leisurely but scared. We stayed away from any race and sat where we could find a seat without struggle. We had to live like a tongue between jaws and teeth. We could not afford any controversy. Our only goal was a B.Ed. degree. As time passed, more crowds started coming to the last bars, and we reached the front benches with no struggle.

We did not ask the teachers any questions to avoid problems. We used to listen to whatever we were taught silently and return home. We had to take the exam on our preparation. Teachers did not play the role they should have. But when a teacher asked me something, it was impossible to remain silent. Prof. Manokant Sharma was the first to ask me a question. The gentleman taught us the Teaching of Social Studies. After college, he used to sit on his outlet to deal with wood.

He accidentally asked me a question in English. I was sitting on the last bench in his class. His intention might have been to impress the students, especially the girls. Second, the students sitting on the previous benches assumed they needed to be more assertive in their studies. Those who sit on the last benches because of the fear of their teacher or to hide their academic drawbacks. I have already mentioned that my case on sitting back was different. I got up and began to respond non-stop. My answer demanded the professor's involvement and comment as he shared. But he was not ready to dialogue in English. He stated, 'Speak in Hindi so other students can understand your point correctly. I followed him to respond in Hindi. I deliberately used uncommon words in Hindi in my response. There was a strange stir among all the students, and some laughed, turning sides. All eyes were fixed on Professor Sahib's face, and the gleam in Professor Sahib's eyes got lost.

Manokant Sir seemed dismayed during that dialogue and couldn't react normally. The professor's frustration was evident because when the students asked the book's name to prepare for the examination outside the class, Manokant Sir answered, 'Why did you ask me? Go to ask the book's name, too, from Ish Kumar.' He was also annoyed with the students as they laughed at his desperation. Girls were equal participants in scenes taking place in the class. After that incident, the attitude of the defiant students towards me had changed completely. Some fellows had the courage even to wish and salute.

Such an incident took place with Prof. Shashi Kant Sharma. He used to teach us education technology. He planned a lecture where some students had to voluntarily offer a demo lecture. I waited for the students to accept the offer, but none agreed, perhaps because of hesitation. Ultimately, I stood up and gave my approval. The next day, I lectured before my fellow students in the same class. Prof. Shashi Kant Sharma was also present in the class. It was clear from the students' attention and the calm atmosphere in the class that they were satisfied. Otherwise, the students must be able to play pranks with the teacher, and I was not a teacher but the one among them. There was a question-answer session after the lecture. Professor Sahib was also among those who asked these questions. I conducted it satisfactorily. The students applauded when the process was over, and there was a loud noise in the class. My fellow students uplifted me in the air after the teacher had departed. Some colleagues commented that I had taught better than Shashi Kant, Sir. I am curious to know how genuine their comments were. But beyond denial, I was comfortable in college after these two episodes.

I interacted with the department head, Mrs. Chandrakala Sharma, several times in class. She had a pet remark: 'If you have questions, come in my room after her lecture, as the discussion would result in losing the entire class's time.' I knew the reality of her paradise and her strategy to avoid any discussion. So, it was pointless for me to visit her after class. One professor needed something to teach but to dictate her notes without explanation or discussion. Only two professors among the faculty members, Mr Trikha and Mr Sharma, always went with the teaching standards. The students appreciated them and had the liberty to interact for their satisfaction. Some roguish students often ask me, 'Tai Ke Bete, Ek Din Is Professor Ki Klass Le De, meaning son of a grand untie, take one class with this professor, too.'

They wanted to enjoy finding a professor in an embarrassing situation through me. Perhaps they thought that I deliberately did the work of trapping my teachers. I always told them one thing: 'I aim to respect my teachers. I don't communicate with a professor because I want to demean them. Even today, I stand firmly with what I had confessed then. Their inability to do justice with their profession was their problem, but I never intended to take advantage of someone's helplessness. I want to recall Professor Manokant again, who settled his score by minimising my teaching practice marks and pushing me a little farther away from the first division. Whatever he did, it may be his level of satisfaction, but I still respect him as one of my teachers. Thanks to all my professors, I achieved a B.Ed. A degree in 1992-93 and a promotion based on it.

Although I got my B. Ed, degree, and I had a Master's in Political Science, making me eligible for the lecturer post. But a long queue of my seniors to get promotion in the Political Science was there. There was ample scope to get a promotion soon in English rather than Political Science. So, I decided to obtain a master's degree in English from Himachal University because there was a semester system to help the applicant get better opportunities for preparation, which is essential for scoring a better percentage of marks.

However, the semester system could have worked better. Twice, I could hardly get the exam date sheet a week before. I passed the examination in the stipulated period in 1994-95. However, the purpose of choosing Himachal University for a better percentage was defeated.

My dream of a Ph.D. in English Literature was also defeated. I, too, had a second option for a Ph. D. after qualifying for an M.Ed. However, the circumstances did not turn out to be favourable and enhancing educational qualifications became a legacy of the past. I don't have any particular regrets because I have been making up for this loss with my literary writings. It is worth mentioning that my teacher, Dr Dev Kumar Chauhan (Dr D.K. Chauhan), who had taught us Hindi at Satyavati College, gave me some advice just a few days ago - 'You have so much work to submit to any university to award you Ph. D.' I said- 'Sir, I am unaware of such a university. Anyway, what difference is it going to make, Sir?' That's all to end up the issue.

Doing an M.A. in English Literature was challenging. My cousin Om Pal Singh was part of our family from 1974 to 1978. He was a regular student of M.A. English at Jain Degree College Baraut, U.P. He took a room in Baraut for his studies. He didn't have other family responsibilities like me, but he could not pass even M.A.'s first year, so he surrendered and came to stay at our house. But when I saw M.A. English written with his name on his books, I wished

I would write something like that with my name when the time is ripe.

I had to achieve a master's degree in English Literature without ignoring my responsibilities to my job, wife, children, and joint family. Private tuition had become the most considerable compulsion in my Balram Nagar, UP house. The condition of the electricity supply was miserable in my area. One incident in particular I remember was that I was reading something, but it was going over my head. I would stop reading in between and read again repeatedly, but I needed help getting into the message.

Meanwhile, I bathed twice but kept studying, wearing a vest-lungi without sponging my body to relieve me from the extreme heat. It took seven to eight hours to grasp the content, which was not lengthy. But when I realised it, my relief had no bounds. It was as if I had won something great. Though it took a lot of time to comprehend the content while preparing English, there was no compromise with the target. At last, I won the battle. But I do not know why, even after doing a double M.A., I felt no urge to write anything with my name as my cousin Ompal Singh would.

I can't resist the temptation to share another exciting anecdote about my M.A. in English. When I joined a school in Dilshad Garden, J & K block, to serve, I had acute pressure to repay my debts. I was bound to purchase a flat. Hence, I had no option left but to give private tuition. Once, my exams fell during my students' exams. I could not go against my students whom I had tutored since the beginning of the session. So, I continued with the tuition and put my exams at stake. But as I said earlier, when your intentions are noble, the whole universe is there to help. It worked with me as a boon for me.

As usual, I was going to school, taking my son and daughter on my scooter. It slipped in the middle of the road, and we fell scattered. Thankfully, no vehicle was following us from behind. My knees and elbows got chipped, but there was no such thing as a fracture. We returned home. When my students came to know about my accident, they visited my house to learn about my health. Seeing my condition, they said: 'Sir, take a rest. You need not worry about us. We will take care of our studies ourselves.' That is how I could save my moral values without denting my students' faith in me. Lying in bed for about ten days allowed me to revise the syllabus that I had gone through several times.

By the time I got my master's degree in English Literature from Himachal University, the departmental promotion process had started, too. It took a year, and I joined Sarvodaya Bal Vidyalaya Timarpur Delhi in 1998 as a lecturer (English). Here, I served for fourteen years, and I was promoted to vice-principal in 2013. I served in Sarvodaya Bal Vidyalaya Burari till August 2018. Thus, the journey of learning that began during my service for my educational and professional growth came to a complete halt. To conclude, my part-time journey as an author continued side by side since 1999 and has now turned into a full-time job.

---OOO---

CHAPTER NINE

My Flaws: My Learning Labs

A person is a blend of distinctive merits and flaws. The dominating trait of the two that governs one's mind is the deciding factor of the individual's personality. It, too, has a set of strengths and weaknesses. Those we consider excellent and most significant are not free from flaws. In such a condition, the scale of the merits is so high that it leaves negligible space for the flaws to dent their merits. Contrarily, if the scale of the flaws is much larger than the worth, the person gets out of the trait of nobility and falls into the trap of demerits. A person's true and ultimate identity is based on his overall assessment, not on one quality or the other.

Here, I present a comprehensive list of my flaws. It is a moral obligation and a genuine need that I love. I am familiar with some of my flaws, which I am bound to share here. But I am well aware that my acquaintances must have noted some more. They can add them to the list of my flaws to make my pen portrait more authentic. Let's embark on this series. As a child, I was timid and somewhat submissive. This can be seen as a blend of introversion and my weaknesses. I have a defining experience: I was a fourth-grade student in a primary school in Kundli, Haryana.

It might have been around Republic Day. One day, my class teacher, Madam Asha, was writing the names of some class students. I eagerly hoped she would write my name. But she kept ignoring me. She didn't write my name even when I asked. She said, 'No, not you.' I was upset to hear this. I was one of the finest students in my class, and Madam gave me special attention. But my disappointment faded when I learned those names were of students singing Qawwali. I didn't feel bad because I knew and accepted my weakness, finding peace in my shortcomings.

Submissiveness did not mean I ran away from work or sat idly on the last bench in the classroom. In other concerns, my activism was no less. When a teacher asked questions in the class, they would first ask those students who seemed confused or used to avoiding eye contact. Or who were poor in getting their teacher's trust. This is not a matter of boasting but of telling the facts. My turn used to be among the very few last students in the class who were expected to have the correct answer. It's not like I was a giant killer. I also made mistakes and got punished. As a science stream student in class 9th, I had an issue with making science models. Our teacher guided us in making an aluminium leaf electroscope. Here, by 'us', I mean a classmate of mine, Ajay Kumar Sharma, and me.

This model was selected first for our school, zone, and district science exhibitions. After this, it was chosen for Inter-District, i.e. the state. This exhibition was held in the Teen Murti Bhavan, New Delhi courtyard. Students from all over Delhi participated here. There, I saw the students speaking fluent English for the first time. I saw their body language and confidence. It differed from the countryside schools, like ours, in Singhu village. Our teachers also needed to show more courage when speaking such English. Anyway, we were students of Hindi medium. After coming there, I developed a habit of writing in English whatever I studied and revised from my Hindi edition books. How far it was grammatically correct English or not was fine. I wanted to train my mind to think and write in English. Our model did not get any state award, but we got the participation certificate. Getting a state-level participation certificate under odd and backward circumstances was an issue of pride. I still look at it from the same perspective; even today, it symbolises hope and optimism for the future.

There was an incident when I became a primary school teacher at the Municipal Corporation in Delhi. I was sent to a centre in Sarai Rohilla to participate in an in-service training programme. There, I was asked what my name meant. I shuddered. I said I don't know.' I had never thought of it from this point of view. I had never had an occasion before that I would feel about the meaning of my name. I had never come across any such discussion during my school days.

I just learned that every name has a meaning. I consider it my fault rather than the fault of my family and teachers. I want to see it as a need for more logical thinking in me. However, when I returned from the in-service training program, what I learned from my peers became the workshop of my life. After being promoted to the post of TGT, I was in charge of 'co-curricular activities' in the school. I wrote poems and essays in Hindi and English for my students on various occasions. I did not miss any opportunity to express my views in the morning assembly.

One more incident from this in-service training program had a tremendous impact on my life. This workshop also had an activity in which some slips were put in a box. Each slip had one task written on it for the participants to perform. Most of them were performing accordingly. I had to say something about my mother. I was newly appointed as a teacher, and the tail of my meekness was still fixed on me. The program attendees were very experienced and talkative, and were Khalifa-type teachers. At this point, too, I had my incompetence in making a speech about my mother and faced great humiliation.

Though a crude embarrassment befell me due to my flaw, I did not surrender to it. Nor did I fall prey to any inferiority complex. I was determined not to let it have a ride on me again. Hence, I actively participated in all our departmental seminars. I was confident that hardly any subject expert who had not compromised with the circumstances during the discussion left. My intention was always constructive during the dialogue. It has always been something to learn and something to teach new. It would be unfair to call it a frivolous mess.

One of the most significant episodes that destroyed my submissiveness was from Vigyan Bhavan, Delhi. The principal, vice principal, and two senior teachers from each school of the Delhi Administration attended the program. Along with them, hundreds of officers from our department, including the joint director, were present in Bhavan. An expert was talking about child abuse. While defending the girl child, she made an irrational or rather irresponsible remark against the boy child. There was no reaction against it in the auditorium. But I could not stay mum on such an issue. I raised my hand to respond. I put my point of view in English, the expert's tongue, facing the crowd of about one and a half thousand. There was no reaction in defence of my counter. After the session was over, our deputy director patted me on the back. The audience, even those unfamiliar with me, were present in the hall, approached me and kept admiring me when they came to the gallery to have lunch.

When I started writing essays on critical or contemporary topics for the popular literary Hindi journal on criticism 'Apeksha' (Quarterly), the post-mortem of the specifics of the subject began. There were calls from many unfamiliar friends from outside Delhi regarding my writings. They asked how far I had studied philosophy. It was a matter of surprise for me. I usually told without hesitation - 'I have not read any philosophy. I studied Hindi till the 8th standard. As a science student, I had qualified it as elementary Hindi at the beginning of the session of ninth grade. The only thing about my writing is that what I see around me or read and write is based on my writing experience. Nothing more than this.' There was a phase when I did not know the meaning of my name, and now the case has come to the point where people talk of my reasoning; some were compelled to ask for my education in philosophy. This change results from my continuing to fight against flaws rather than fear them.

I received the biggest compliment from my friend Mr Mukesh Manas, an associate professor at Satyavati College, regarding my writings. He had read most of my papers and was very impressed. He responded several times: 'I constantly see a tendency in your writings that you conceptualise things. I notice a newness in your writings. I announce that your report will also be featured for English titles.' I often responded, 'I don't try to do anything like this deliberately. This is a self-developed trend in my writings. It is a matter of great sadness that he has been the second person to know me well and is no longer with us today. The first person was Dr Tej Singh. No one can understand me better than I can to write. Although I have Tej Pal Singh' Tej' as an asset among those who understand me, he has no match.

I have easily defied the flaws of the in-service training program. However, one major drawback stuck with me during my job at MCD. I have already mentioned Mr Tara Singh Vedi, School Inspector (Physical), who lived in Ghonda and was addicted to non-vegetarian food and drinking. Coincidentally, my colleague in Yamuna Vihar school, Mr Sant Ram, also resided in Ghonda. I treated him like an elder brother and visited his house occasionally. Santram, too, was fond of drinking. I am still determining precisely which day and how I entered the drinking club. Anyway, I started attending parties with non-vegetarian food and drinking. I could get rid of it when I was promoted to the post of TGT in the Delhi Administration.

During the sports competitions, Vedi Ji used to take us to his house, and there would be regular drinking, causing us to drink. Later, it turned contributory. Today, I understand two reasons for joining my drinking circle. One is the company of my elderly brother Santram, and the second is the persistent and polite insistence to join the company, which was so strong that fish could not live without getting trapped. Since the route to my house was different, there were occasional rounds of Mr Vedi Ji's residence, but Santram had few options to stay away. Another reason for being part of this club was my sports addiction and desire to stay close to the boss. Like me, most sports associates were associated with this group for one reason or another.

The other senior school inspector (physical) also actively participated when MCD's central sports competition was held. He was a Jat by caste. The games used to take place at the MCD sports ground near the Old Delhi Railway Station. There was a big hall for indoor games. It, too, had a small office nearby. During the games, a bottle of whiskey, a glass used for drinking, a jug of water and snacks were kept in one corner of the office.

While different types of games were being conducted in the field, the liquor troop watched the game in herds and kept gossiping. The sports boss pointed to one sportsperson with an eye gesture to go to the office on his turn. This was followed faithfully by making one peg, drinking and eating salty, gram, etc., and rejoining the group at the playground. The sports and the game of drinking went on simultaneously, with gossip about how both games were successfully conducted.

In the end, non-veg arrangements also took place outside the grounds or sometimes at the sports office. There was no caste, creed, or hierarchy issue on such occasions. It is such a foolproof platform even today, where consuming alcohol debases all the caste and religious barriers to ensure real socialism, which no other platform can claim so confidently. The liquor gatherings are probably still above the wicked walls of religion and caste. I am making the statement in a light mood that real socialism can be seen in liquor-consuming guys, but that does not mean I encourage consuming alcohol. The cost is too high, and no society ought to afford it. I am just showing the mirror to the caste and religious fundamentalists. A strange scene is seen when someone who does not drink finds himself like an untouchable in intellectual gatherings where drinking turns out to be a standard feature. In such gatherings, I, too, find myself isolated and somewhat backward these days.

To lighten the burden from my head, I wish to share one more example of the extremity of the issue. It is about when Mr Raj Kumar Bharadwaj and I were the coaches of Tennikoit in Delhi. We were taken to Hyderabad to play the National as players. Our school inspector (physical), Mr Tara Singh Vedi, joined us as our coach, and Naseem Akhtar Siddiqui was the president of the Tennikoit Federation as manager. We stayed there for three days. By the grace of both our bosses, we did not get vegetarian food. Whether it was breakfast, lunch or dinner, there was no option left but non-vegetarian food. It was impossible to have evenings without whisky, the strong urge of bosses. They always had strange excuses for drinking. I feel a peculiar wildness when I glimpse the episodes of a bygone era.

While writing about the multiple episodes of consuming alcohol, I recall there was no opposition from my father or anyone else in the family. Neither did my wife. My father has been a staunch Arya Samaji and has been running campaigns against drug addicts throughout his life. He organised oath-taking ceremonies. Maybe it was because I was not an addict. My drinking did not cause any trouble in the family environment. Neither frivolous talk nor any spectacle in the street or on the road occurred. But whatever it was, it was in no way justified.

If my father had interrupted me or issued any oath, there was nothing to go against. It will not be wrong to say I have taken undue advantage of my father's decency. I am incredibly sorry for the wrongdoings I got trapped in. Nothing can make it right now but to repent over the wrong deeds. The time doesn't have a retake facility. Readers of my life are privileged to comment, 'The cat, having eaten a hundred mice, goes on a pilgrimage.' Well, whatever it is, the reality needs no patch-up.

Keeping in view the shortcomings, I do not believe that alcohol is a terrible thing and that those who consume it are all bad and unworthy. If seen in a nutshell, why only alcohol? Anything may be wrong if it is mishandled. Vice versa, if something is termed abuse, it can be applauded if handled sensibly and intelligently. The same happens in terms of language, beliefs and conduct. In today's society, the intoxication of religious and ethnic high-low and bigotry has become so frightening that it has the potential to destroy hundreds and thousands of times more than any other drug in the world. With this, how much damage can the intoxication of power, fame, and autocracy do? It can be seen and understood with the naked eye in this world, which has suffered two world wars. Today, there is no scarcity of such drugs in India that are eager to push the country to the face of ruin.

I do not claim that I do not drink alcohol now. I do, but according to the standards I have set for myself. I do not drink in public, at relatives' gatherings, or weddings. I've never been to a liquor store. I consume it hardly three or four times a year with my brother-in-law, Manbir Singh. Sometimes, I drink it with any of my friends as well. But not even once after Corona. I maintain the quality of the whiskey, and my limited-capacity stand. It has nothing to do with intoxication. I have had drinks several times with my literary friends as well. Therefore, as per the need of the circumstances, I have not avoided making timely deals with drinkers.

I would like to recall Mr Chandrabhan Prasad's episode. Chandrabhan Prasad is a well-known columnist and profound thinker who participates in various TV debates and is an expert on numerous issues in the country and abroad. I have had the chance to visit him on certain occasions. Celebrities from different fields are generally present at his parties. There, I had a good dialogue on multiple issues related to society and the nation. It has been nice meeting him and enjoying various non-veg and drinks on almost all occasions, without which no gathering comes into being. That's why I don't see such a gathering as any evil. This is my point of view: everyone has the right to disagree; It is not beyond acceptance.

Non-veg, drinks, etc., have extra credentials in some gatherings. I want to share a one-time story. Mr Chandrabhan Prasad invited me to a two to three-day program at Lakhimpur Kheri Periphery. This is not today's Lakhimpur Kheri, a victim of politics that remains in the news for the wrong reasons. There, Chandrabhan Prasad was to inaugurate the statue of Lord Thomas Babington Macaulay. He tilted Lord Macaulay with 'Dalit Goddess English' and established it in the school of Amar Chand Johar (Host and Manager of the school) in Banki village. Mr Shyam Dinkar was the convener of this program. Chandrabhan Prasad with DICCI chairperson Milind Kamble from Pune, Ram Babu, a professor of English, Mr S Anand (Narayan Publishing, Chennai), a British national, and I attended the ceremony.

The event was on 25 October. If I'm correct, it was the year 2010. It is a coincidence that I was also born on 25 October. It was a revelation that happened one day during a party at Chandrabhan Prasad's residence. I enthusiastically support Lord Macaulay's role in furthering English and the education system. But I can't accept him as a goddess. On the foundation day of this statue, all the participants addressed the public gathered to create awareness about English. All the participants shared their experiences about how they got acquainted with English and how they found it a tool to make their lives comfortable. The village guys madly joined in the program and made it memorable.

Chandrabhan Prasad's contribution to this episode is commendable. When we stayed at the hotel for the night, non-veg drinks and other types of food were available. There is no compulsion like food and drink in such programs. But the majority fits drinkers and non-veg lovers. I have not shied away from the saying: 'Do as the Romans do' if it is affordable.

---000---

Tihar Jail: A Hail Of Peril

The story is from the year 1982. My job in MCD would have been hardly two and a half to three years. The probation period was over, but the regularisation certificate from the department was still awaited. The job is considered permanent only when the certificate is obtained. If something goes wrong in between, you can lose your job. I got married on June 14 this year. It needed more attention other than the regular joint family requirements. Contrarily, I prioritise something else beyond family. But I had strong links with my colleague Krishna Prakash Parashar, his brother Rishi Parashar, Bhudutt Sharma, Ram Sharan Sharma, etc., the Teachers' Council organisation leaders. It can be called a BJP-supported organisation in today's terms. Several times, they took me to promote the union and its activities, as I had no idea about their political ideology. There was no such animosity towards a rival's political ideology as we experience today. My concern was confined to the teachers' cause as being a committed teacher. My nature and activism could be another attraction. The other reason was the affinity and love of the union leaders for me. It is my version to be with them, but

I don't know their stand in giving me space in their team. Both of my points of view need to be corrected.

Primary teachers struggled to rectify some of the anomalies regarding their salaries. Still, the circumstances forced them to go on strike. It did not work; ultimately, the teachers went one step ahead to get arrested. Krishna Prakash Parashar led the first batch for the arrest. All were arrested, and their services were terminated to pressure the agitating teachers. The government's strategy backfired, and the teachers' arrests accelerated. Those who got imprisoned first were now out serving their fifteen-day term in jail. More and more arrests were made to pressure the government and get the order of termination waived. Consequently, one troop after the other was offered arrest and got suspended from jobs. Hence, the voluntary arrest was the impetus, and perhaps it was the fourth or fifth batch; my friend Bishan Lal Kanojia and I gave the arrest from our school. This group consisted of several hundred teachers. A prominent leader, Bhoodutt Sharma, led the group for the imprisonment.

With garlands around our necks, speeches and enthusiastic slogans made our farewell festive. Savitri, the nursery teacher at my school, made it memorable. She showed sincere concern by inviting me to her room. To my surprise, Savitri offered me the non-vegetarian dish. While saying farewell, I observed her heart was heavy. We were taken on a bus to the Parliament Street police station. We were enlisted and sent to jail for a week. Some more friends left from different schools wearing garlands but slipped away from the police station. I have learned to respect my words since childhood and kept them, whether it led to jail.

There was a ruckus over the food on the first evening in the jail. Our leading food is Dal and Roti. Dal and Roti were in prison, but we did not find it worth eating. Since we were in the tempo of agitation, we raised slogans in jail. The jail administration respected the teachers. So, they solved the problem the same night. They gave us some undertrial prisoners and told us to let them know what to cook and how to cook as per our choice. The jail authorities gave us the raw ration necessary for our food. Some of the teachers stayed in the kitchen to guide and help the prisoners to cook as they desired. Thus, we settled the issue of food. There were fifteen to twenty teachers in each cell. Blankets, rugs and some jail utensils were enough to meet our needs.

Some of our fellows were experienced enough to take packs of cards. They used to play cards and had fun all day long. Wherever you look, everywhere, jokes occupy the atmosphere of the gossip of card players. I didn't know how to play cards. However, my father knew it and played with the neighbours while free. The game in which the trump card is more significant; he used to play that game for fun or as a time pass. But we brothers and sisters were not allowed any game of cards. Even if we stood near the card players, our father would be angry and thrash us. He had a similar attitude towards kite flying. That's why we never enjoyed kite flying in life. Playing cards was impossible for us.

In the village, we used to play kho-kho, Stapoo, Pitthu, hide-and-seek, and Kai Danka (The game was one boy had to touch any of the boys protecting themselves, moving one branch of the other on the same tree. If he kisses the stick, it is placed in a circle marked on the ground before other players reach for it. He could be free from the obligation of following the players if the other player succeeded in doing so first. It was the defeat of the chasing fellow, and he had to keep repeating the same process until he won. We used to play other games like kabaddi, wrestling, racing, and desi hockey in the fields. These games were allowed, and there was no punishment.

On the other hand, I grew up responsible and had nothing to pass the time in the cell but to follow the saying: Do at Rome as Romans do. I also sat with the teams, played cards and learned the game of Sheep (?). Players would comment about me, saying he did not know the game's technicalities but knew how to place cards. He needs to learn the nuances of the game. Specifically, they meant I couldn't have the skill of reading the cards in other players' hands accordingly. Yes, I did learn card playing as much as I could, but I left it there, where I had learned.

There used to be a queue for the toilet in the jail in the morning. This was a big problem for us. As I mentioned, Bishan Lal Kanojia was also a physical education teacher with me. He was a hilarious person. One day, we were standing in the queue. Mr Kanojia was behind me. For fun, he made a strange and innocent gesture and said - 'Brother, let me go to the toilet first. Otherwise, my morale will go down.' It was the pet dialogue of the teacher's agitation.' Hearing it, the teachers in the queue laughed, and Kanojia laughed a lot. This popular dialogue about not letting morale fall was repeatedly spoken during our strike. So, it was on everyone's tongue. Now, the mood of the fun was such that even when someone had to be removed from playing cards, the same dialogue would be repeated - 'Brother, let me play cards. Otherwise, my morale will go down.'

Our day began and ended with fun and cards. Interestingly, there was a volleyball ground for the prisoners to play. How could a dancer control oneself on a musical tune? The teachers made a team to play with the prisoners. Some prisoners were prisoners by name.

Otherwise, they lived there as if at home. There was a Sikh boy who was a student at Khalsa College, Delhi University. He was serving a sentence in a stabbing case. I had also seen mosquito nets, exercise dumbbells, and a container of ghee in his room. The other prisoner was associated with a famous 'Maya Tyagi case' in Baghpat, UP. Maybe his name was Sunil Tyagi. He was Maya Tyagi's brother-in-law and the sub-inspector in the police. He had avenged the murder of his sister-in-law and was serving a long-term jail. They lived in civil clothes as if they were home and had a good life. Perhaps they had all the facilities other than visiting their homes. Mr Tyagi had great respect for us as teachers. We played daily volleyball during the days of our imprisonment and had a lot of fun.

There was also a shop in the jail. If one had to buy anything, one could visit the shop comfortably, but it was a little more expensive. Once, a teacher went to buy something at that shop, and on the way, he came across a prisoner. The prisoner had a blade in his hand. He asked for money from that teacher and said, 'If you don't, I will make a scar on your face with this blade. 'Nothing like this happened, but warnings were issued to all the teachers to protect themselves from such incidents.

We were all having fun but missing the natural freedom. Meanwhile, one day, my wife, Shashi Bala and my fellow teacher, Savitri, came to see me in jail. They brought home-cooked food with them. But I don't know why; seeing them made me feel heavy at heart and awkward. Even today, when I recall the feeling of being cut off from the outside world in prison cells, it causes pain. We were in a group and used to have fun with no bounds. We were also scheduled to leave within a week. The behaviour of the jail officials was also respectful. Contrarily, when I think of the ordinary prisoners who must stay in jail for a long time, they didn't have freedom like us as teachers. They were criminals and had been treated by the authorities accordingly. Their state of affairs disturbed me a lot; even today, it causes pain.

I was uncomfortable when I returned home, serving the one-week term of imprisonment. The home environment did not please me. I felt lonely despite having all my close family members' concerns. I felt the urge to talk to none. My preference for loneliness compelled my family members to ask if I had any problems. I had nothing to say except, 'I am fine, no issues.' When I was in jail, the homesickness disturbed me, and now, when I was at home, the fun and company of jail associates lured me a lot. The temporary prison family sentiments overpowered the permanent family's love and concern. Gradually, the effect of the prison fun subsided, and I returned to my old spirit and life.

A week later, another significant arrest was planned at our teacher's union level. I offered for my arrest again. This time, too, there were roars of slogans, speeches, and displays of garlands. We were boarded on special DTC buses to take us to the Parliament Street police station. We were enlisted again for imprisonment, but instead of being sent to jail, we were released to return home. It was the journey of my imprisonment that came to an end, teaching me new experiences in life.

Today, when I look back on this plot, I realise that taking such risks under an unconfirmed job could be a ruin. I should have avoided such risks. But I must confess that certain risks are beyond my control as a natural personality trait. Discussing another topic before moving on to the school-frenzied topic is relevant.

Once, we went to Darjeeling for the scout and guide's camp. We were returning by a toy train run by Darjeeling Himalayan Railway. We may have to come to Jalpaiguri. The bogie was specially booked for scouts and guides, and I suffered from loose motions. It was summer, so I was in a Loongi and a vest. The rest of our scouts also wore casual clothes for their convenience. Suddenly, our train stopped at a station on the way. Finding it a golden opportunity for medical help, I ran downstairs to purchase some medicine from the chemist. When I returned, I found the train gone. It was as if the ground had slipped from under my feet. My luggage was on the toy train, and I had little money. The most worrying thing about this was that I did not know where we were to stay. We didn't know anything beforehand. Mobile facilities, which we enjoy today, were not available then.

I forgot all about loose motion and weakness. The train was invisible, but I knew the train could be found by running downward to the railway track below, whether the station was there or not. I ran downwards, but it took some time. Finally, I found the railway track below. I stayed there. After a while, the train came, and I boarded the moving train. My struggle materialised, and I reached my destination. The circumstances helped me experience the scenes we witness in movies as extraordinary and miraculous. Going down the steep hill in haste and catching the train was risky, and there was no other option left but risk.

I took the risk to get rid of the troubles. But when I joined Sarvodaya Vidyalaya Burari in the post of Vice-Principal after promotion, it was like a new world of risk opened up. Another friend of mine, Mr SP Singh, joined us here in the same capacity. Our Principal, Mr Surendra

Kumar, arranged an office for Mr SP Singh in the four-storey main building. He arranged my office in a separate building with an adjoining tin shed. These sheds were used for the middle classes. My old acquaintances, Mr MS Bisht, my college mate, Mr Mangat Ram Tyagi, and several other teachers wanted me to stay in the main building to work for the betterment of senior classes. They were familiar with my academic approach. When an officer is transferred or promoted from one place to another, his good or bad deeds precede him than the person himself. I was no exception in this matter.

I started working there with no ifs and buts. The shed building needed water and toilet facilities for the students and the staff. All the students had to go to the main building to meet their water and toilet needs. However, the students would go to the main building for water and use the nearby ruined porta cabin, the exterior of the classroom walls, including my office walls, for the toilet. That's why it smelled so bad. It was highly unpleasing from the point of view of decency, health, and hygiene. I politely requested the principal to solve this problem, but in vain. I thought he was interested in something else rather than solving this problem. It had only been four or five months since I reached there. The period was enough to learn how autocratic and influential he was. Eventually, I got upset for not paying attention to my request, an essential student need. Hence, as the next step, without hesitation, I put forward my problem through e-mail to keep it as a record of my concern. I mentioned the names of two teachers categorically, in whose presence I had addressed the principal to solve the issue previously, to stand them as witnesses if needed.

It was a strange experience for me that both the Witnesses discussed why their name was written as a witness only to remain in the principal's good book. However, they knew my concern and need for the hour. The episode taught me to avoid having expectations and support from the spineless guys. Corruption prevails everywhere because people cannot stand up for truth and justice, even if they are free from harm. Often, the police also blame the public for not standing as witnesses to put the criminals behind bars. The case of the police is different as we see the police harassing the witnesses unnecessarily.

It was not so in my case. When I got no response from the boss, I sent the reminder again. Since the issue had come up in writing twice, Mr Surendra Kumar was forced to answer. Hence, he responded in writing, but following his tyrannical trait, the boss reacted with no concrete facts but to divert the issue of baseless narration. I was not to let him succeed in abusing my sincerity. I countered the rubbish he had spread to digress the issue's intensity in his defence. The writing trail began through e-mails but did not have a break.

It is beyond doubt that our principal was an authoritative person. It is still there, though he is retired now. He has been and still is strong physically and financially. He has a good grasp of English, too. It is a plus point for an officer's departmental correspondence. In its absence, such an ability of many officers could be improved. His arrogance did not let him stay free when he attended the official meetings with other zonal and district officers. He never allowed me to participate in departmental conferences and even did not bother to share the minutes of the meetings. He still needs to share the official password to familiarise me with correspondence between our school and various offices. He kept me completely away from the admission process, the HOS Supervision Diary, and the activities of the Vidyalaya Kalyan Samiti. All these were said to be in our (vice-principals) possession during our three-day workshop at Thyagraj Stadium.

I intend to familiarise myself with the abovementioned information so that I can respond to the authorities in the absence of my boss, Surendra Kumar. It was mandatory for me to know how to contribute to the furtherance of the institution's academic environment and to deal with the teaching staff accordingly. I knew well that my Integrity and honesty would only be questioned if I didn't know the primary information about the institution where I was the second boss. My position in my department could have been of an irresponsible officer, and it did not match my personality. I can cross any limit and work hard for my image. Because of this, I always arrived between ten and eleven o'clock compared to the scheduled time of the school, i.e. 12.30.

Another side of the coin is that I wanted to play my role in improving the school environment. But I was unable to do anything. I had to remain a mute spectator to the problems of the teachers working under me. However, I was not ready to make any compromise in the matter of getting them to work. I was still waiting for an answer about whether any teacher wanted me to have any information regarding admission policy or other issues. This situation was painful, and it was hard to bear this much for someone like me who didn't give up. That was why the tussle of writing had come into existence.

I didn't know why he was doing all this. It could be his ego or his autocratic style of functioning. It could be the arrogance of his ethnic superiority. Nothing could be denied straightforwardly. But I do not allow anybody to make me a victim of any oppression. Generally, I am not inclined to look at any event or person through the lens of caste. In this case, I also never got any illusion that my boss was treating me like this because of my caste. I only meant to eat mangoes, which had nothing to do with kernels. It was simple to learn that his behaviour was not just. It hurt me because of the anti-school environment. So, it was my moral and official responsibility to resist, and I did it with gusto.

Yes, it is necessary to recall Mr MK Pathak, a teacher at my school, to understand the episode better. He was a staunch believer in his hard work and ideal path. He had also qualified for the PCS exam several times. It is a different matter that he could not reach his final goal. He was impressed with my working style and said to the staff aloud in his alluring style,' Before Ish Kumar sir came, the building in the middle section was like a sanctuary, a protected place where animals and birds could roam without fear. He metamorphosed it around.

This MK Pathak was the only teacher in the staff of over a hundred who could stand against the principal with the spine. I loved his genuineness and frankness. He even called me his mentor at my retirement party. During this dispute, one day, he told me, 'Sir, why don't you go to the SC/ST commission? All his viciousness will get settled.' I said, 'Dear, I do not need to go there; I will deal with him and his company alone. Do not be upset.' Even today, Mr MK Pathak mentions my confidence and high spirits everywhere when relevant.

I return to the initial point again. Why my principal did not want to share any information with me was not rocket science. Every teacher of the school knew the reality of our principal's paradise. There were loopholes at each step of his style of functioning, but the teaching staff of more than a hundred teachers did not dare open their mouths against his malpractice. My subordinate teachers, unfamiliar with my dedication and sincerity to duty, discussed that the struggle between the HoS and me was to get a share in the robbery of school funds taking place there and nothing else.

Such perceptions among the teachers had a solid ground based on their past experiences. The existing principal, Mr Surendra Kumar, carried the legacy of fraud. When he joined Burari as the principal, he had claimed his honesty too loudly to betray. But now, his hypocrisy had no bounds. That's why the staff members doubted my Integrity. His pomp and show of honesty were to create a perception that his blacks may look white. I want to share an incident to learn the image of school principals in terms of honesty. Once, a friend (the name is not appropriate to mention) was in a meeting with the director of education. In that meeting, the director remarked, 'Jitne Principal, Saare Chor' means all the principals are thieves. This was the terrible truth of corruption in the Delhi administration.

Here, I am not talking about exceptions. I am talking about the overall perception. Whatever my boss's image was here, it was crystal clear to all. Under such circumstances, my staff members' putting me in the same category of crooks was in no way strange. I blame none for putting me in the category of fraud.

I didn't care what the people thought about me; I cared about being honest to my conscience and focusing on my own business. I did not need to give unnecessary clarifications about me and my actions. Patterns are an essential part of my personality. The work should speak louder than the person himself. I follow the same in my writings. People say this is the era of publicity. Without publicity, none can win the race of popularity and success. People need to take them seriously in the digital world.

My daughter once commented, 'Papa, your twenty-four books are available in the market. The identity and recognition you deserve is very far from known. You post one thing on Facebook and think it is enough; you have no role left. It doesn't happen like that. Unless we constantly talk about our work in one form or another, it will result in nothing.' I agree with my daughter to a certain extent but fail to follow such a pattern. My conscience resists against it as whatever I write is in the interest of society and to the best of my satisfaction. Running after publicity is like making my conscience and me as if a product for sale. I love both, nonetheless. Hence, I enjoy my freedom of speech and writing, an excellent source of inspiration that keeps me energetic and enthusiastic to move on freely. I don't need any second opinion to compromise my freedom, whether related to my school or personal affairs.

My principal was the 'Pradhan Sevak', which means chief servant of our school. His mannerisms were similar to today's 'Pradhan Sevak' of the country. What he made black or white was the ultimate truth. Whatever the rest of the school staff was, if we try to define it based on the working pattern of the existing regime, it was a group of the commoner, each member of which was merely to be yes men or back-stalkers and nothing else. But in both cases, his voice did not reach the ears meant for it. That's why our boss was the autocratic and uncrowned king of the institution, accountable to none. The staff used to call him Daroga, which is the word for police inspector. This title was so popular that the word 'Daroga' often came out of people's mouths, even when dealing with him. But he didn't mind it. Perhaps he had accepted this identity. But I never addressed him with this title. In my dealings, I called him 'Sir' and used the word 'Sahab/boss' in conversation with the staff. Using the word 'Daroga' did not match my personality.

I was neither of the two—a backbiter or a dumb who stays silent when justice demands resistance. I was vocal in my dealings and writings but never crossed the limits of decency and discipline. My staff and even my principal, Mr Surendra Kumar, never forgot to mention it as a remarkable personality trait. It stayed the same in his absence. We lived together for four years, but the official dispute never became ours. Even today, our mutual relationship reflects no sign that we ever had any official dispute.

My correspondence against the boss' acts of functioning became a topic of discussion among staff members. It was a feeling of unintentional pleasure for them. During these episodes, hardly any teacher might have stayed mum in sharing loopholes against the principal. But no one was ready to be a witness to ensure justice. I listened to them patiently but didn't respond accordingly against the boss. Some teachers even commented: It is the first time that an educated Vice Principal, i.e. me, has come to the school and learned how to write and address the issues with a spine. I knew that my staff was using my shoulder to fire their gun. However, I was focused on the betterment of my students and the school, away from personal grudges. I never allowed my cause of action to change centre.

I had accumulated a lot of material through my e-mail. Meanwhile, the principal, Manju Sharma, officiating as zonal deputy director, jumped into the dispute to intimidate me. On August 14, 2013, Madam visited my school during the morning shift. She also wrote the school report for the evening shift at ten o'clock in the morning. When I reached the school at about eleven o'clock, the principal told me that Madam had supervised the school and called me to meet her at the office. Coincidentally, I had already waited for her to address my problems in her office while she was writing the supervision report at my school. I had a written draft which I had to hand her over. I returned to Madam's office and presented the detailed report to her. Later, I also submitted it to the office diary.

During the discussion, Madam repeated many times in apparent words - 'You are right, and your points are valid. I agree, but you have to move in with your boss.' But how? She had no answer to my 'how'. My boss had a win-win situation. My boss and Madam had a friend-like relationship. It should not be said, but it is a compulsion. Their relations were like thieves and cousins. Due to this connection, during her visit, she wrote in the Supervision Register at ten o'clock about Surendra Kumar's pridefulness: "There is a lot of pressure of admission in the school, and the principal is doing his best to maintain the school. Classes are going on in the open Veranda. Cleanliness is up to the mark. All efforts are being made, and the principal's actions are highly acceptable.

In conclusion, the principal is fully capable of running the school. Ish Kumar was absent. Significantly, no Gangania suffix with my name is in the official records.

The boss was excited that Madam had lavished praise on him and wrote about me being absent two hours before office hours. She wrote nothing about Mr NP Bhardwaj, another vice principal who worked with me, who used to come only at 12.30. Secondly, my principal got the DDE zone's report signed by me in his support by handing over a photocopy. The readers may call it Vernavaad, Casteism or the cheapness of his arrogance. They can draw their conclusions at their convenience. But I did a postmortem on the foul glorification of Madam Manju Sharma, seeing the students sitting in the Varanda before the school began functioning. How did she conclude that the cleanliness was up to the mark before the commencement of the school? How did she measure the admission pressure, and how did she decide my boss's efforts were highly appreciable and that he was capable? That's why I had titled the two as thieves and cousins.

This was the hypocritical pattern that the HOS, Mr Surendra Kumar, followed regarding the supervision of the class and teachers sitting in his office. This kind of abuse of power is seen everywhere throughout the country. Nowadays, CBI, ED, Election Commission and in some ways even the courts are not free from misuse of powers. It is a serious issue that is tarnishing the country's image worldwide. It is another issue of debate to find out which community or class these enemies come from. The answer is well-known: Has black covered substantial space at the bottom? I never believed in such disgraceful practices. Even when I happened to be a HOS, I would reach the office about two hours before school, between ten and eleven, to attend day-to-day correspondence. I did not compromise the teaching hours with my office work.

I reported this fraud and autocracy of the two to the deputy director (district), Mrs Tandon. A memo against my boss, 'Manju Sharma, with specific guidelines, was issued to sort out my grievances. However, the principal needed to be more egoist and ready to follow, though the memo called him an unbecoming government servant.

I had yet to file several RTIs to get more and more information about his misappropriation of records directly in my name. The data I received had substantial evidence to represent my grievances to higher authorities. The situation worsened when DDE (Zone) Madam Manju Sharma's image was tarnished by wrongly supporting my boss. Possibly, it was the year 2014 when my boss applied for a transfer; Manju Sharma probably felt lost along with my boss, Surendra Kumar. She told me with great gusto,' Surendra Kumar is getting a transfer, I will visit the school regularly, and now I will see your competency.

This case was widely debated, and I got feedback from different corners. One of my colleagues from my previous school commented: Ish Kumar's job would not survive. Even in my school, Burari, there was frequent talk of decisive action against me. Perhaps at the behest of Madam Manju Sharma, my boss put up my file to higher authorities to surrender me. It fuelled the rumours against me and created a strange atmosphere around me. I had no problem with this move as I had to do my job rather than slavery. Eventually, it was rejected by higher officials. This was a problem for my boss and Madam Manju Sharma.

My boss got no transfer, and his confidence and attitude lost ground because of the repeated defeats. His retirement was drawing closer, and perhaps he had realised the possibility of being trapped. The issue had now been glimpsed at our headquarters. It had become quite a headache for him. In the meantime, the building of our school was declared dangerous, and there was a campaign for months for alternative seating arrangements for the students, but the result remained the same for three days. But Madam Manju Sharma would call me several times for letter drafting for other departments. She, too, was polite enough now and shared sweets, tea, snacks, etc.

But when it came time to review my APAR, i.e. Annual Performance Assessment Report, her suppressed revenge burst out. My boss, Surendra Kumar, with whom I had a dispute, gave me a grade of 6.4 and coined significant remarks: 'Good mannered, good relations with the public, Polite in public dealing'. He concluded his remarks by mentioning me as hale and healthy with a sound physique and mental health, and 'Integrity beyond doubt. Finally, he concluded with the words: The officer deserves the position he possesses.' But Madam Manju downgraded it to 5. Generally, a superior officer is to upgrade, not to downgrade. This was an adverse grading from the point of view of future promotion.

It was about when I was drafting letters for her, sitting in her office in a cordial atmosphere. I told her, 'Madam, why did you downgrade it? She said- 'Ish Kumar ji, what difference does it make? I work so much, and I also got a grade of seven.' She was stuck to her retaliation and did not listen to me. I requested her to review it officially. I wonder if the villain inside her appeared in the open. She sent my original APAR back to school and directed the principal to tell all the episodes of creating problems in the school administration and hampering the administration.'

This dispute began in August 2013, but I lodged my objection at my headquarters on October 13. I attached 26 documents to prove my point. Meanwhile, the office demanded a report. Madam also sent this report to our school to teach me a lesson with my boss. But this could not happen because my boss was smart enough to feel the direction of the wind.

He gave me the file to go through. He, too, refused to follow Madam's directions. While it was happening, I got scary news but didn't feel scared. The reason behind my fearlessness was: 'My aim is selfless. Whatever I am doing is for the betterment of my students and the institution I am accountable for. It is for the rights the department ensures. Finally, each of my moves is against malpractices. Why punishment?' This attitude has been my energy source; It encouraged me to fight with no fear, whatever the consequence.

Until the APAR controversy in 2014, I was deputed to the morning shift as the HOS. I was bearing all the additional responsibility regarding the new construction of the school. Then, Madam Manju Sharma was determined to keep me on the morning shift. She even commented in my favour, 'You are very bold and skilled in solving the problems of the school.'

This was an issue from 2015. Madam Manju was adamant about keeping me there. It was the time of Mr NP Bhardwaj's retirement. Hence, Mr Surendra Kumar demanded my return to my parental school. But after a lot of controversy, she was again forced to show herself as an opportunist and argued for sending me back to the evening shift. Her plea was: 'Since this school is for girls, Ritu Bhatnagar should be made HOS.' However, Narendra Chandra had previously worked as the HOS in the identical girls' school before me. There was no question about a male boss working in the girl's school.

In about two years, I also wrote six letters to the highest official of my department, the Director of Education. Madam Manju Sharma got exposed all the way. There is a saying: no matter how brilliantly a lie is told, ultimately, it is destined to face defeat to let the truth win. Moving ahead of her lies and the misuse of her power, Manju Sharma had come down on a criminal offence in a way. She changed the note sheet of the file related to this dispute. Surendra Kumar had accepted my demands, but now my case and Madam Manju Sharma's case dragged on for so long that a week was left for her retirement. She was not getting Vigilance Clearance. Zone 7 DDE Madam Neelam Sahrawat and Zone 8 DDE were jointly appointed as Inquiry Officers. Although they were officers of three ranks above me, they requested me - 'Ish Kumar ji, the one who forgives is great. She is older than you, forgive her.'

My only answer was - 'I have never made any complaint against her. She went on and on against me. Whatever I have written is in self-defence and nothing else. I never wish her to suffer. If you ask me to write and give something to help her, I will not do that. It may go against me. Yes, you can write whatever you want in her favour to save; I will not take the matter further.' It was followed, and she probably got vigilance clearance two days before the retirement date. I am not happy with what she passed through. But I have not compromised with justice; I am so glad. I could have paid at any cost if my stance was wrong. After that, I got to work with Madam Neelam Sahrawat and Pramod Kumar Ji. But our relations have always been cordial, and we worked very enthusiastically.

A similar risky episode happened in the case of my DDE (District), Madam Osta. Education Minister (Delhi Govt) in the School of Civil Lines, Mr Manish Sisodia, had a meeting. This included VKS members, as well as HOS and MLA representatives. The MLA representative of my school, Vikas Bharadwaj, complained that a blind teacher was forcibly sent to the Burari School while there were already ten- or fifteen blind teachers working in the school. When asked, Madam Osta gave an evasive answer. Perhaps the minister wanted more from her reply. When he asked me, I told him the whole truth.

The next day, an explanation came to Madame Osta's office from the Education minister's office. When I reached the school, I got a call from Madam Osta's PA to report to the office immediately. Till then, I had completed documentary proofs of the joining of the blind teacher in question, like a statement from the blind teacher, details of a mobile conversation with the dealing head of the Madam's office, a statement of the dealing head of my office and a comment of nine-vacancy made by me on the teacher's joining letter. I wrote a letter and attached all the documents herewith. When I reached DDE's office, many officers and Babu were sorting out the issue.

On seeing me, Madam suddenly roared at me - 'What did you need to say that there was no vacancy? I had posted him to help a blind man.' Before I could put my point of view, she said,' You have done this intentionally. You could refuse. I refused, too. What do you think of yourself? Now I have been asked for an answer; tell me what answer I should give.' I handed over my drafted letter to Madam and said sorry. I said, 'Ma'am, I only said what was the fact. You could respond as I had done, couldn't you? She said: I will come to your school and see what else is true there.

Another bitter truth is that, having gone through my letter, no one in the office could argue against my stand. Therefore, no case was made against me for speaking anything else. Apart from this, my episode and Manju Sharma's episode created a different picture in the minds of other officers. They used to refrain from showing their officer-ship to me. I used to be very simple but needed help to settle for the right.

Working in the Delhi administration, I find a particular trend. Here, the officers give some orders orally. Still, when any issue gets complicated, all the responsibility is placed on the officer who would have obeyed such orders orally. Ignoring the verbal order of an officer or making a written demand was also not free from the officer's temper. I have never taken such a risk. But I found a great solution to this problem. Whatever verbal order I would comply with, I used to send the compliance report to the office by e-mail, citing the oral order. I kept a copy in my record so my officers could accept what they had ordered orally.

This action did not give any officer the courage to say why the compliance report was sent or why it was not required to be sent. I did not limit this record-making habit to my officers. I made a record of every activity that I suspected to be a dispute. This tendency has played a tremendous role in my life and kept me safe from controversy and risk.

I am trying to figure out what Madam Osta wrote in her explanation to Mr Manish Sisodia, the education minister. Or was the minister satisfied with Madam Osta's reply? I need not bother with anything from the stress of that episode. But one thing scared me a lot about the education minister. Whenever the minister visited any school, he often strongly reprimanded the HOS and the staff. He was unsatisfied with it; he put the video on social media to expose them. I wonder how significant the faults were that the HoS faced shame in public. But I was deeply hurt by his public humiliation.

Watching such insulting videos, a thought began to take shape: if the minister came to our place and followed the same trend, I would not be able to keep quiet. Each video strengthened my resolve. After all, the minister made a hasty visit to my neighbourhood school one day. A small door would open in my school from the boundary of the same school. The minister, along with his team, entered our school secretly.

When he started visiting the classes, after some time, I learned that the minister was visiting the school. I left my office and went to him with ease. He talked about the Happiness Curriculum in junior classes. Not only did he speak, but he was like a lawyer, cross-questioning the students. We were working on the ground level, so the answers were commendable. I was amazed by the spirits of the students. Something needed to be fixed with the library, so he examined the library very keenly. He got a good response to whatever he asked. He didn't visit other classes, then.

He came to the office and had a cold drink. He is famous for not eating or drinking anything in any school. But we didn't have anything like this here. People may want to hide their flaws under the guise of food and drink. That's why I like the minister's focus to shift from the school's drawbacks. But I didn't feel like hiding anything. When Education Minister Sisodia Ji left, he shook hands while sitting in his car. He looked into my eyes and said, 'Ish Kumar Ji, you are doing a great job. Well, done.'

The minister left, but our DDE, Madam Osta's office, kept making calls asking what had happened. Our school fell under her domain. She feared something might go wrong as our school was more immense in the North and had the district's most significant strength regarding students and teachers. If something went wrong here, the blame could have fallen on her, too. I briefed her on the whole incident. She was pleased. She also shared the information about this visit during the HOS meeting. All the HOSs asked me questions in their style. After all, Madam said: let's wait for the report. But this time, neither report nor video was put on the net. It was a relief for me and the officers of my zone. That's because if I had a mess here, it would have caused trouble.

At every stage in my life, such incidents have been scattered where I have got an appropriate, rather soothing response for my hard work. The teacher and school assessment depend on the students. In other departments, evaluating a person's hard work depends directly on their work. If your efforts are sincere, then they give positive results. Thanks to this thinking, I have never faced dismay as a teacher and HOS. After the minister's visit, the thought of any tussle with him had left my mind forever, and the rest of my service period was without such worries.

---000---

CHAPTER ELEVEN

Passion for Solidarity And Scientific Spirit

Is it enough as we know our parents? Or is it sufficient to know about our children? The questions follow me time and again. The process of knowing each other never ends; it should not be. The same applies to anybody else we claim to see, including ourselves. If this process of knowing ends at some point, we cannot enjoy our kinship as energetically as possible in its continuity and newness. The method of knowing should not be confined to the family. If the process of knowing extends beyond the periphery of the family to the society, nation and the universe, it makes our global citizenship authentic. Finding one's constructive role in the whole process can serve humanity excellently.

I have taken refuge under literature's umbrella to know myself from a global perspective. It is to be discussed in the episode related to literature. Here, I want to be confined to the family. Although my parents are not with us today, still the desire to know them keeps haunting me. When I talk about my journey of adventure to Tihar Jail and look back, my memories take me to Kharkhoda, Haryana. My father got his transfer there. He needed a house to live in. There was a big vacant house near the Chaupal. In front of it was a very long courtyard. My father talked about taking it on rent. But people said that there lived a Dhol-Kadiya, a ghost with white clothes. There was a threat to life.

My father was adamant about his insistence, and he said, 'No problem, still I want this house.' Finally, he got the house on rent. We, the family members, were not yet with him. That's why my father spent the first night there alone. In the morning, many people were curious about the night my father spent there. They wanted to know whether Masterji was safe or not. My father probably knew the psychology of people. He did not say that there were no ghosts. Instead, he said – 'Yes, the ghost in white clothes had come at night. The ghost and I had a lot of tussling. The ghost could not stay for long and ran away, scared.

My father also told them he got the ghost to do sit-ups and got a promise: it would not return there again. My father often talked of the story and laughed at people's ignorance. Such courageous tales of his stories gave us the courage to fight against blind faiths. Whether the villagers learned anything from this incident or not is far from known. After that, we stayed in the same house with family; again, no one felt the need to see ghosts in our home.

My father got this courage from Arya Samaj. He was a sincere follower of Arya Samaj. When we were young and used to get scared at night, our father made us repeat Gayatri Mantra. He would assure us that we would have no nightmares if we recited the Gayatri Mantra before sleeping. We followed it faithfully before going to sleep. Whether the mantra did anything is uncertain, but we trusted my father's word, making us sleep without nightmares. I believe that the business of amulets of tantric flourish on such beliefs.

This is the psychology I see behind the Babas engaged in Jhad-Phoonk or tantrums. But since reason and prudence became an integral part of my life and since I made my righteousness my protective shield, I did not feel the need for Gayatri Mantra. Chanting a rosary is also a way to escape the whirlpool of thoughts of doubt and fear. It works on the principle of placing a bigger image for a person to focus on, only to divert his attention from doubt or fear. It helps dilute negative thoughts and relieve a person from agony. Dhyana yoga is also one of the most popular tools; that is my belief.

The practical aspect of Arya Samaj, which I appreciate, is ethnic equality and the denial of idol worship. I like Swami Agnivesh's reasoning, but when there is talk of some unique benefit or extraordinary relief from chanting specific Matras, I have lost the gleam of relief. I do not like it when mysticism about atmosphere purification is established by denying the reality of air pollution from Havana. I object to it when Arya Samaj claims to sail the boat of life by carrying the Vedas on our heads. My father had learned and memorised mantras by heart and preferred weekly Havens. The entire house was cleaned before performing the Havan. This weekly cleaning issue fascinates me, but we feel sorry for not following this practice today regularly.

I am curious to know how much my father understood the meaning of the mantras uttered during the Havan. Never thought of learning. Having completed the recitation of Mantras and before Shanti Path of the Havan, he used to offer a prayer in his simple and common Hindi language. It was something like this - 'O God! O great father! Our family members have come under your protection. Please accept our greetings. We need help understanding that we make many mistakes in life due to ignorance. You must punish us accordingly. But we request you to give us the strength to bear it. O Daya Nidhe! O treasure of mercy! We hope you will listen to our request and show your kindness.' Ultimately, he wished for happiness for the family, neighbourhood, country, and all living beings in the name of a more prominent family. He hoped he would certainly listen to his prayer. Om (ॐ) Shanti.' After this, we collectively recited the Shanti Path we had learnt.

I am proud of my father's self-reliance. Even when we struggled to meet our family's needs, he never resorted to seeking help from any deity. He did not visit temples, Dargahas, Gurudwaras, or Churches to complain about his miseries. Instead, he believed in his work and wished for its fruits and rewards. This principle of self-reliance is something I deeply respect and follow in my life.

There is no need to pray for mercy for your actions. Getting a reward or punishment for your deeds is a natural phenomenon. Then, why to beg? That is why I do not believe in the power of any temple or mosque. It is the willpower or intensity of faith in yourself and your actions to be optimistic. I leave no effort unattempted regarding my possible role, whatever field it is, harming none and always getting contented.

It is worth mentioning here that I have also visited so-called pilgrimages or holy places. I have seen them as tourist destinations since I have a strong scientific temperament. I have tried to study the minds of those keen to surrender themselves before deities. I have observed a remarkable change in me; my activities automatically become food for critical analysis.

I had a bitter experience; I went to Vaishno Devi twice in the eighties with several of my relatives and their families. Even for the first time, I did not go on there out of faith because of the influence of Arya Samaj. There was a Langar, which means free food, from the late Shree Gulshan Kumar, a singer. We ate Langar, and three and a half hundred rupees disappeared from my pocket. We bought dry fruits, sewed our bags, and left them with the shopkeeper for further comfortable shopping. While returning, we picked up the goods and returned home. The walnuts turned out like a stone ball when we opened the bags. Hardly anything came out with the help of the needle. The episode made me realise the place was fit for the crooks alone to make their wishes come true.

I had to go to Vaishno Devi once again with my in-laws. We stayed at Dharamsala with a commitment to buy Prasad (blessed food) from their shop. When it was time to buy it, they insisted on buying at least twenty-one rupees per person. The matter was settled somehow, and we reached the doorstep of Vaishno Devi temple. The visitor's line was long enough, and we had yet to take a room for luggage, etc. I had no intention of visiting. Hence, I offered to stay with the luggage outside to make the group free to get in. I got back home from the door of the goddess. The stories took place before my joining Ambedkarite literature.

As an Ambedkarite, there is another story to share here; it happened that once a friend of mine, Mr MS Bisht and I planned to visit Mumbai with our families. His family consisted of four members: a husband and wife, one daughter, and a son. His son had been my student; he was somewhat of an atheist like me. But my wife was interested in visiting the temples with them. The biggest issue took place at the Shani Shingnapur temple. Only men had to go there wearing yellow clothes and offer oil on the stone figure like Shivling. Mr Bisht was not ready to go alone, and I had no option but to accompany him with too many ifs and buts.

During this journey, we visited Sai Baba at Shirdi. Based on my experience, whether someone believes in or not in the world of deities and places of worship, one can witness the reality of religious empires; you need to keep your mind and eyes open a little. That's it and nothing else. On the same pattern, if we need a wholesome image of an issue, the literature supporting and against it must be gone through. So, our brethren need to study beyond Ambedkarite icons.

Regarding my brothers' and sisters' beliefs, one of my brothers follows Christianity, and one brother lives in a temple and has his own beliefs. He is entirely devoted to the temple culture. A brother has nothing to do with the world. He is beyond the human world and humanity. Both the sisters are part of a simple worldliness. They do not have any personal views or concrete beliefs of their own.

I must call myself a liberal atheist. Liberal in the sense that I put my point of view freely with no prejudice without hurting the sentiments and belief systems of others. One more noteworthy thing is that nothing is permanent in this world, especially the belief systems. For instance, In the beginning, I followed my father's Arya Samaj. I followed Ambedkarism from 1998 to 2018. I realised I had entrapped myself in a realm and got suffocated. So, I set myself free to be no longer a slave to any one ideology, any person's philosophy, or any book that emphasises following a specific pattern of beliefs.

As a result, I felt somewhat isolated from my literary friends. The present situation opened doors to Ajivakism, Stoicism, and many more and helped me find a lifestyle that can address contemporary challenges that are getting worse. In this connection, I would like to share that my father was an Arya Samaji under whose shadow we were brought up. But today, if I say that our family has no relation with the Arya Samaj, I find nothing wrong with it.

Nowadays, there is a strange debate among my friends about instilling in a child Ambedkar's and Buddha's ideology since childhood on the pattern of other religions to be a permanent part of their personality. Their suggestions need a beginning or end to the activities to fulfil this objective. They seem in haste to get the desired results, ignoring the child's psychology and sentiments. They consider Buddhism to be a part of it. I find this tendency no less fatal than any religious fundamentalists. It is a torturous act against a child's innocent mind. I strongly condemn such moves against children's freedom, which is essential for their genuine outcome of mind, body and faith.

At this point, the families must provide an atmosphere suited to the scientific temperament. It is cruel to make their kids the carriers of their beliefs rather than the frustrations of their failures. Who are we to decide even the breathing patterns of our kids? Who are we to make our kids slaves to our support? Why don't we let our kids decide what to read and follow based on their understanding? Does merely giving birth to a child give us the right to enslave them to follow as a feudal lord? We need to find options, as I saw. I share the same point of view with my students. I have never tried imposing my opinions on my students. I have left each issue open-ended so that every student or individual can come to any conclusion.

Today's world is full of caste, religion, race, and region disputes. The family is the pivot that nurtures it in one way or the other. The family leaves no space for the child's autonomous and discretionary thinking. They waste no opportunity to impose their thoughts on the child's mind. The irreligious thinking of the so-called religion is working in preparing the fanatic thinking of the parents. Those who do politics of religion and business of religion turn an innocent person into a devil. Consequently, religion is neither a friend nor a guide to man. It has become difficult nowadays for religion to become a tool of peace and prosperity.

Today, the picture of religion is like that of making a man addicted to opium, whose intoxication kills wisdom and mortality. Man does not even know how big an enemy of humanity he has become. It was the religious authorities that put an astronomer and great scientist like Galileo under house arrest because he had told that the Earth revolves around the Sun, not the Sun, based on his research. The religious autocracy and cruelty took his life in detention.

I regret that the 'business of religion' is flourishing on many of Galileo's graveyards in India. It is the so-called religions and religious books that separate human beings from the human race to form a caste. Religion is making everyday living human beings Robots. Robots because religion does not allow reasoning. It only advocates following faithfully. Fatwas are issued against those who refuse to be robots and argue. These fatwas create a hollow of disgusting inequalities. Hence, there is bloodshed of human beings and humanity all around. That's why I find comfort in living without any religion. I cannot explain how others get their comfort. I prefer freedom irrespective of any majoritarian or minoritarian strata. One must respect others' freedom as one expects from others.

Whatever a parent does is in the child's interest as the intention is beyond doubt, but it is not so regarding capabilities. There is a limit to the dreams of parents. My father used to teach us to shoot arrows in childhood. When my younger brother was in class 7th, and I was in 8th, my father taught us to make shoes and slippers. But I still don't understand why my father didn't dream of something better regarding our careers. I am not doubting my father's foresight, but it is the question that haunts me. What my father dreamt of about my brother and me is the past, and we became what we deserved, but every parent should dream big and support them to achieve.

Beyond doubt, my father was a sincere person. But how he lagged in planning our career is still a concern for me. The circumstances of our village might be responsible for inappropriate assessment. He used to go to his training centre in the morning and return in the evening. In the evening, people's visits were very common to our house. The cleaning and preparation of the Havana on Sunday was like a festival. His world had become like a bondage to his job and village life. Maybe that's why he couldn't dream big for us. The realisation or non-realisation was a secondary thing.

If my father had taken back his Tagore Garden house and decided to settle in Delhi after retirement, the picture of the whole family would have been different. I realised the importance of city life when I joined Satyavati College (Evening), worked in Haryana, and told him my preference to live there. It is not that living in a town is unwise or a crime, but ignoring better opportunities is also not justified. But on the pattern, better late than never, we left the village. Even though we had not even imagined such circumstances as were responsible for our leaving the town.

It was not the first time we had left our village, but changing our residence every year for my father's job was obligatory. We had nothing like that of our permanent township. Later, it became an inheritance. Father left his village as a child and went to Kumar Ashram, Meerut, where we did not have anything like agriculture. From there, he shifted to the hills to Nehru Kutiya Delhi. Our family moved from Nehru Kutiya to dozens of new villages in Haryana each year as the demand of my father's job. The father settled down permanently in the Kundli village to eliminate the migration. The situation turned unfavourable, and we shifted to Khekra, U.P. From Khekra to Balram Nagar, Ghaziabad, U.P. My family stayed there, and I moved to the East of Loni Road, Chitrakoot, Delhi. After thirty years of stay there, while reviewing my autobiography, I live in Habitat Society, Vasundhara Enclave, Delhi-96. When I look at my escape journey, it seems strange. But it is the need of the hour and not a drawback but a journey for advancement.

This migration journey was not limited to changing my residence. The ideological shit, for the better, does not seem to have an end. Earlier, I was an Arya Samaji with my father. Today, I am an atheist. In literature, for some time, I was Dalitvadi, then Ambedkavadi and Ajivakvadi, and now I am free from any Vaad, which means ism. My writing has become 'Na Koi Vaad, Na Koi Vivad, only Samay Se Samvad', i.e. neither any ism nor any controversy but a dialogue with time. If I take the example of my literature genre, I first entered the literary world through poetry. Then, the literary criticism remained my passion for a long time. I wrote stories, and it journeyed to the collection of stories and then a novel. Now, I am writing an autobiography. Everything is going on simultaneously, keeping hand in hand. This escape is not a total escape, leaving one thing to another. The escape is not to be confined, as the sky is the limit of my Karma Bhoomi, my ideological flight to enjoy.

I want to recall my father again, as he never compromised our education. Even during a terrible financial crisis, my father did not tell us to leave our studies and work to earn, focus on the buffaloes' care, or make it a full-time livelihood. Although we two brothers knew how to make slippers, our father did not do any such work to promote his skills, for which we had to become his associates. He had only one dialogue - 'May it be that I have to sell the house's utensils, I will not ask you to leave your studies.'

We are keen to multiply the legacy with no bounds regarding our children's education. I lived in a joint family, and no suitable school was nearby. So, the first class needed a better start. When DAV Public School opened at some distance, I admitted both children to DAV school. Mohit was older; he studied in the third grade, and my daughter Pooja was in the second grade. Since I was an English teacher, the English medium was fine. I took them for a regular morning walk to improve their physical and mental health. Instead of cramming, I motivated them to thoroughly understand and express their thoughts in their language. Even if there were mistakes initially, we didn't need to be afraid of them. I knew the inaccuracies in the language would diminish, and the journey to accuracy and evolution in the language goes on, and there is no ultimate end unless we surrender. The same pattern was followed by Mrs Bursley, the principal of Green Field Public School, the best across the Yamuna. When my children came to classes VIII and IX, I got them admitted to this school. Even with nursery kids from non-English families, Mrs Bursley's instructions were to speak English. She strictly followed it without fail.

On the one hand, the conditions in this school were much better in terms of education. On the other hand, the spoiled children of the money-minded people were a threat to the educational environment of the school. When I would listen to the stories there, I often felt that I had made a mistake by getting my children admitted there. Since my children were from a different environment, they were neither the victim of poverty nor spoiled children of affluence. As I observed, my children, too, were affected adversely by the environment to some extent. Their focus diverted to other non-essential things that hampered their academic outcome.

I preferred both my kids in the science stream and biology so that they could get more options for their careers in the medical field. My son appeared in medical entrance tests but couldn't succeed. Eventually, he was admitted to an M-Tech in Biotechnology Integrated Five Year Course at Bundelkhand University. But his entire troop left the university after B-Tech, and the MBA ghost occupied everyone's mind. My son qualified for the test but didn't join. After this, he did an MSc (Bio-Chemistry) from Dehradun Para-Medical College. After this, he did his PhD after JRF and SRF. Precisely, the same was the case with my daughter. She earned a BSc in Zoology (Hons) from Acharya Narendra Dev College (DU) but left it to join Medical Microbiology from Dehradun. She completed her MSc in Medical Microbiology from Ambala Medical College and, finally, PhD from Santosh Medical College.

I mention all this because I have never imposed my will and decisions on my children when choosing their careers.

It also doesn't mean that I left them open to do anything. I have never been free from sharing my opinion. What they had to do, or not, has been a discussion for the whole family. Once the decision was made, it was accepted as the decision of the entire family. Whatever its consequences were, it has been the collective responsibility of the family. There was no space left for blaming anyone in case of failure. This process did not apply to studies alone, but the same pattern was adopted in all the family affairs.

Once, my daughter's health turned out to be very bad while doing her M.Sc. The doctor advised her not to take long-term courses like a three-year MSc, but my daughter was firm in her decision. She was adamant not to surrender. Eventually, the whole family stood by her assertion. She fell ill often, but the family stood by her, and she got out, achieving what she was determined to. The same problem arose for her PhD, but the collectiveness of the family came with flying colours.

As a child, we had read the story of a farmer and his four sons. He gives the message through the story that if you remain alone or scattered, anyone can harm or defeat you. My family naturally followed this policy to stay united and achieve the desired goals. This unity of ours defied that doctor's opinion: If you do not keep her away from stress, you will lose her. We, too, believed the same, but we had solidarity in our family, and ultimately, it proved the doctor wrong.

This issue of family solidarity is not our invention. We have inherited it from my parents. Our family's unity was unquestionable when our existence in the Kundli was at stake. The family challenged all the crises based on solidarity to defeat the ruin chasing us. I want to give credit to my parents for this. I know a little about my forefathers through rare tales, as we have seen none. It is comforting that my maternal grandma witnessed a remarkable example of solidarity in the family. About seventy-eight years ago, she had four iron and cemented roofs, as seen in railway quarters or other buildings. They owned no agricultural land or business but had hard labour and solidarity.

However, we have grandchildren today. We enjoy collective decisions as usual, which are carried as a legacy. This unity works even when selecting each other's dresses for different occasions. Decisions on how to treat young children and how to take care of them are also taken collectively and followed faithfully. I am proud of my family and its legacy. I sincerely wish my future generation to enrich their inheritance so that they can accomplish everything with a sweet smile. It is on the readers to follow it if they find anything convenient for their betterment.

---oOo---

CHAPTER TWELVE

Proud To Be Beloved of The Universe

We have heard the stories of miracles around us; perhaps nobody has seen them happening. The whole business of religion and faith is based on miracles. They depend on the fulfilment of wishes. It is seen in the form of the omnipotent so-called supernatural forces. Whatever seems impossible becomes possible because of supernatural powers. The art of making the impossible possible with supernatural powers makes them God, Allah, God-Goddesses, etc.; it makes them almighty, omniscient and omnipresent. I don't know about any other people, but I have yet to learn about the reality of the existence of these supernatural powers. Knowing how they do miracles is beyond the understanding of a simple guy like me. These are the subjects of scholarly people that I am not. I have no hesitation in admitting my ignorance.

I have little knowledge of this world of mine. But the little knowledge and whatever happened around me forced me to conclude: The whole universe is with me. I felt like a miracle in my life. But I do not consider it a miracle because even if there is a miracle, it is the prerogative of supernatural powers. Why would they do miracles in my life when I never visit their shelter houses? I do not make any such complaint to them either. But I find something incredible, like a beam of positivity and solace in me. I am writing this because it is a source of my energy, a lighthouse of confidence and positivity.

As a result of thislight beam, the whole Kaynat, the creation, is with me like a boon to success and satisfaction. The realisation keeps me determined to work with dedication without worrying about the result. I need not think about which door to open or shut for the future of my journey to success and solace. Whatever I encounter, which may seem unpleasant to others, does not let me lose my belief: It is all for the best. Sometimes, I find one door of life closed, and another opened to my enthusiasm. 'Failures open the door to success' is a slogan to preach, but I live it practically in real spirit. It is a privilege for the reader to see it in terms of 'grapes are sour'.

Looking back, I was admitted to Chemistry Honors at Kirori Mal College, University of Delhi. Still, I had to leave everything to prepare for the NDA examination. It was a significant loss to lose one year of my study period. But it doesn't bother me anymore. I see this in my favour as well. Even if I had done a B.Sc., getting a job would have taken at least three years. Getting a job after completing my B.Sc. was not easy. It could have taken some more time to prepare for a particular job. My critical economic conditions did not afford more time and money to invest in my studies. Completing my diploma in basic training from Jamia in 1977 increased my job prospects, and I got a job. It was crucial for the survival of me and my family.

When my wife and I were enthusiastic about our love materialising in marriage. It can be termed our ignorance that we had aspired to have two sons and two daughters, i.e. four children. Perhaps I had not even thought about how to handle the responsibility of their upbringing. But when my daughter, the second issue, was born, my wife was diagnosed with a tumour rather than a cancer in her stomach, ruined lofty castles of pleasure in a single stroke. Our victory in love turned into deep mourning. The doctor told us about radiotherapy, chemotherapy and the suspension of ovary function, which meant she could not become a mother further. The thought of my wife's survival eradicated the idea from our minds about whether Shashi would become further a mother or not.

The news of cancer had broken me badly. During the treatment, my wife was staying at her paternal home, Kotla Mubarakpur, near Safdarjung Hospital; I would cry wholeheartedly in the deserted streets at night. But in the presence of the family members, I tried to look and behave normal. We tried to console each other but were internally stricken. The cancer treatment was completed and followed up over the years. Finally, the doctor said- it has been over eight to ten years, and the chances of reappearing of the cancer are negligible. He advised us to visit at regular investigation after certain intervals. We followed the same and defeated the cancer. The most significant role my wife played was her courage. It did not let the terror of cancer attack her psyche. She took cancer like any other common disease and defied it. But today, it is not like that; now, she is scared of even minor health issues.

Cancer-like trouble came into our lives, and we had to struggle hard. In a way, it came with a blessing, too. If my wife hadn't suffered from this disease, we could have had more children. We couldn't bring them up with the same dedication as we did with Mohit and Pooja. That's why I call the cancer in our life solely as a curse but a boon as well.

It inspires me to believe that something in the universe evaluates and judges our actions. I do not see this judging force as a supernatural or God.

My family was left small because of cancer. It would be better to call it a boon that we got the benefit of a 'small family, happy family' without asking for it. We were able to spare our children enough time. Obviously, our children saw us playing our role in the joint family since childhood. Today, my son and daughter are married and have their own families and children. But everything in the family is as it used to be while living under one roof. Understanding our responsibilities towards each other and seeing the family as a unit continues even today.

Regarding my daughter-in-law Preeti Rajaura, now Preeti Gangania, and son-in-law Pradeep Kumar Singh, we never realised from their behaviour and conversation that they had their upbringing elsewhere. I would feel proud to say that I think about my son-in-law and daughter-in-law as if they, too, were born in the same family. They have been brought up under our supervision in the same way as Mohit and Pooja. Because of this, every family decision is made with consensus. We share our sorrows and joys together as if one unit.

It does not mean we don't have controversies—they do but within certain limits. They are to be sorted out dignifiedly with mutual consent. Whether it is the elder or younger in the family, none feel the need to impose their will on others. Everything proceeds on mutual acceptance. I am proud of this legacy growing in my family's creative direction. But yes, it is to mention categorically that today's facts guarantee nil for the future.

In the same light, I see my family's escape episode from Kundli. My parents loved the village. They had many dreams about the house. For instance, their four daughters-in-law would come to the same house. Their children would have fun in the house and courtyard. There would be a lot of activity in the house. The daughter-in-law would cook food at the Gobar Gas Plant. We would enjoy the shade under the Neem tree. The daughter-in-law would sing songs while swinging under this Neem tree in the month of Sawan.

The parents' dreams were for daughters-in-law, children, and grandchildren to enjoy the joint family. However, they had not dreamt that their kids would grow up and the situation would not be the same. While my parents talked about such plans of ecstasy, I, too, had no idea of finding any dent in their flawless journey of thoughts. I simply enjoyed what I heard from them in leisurely hours. I needed to be younger to think of such a plan. The rest of the family members would enjoy the dreams of our parents.

These were dreams that had no end. Anyway, dreams have no end and probably shouldn't be. But in their dreams, there were no dreams of children's education. Nor were there dreams of migrating to other places for the job. They did not even dream of traffic chaos and waste of time. They needed to learn about getting a job at such a place where daily ups and downs were not feasible. They did not even think of working daughter-in-law for their sons. I have already talked about the sad incident of leaving the village. Leaving our town without such a tragic accident may not have been easy. The family took the terrible departure too as a blessing, so until her last breath, my mother would bless, raising her hands towards the sky to those responsible for this dreadful episode. She used to say: If they did not treat us like enemies, we could not leave the village. If we had not left the town, we would have had the same plight as the other people in that locality after leaving our village. Our lives would have turned into hell, facing courts and even life imprisonment as well.

The issue of migration from Balram Nagar, Ghaziabad, UP, has also been similar. Although the distance of my wife's school, Amar Colony, Delhi, from our residence in Balram Nagar, would have been hardly three to four kilometres. But this road was often broken, traffic jams were common, and no permanent solution had ever been found. One day, the rickshaw overturned on the way, and my wife had to return covered in the mud without attending to her duty. She was adamant not to stay there anymore. Some of the actions of my younger brother's wife added fuel to the fire. Ultimately, the decision to migrate from Balram Nagar was taken in haste.

If she had not fallen in the mud on that day and had not had a rift with my brother's wife, buying the flat could not have materialised. Another factor responsible for purchasing my flat was my daughter's friend Priyanka's father, who had discussed his plan to buy a flat with us. He told us that later, the flat rates would go high with the coming pay commission. Both her parents were doctors. They missed the opportunity to buy the flat then and even later because the price had increased significantly. When the decision to purchase a flat was finalised, we made speedy efforts to raise funds. We bought it, even though all the money was in the form of a loan. Well, we became the flat owners and shifted on April 14 1994. Gradually, in three to four years, all the debt was settled.

There was controversy behind this purchase as well. My parents and family were unhappy with this decision as it was a matter of separation from the joint family. By the way, all our responsibilities towards the family had ended. However, no parent wants their children to be separated. After the purchase, my wife's school was within walking distance. Time was saved for my children's studies and for me to travel to and from the job.

Regarding the share in the land, house, etc., of Balram Nagar, I was determined to leave everything for the family. Later, when my separation from the family subsided, things changed for the better, and my parents realised that they had two houses now instead of one at Balram Nagar. They appreciated that my decision to have a separate house was correct. It confirmed that circumstances always turn out to be favourable for me as beloved of Kaynat, the universe.

I could not get this flat so comfortably. It, too, has a story. While I purchased the flat, I served at the school in Gokalpur Village. Mr Keshav Ram Gupta used to be our headmaster. Suddenly, he was transferred to Dilshad Garden. He was very impressed with my commitment to the job. He transferred me to his new school of posting, J&K Block Dilshad Garden. There was a lot of scope for private tutoring. I have always been, and still am, caught up in working hard. Just then, what was it? I got busy with my work, and by 1998, all the dues were settled. This year, I moved to Timarpur Delhi as a lecturer (English) on promotion.

Along with leaving the school, I also gave up private tuition forever. It is certain that if Kesho Ram Gupta had not taken me to Dilshad Garden, the dream of owning a flat would have come true too late. The period of hardship could have been a little longer. I could not send my children to my desired school. In this whole episode, I did nothing to make things favourable.

Being with the entire universe was a different experience. At this point, my children had come into a higher class and had no special need for my guidance. They moved to their self-studies, and I had no pressure of any loan to settle now. There was no question of private tuition, too, as I have never been a money-monger. This was when I got the one door closed that was no longer worthy of it, and a new one opened automatically. It is the world of literature. Neither did I think about it, nor did I plan to enter anyway. I have already shared the story of my literary entrance. It started with Dr Jai Prakash Kardam, but he used to bring out his annual journal, 'Dalit Varshiki' once a year. So, there was no notable scope there. It is worth noting that I published my first book, 'Har Nahin Manoonga'; the translation is 'I will not give up'.

Then, a new door outstretched, and the circumstances brought Dr Tej Singh closer to me. Together, we published a quarterly magazine called 'Apeksha'. With this, a series of studies and writings came into existence. We worked together for eight years. I was attached to the selfless work as expected. Even thought of any benefit or favour never struck my mind. Still, selfless efforts materialised, and I was recognised as a writer nationwide. I will share my entire literary journey in another chapter to come. I am sharing it here to state that when one path is closed for me, another better door stays open. That is why I do not need to worry about my future activities, as the tracks automatically take me to a new destination.

These new avenues keep opening one after the other. Earlier, I entered literature through poetry. Then, I entered the field of literary criticism with Dr Tej Singh. To solve the question of identity, I took out Aajivak Vision magazine. After separating from Dr Tej Singh, I published my story collection, 'Intuition'. It was a unique experience in itself. It took off my spirits, and I wrote a novel within four months. It is also a strange coincidence that I got a call from Kuku FM Radio saying they wanted to launch my book in the audio market. Its audio opened a new path, and Kuku FM launched my story collection, 'Intuition' audio. My friends said your work should also be in English. This will make the canvas of your literature global. I grabbed the opportunity to rewrite my stories, novels, and poems. A new literary world opened for me go ahead.

In my family lineage, no evidence exists of anyone being an author. I am the only one who got the opportunity to break the rocky ground of literature. This opportunity is nothing less than a tremendous boon for me. My post-retirement life served as icing on the cake. On the contrary, some of my friends are troubled by their post-retirement lives. They have yet to continue their reading and writing habits or hobbies, such as social work. So, they are compelled to kill their time in worthless activities. Their concern is how to pass the time. On the contrary, I have so much scope for creative work that even twenty-four hours a day seems inadequate. Literature is a blessing that has become an integral part of my life and a reliable companion to my isolation.

As discussed earlier in the previous chapter, the door to the B.Ed. was opened for me differently. Visiting my friend, Mr Om Prakash, to share the information about B.Ed. summer course, by grabbing the opportunity to pass the entrance test, and finally, the support of our principal is one of the classic examples of the universe with me. The issue of my MA (English) degree needed to be explained. I would like to recall this episode in the present context. As I have mentioned earlier, during which one semester of my MA papers was to be held in March. At the same time, my students on private tuition had board papers. The problem I faced was that continuing with the private tuition would put my MA (English) degree at stake. My morality would be at stake if I focused on my MA at the cost of ignoring my board students. Choosing one of the two was a tough decision to make. There was no option left but to pass through a dilemma.

I could not afford to put my morals at stake, so I sacrificed my MA (English). The turning point was when affairs stood with me as a boon and protected my morals and MA (English). As usual, one day, with the dilemma, I was going to school with my two children on a scooter. My scooter slipped on the busy road, and all three were scattered like lifeless objects. My hands and feet got chipped, and there was minor bruising, but there was nothing like a fracture. Remarkably, my children were free from such minor issues.

It was also a matter of comfort that no vehicle came from behind, which could cause severe damage. The information reached the school. Some bright students visited my house to talk about my health conditions. Out of sympathy, they said, 'Nothing to worry, sir. Have a rest. Whatever you have taught is enough to prepare for the exam.' It took me a week to recover.

Meanwhile, I prepared for my syllabus during bed rest; the students handled the examination well. Eventually, I got the degree, and my name was on the list of promotions released from the directorate of education. Now, I got promoted to Lecturer (English) in 1998. I was the first among my peers to get promoted before them because of my English. Had I depended on my political science master's degree, it would have been too late. Even the dream of promotion to the post of Vice-Principal would have been a dream.

I would like to share another incident from the Gokul Pur Village school that chases me repeatedly. This school was co-ed, i.e. boys and girls studied together. A girl in my class was talking to a former student named Shekhar near the tin boundary of my school during working hours. This girl was a little bright and ahead of her age. I called her and enquired, but she needed help answering the questions. I scolded her and said, 'After school, I will accompany you to your house; I must talk to your family. As usual, I went to different tents to take my regular classes. About an hour before closing the school, one of my students told me the girl was missing. It was a matter of grave concern for me, and I felt a strange fear inside because the issue was related to a girl. The position of a girl and a teacher is almost the same regarding sensitiveness. If their behaviour has slight ups and downs, their character is the first thing to target.

As I had told the girl about visiting her house, it was more a threat than a reality. But now it had become mandatory for me to see her home. I took a school child to her house. She had a sister-in-law in the house. Her parents were probably not alive. I told her about the incident and shared my landline number and home address to contact if needed. They did not call me, but two or three people reached my residence at night. Among them was the girl's brother. He informed me that the girl had not arrived home. I also shared all the details with him, and they returned. I am curious to know how satisfied they were with what I had shared with them.

The girl did not reach her home even the next day. That's why her brother came to school with many people. Some of the teachers at my school had a grudge against me unannounced. They called them to conspire and said that only I knew where the girl had gone. They said - he is the one who comes to school suited-booted with Tie-Shai every day. Undoubtedly, the conscience of the troubled does not work correctly. The same thing must have happened to them. They were destined to go to the police station as it was the question of a missing girl. I don't know what they said about me to the police. But a sub-inspector and a constable came to the principal's office in the afternoon to investigate. I was called but not allowed to put my point of view. They told me to go to the police station to explain. I requested to visit the police station the next day because it was my son's birthday. They flatly refused.

I reached Gokul Puri Police Station with two colleagues, Mr NC Tyagi and Mr Padam Singh Kasana. Now, the fear in my mind was taking shape. The concerned sub-inspector was not on the seat. He was out for lunch. He sent tea for us. While sitting, I tried to look normal but suffered something unpleasant. The inspector came after lunch and said smiling: Master Ji, you may go home. The girl's brother had just told me the girl had returned. She had gone to her maternal uncle's house out of fear. I breathed relief and departed.

The point of the discussion is that if we had met the sub-inspector before lunch and he didn't know that the girl had returned home, he could have shown his typical policeman attitude. He could have misbehaved, but it did not happen because the truth and the universe were with me to come clean. We celebrated my son's birthday as usual. My faith gives me energy and motivates me to follow righteousness.

When I talk about the police and the police station, another incident knocks on my memory. As discussed in detail in another chapter, my maternal uncle possibly lodged a complaint bearing the names of my father and two of my younger brothers. I was set away from the clash, though I was the eldest among brothers. They were genuinely innocent; they faced a lot of trouble at the police station. The family, too, had sleepless nights. Ultimately, the case proved fake, and all my family members were innocent. Why they had to suffer is still a puzzle that needs a solution. But being kept free from direct hits pushes me to comment: It is another classic case for me to claim a beloved of the universe.

My struggle against the autocratic and mala fide approach of my Principal, Mr Surendra Kumar, and Deputy Director (Zone) Manju Sharma was no less risky. I did not compromise with my superior officers for justice because of my fair intention and selflessness. My honesty was my strength, keeping me energetic to fight against evil. My purpose in recalling the issue here is that this issue is a witness to illustrate the whole universe being associated with me.

It is essential to share another incident from our own school. When I became HOS, Head of the School, instead of doing the job of a Principal, I had to comply with the jobs of two Vice Principals and one Superintendent (DDO), four posts due to a staff shortage. I had no problem with any work except for the DDO ship. To solve the problem, I had a teacher named Basant Kumar Singh. He was very amicable when dealing with official matters. He didn't let me know if I had any issues with DDO-ship. He was accompanied by another companion, Shivshankar Puligundla. He had a wonderful experience working at the Headquarters. Both of these proved to be troubleshooters for me. I am grateful for the unparalleled cooperation of these two. I put this episode as one of the fine examples to claim that the universe supported my righteousness. That is why I could justify my multiple jobs brilliantly.

Regarding my writing, some of my colleagues often ask me why I write on the ruling party's critical issues so bluntly. Why do you make a crucial satire about religion? Nowadays, the political mood does not allow to comment on politics and religion. Why don't you understand? It is just like inviting a bull to attack you unnecessarily. Their logic is authentic and practical in today's environment, but I wonder why I could not stand with my well-wishers to this day. I agree that the dangers are great because of the current regime. It pains me a lot if I do not discuss the issues that bother me. It forced me to look at the life struggles and spirit of sacrifice of personalities like Bhagat Singh, Netaji Subhash, Dr Ambedkar, Phule couple, Periyar, Nelson Mandela, Socrates and Tathagata Buddha, I feel like a pigmy relatively worthless. I feel embarrassed about being a human. To console myself, I record my consent or dissent in any genre of literature. I have no option but to go ahead, whether the affairs favour me or go adversely. I am not straining my mind about what shape the circumstances will take place as I have a strong faith in the universe as my sole companion.

I also keep my marriage in this category; the universe is to shelter me. I have discussed the episodes of my association with girls. The marriage issue was of prime importance in some cases but was in vain. The episode of the struggle for the marriage between Shashi's family and mine was long, full of challenges and upsetting till the end, but ultimately materialised. It symbolises my genuine desire: 'I wanted a working woman as my life partner within the target of twenty-five years of age. The boy and girl should know each other appropriately before entering a marriage institution. Such a marriage can be happy, prosperous, and long-lasting.' At this juncture, it is established that if the wishes are grounded, the intentions are noble, and the efforts are honest and sincere, the wishes often come true. My journey of married life of more than forty-two years with mutual wisdom and solace was not possible without the blessings of the universe.

I do not favour beneficial events like a boon. I do not credit them as a product of luck or God. However, I accept the role of determinism to some extent in my struggling life and its optimistic results. This determinism is not fatalism. Often, people call it fate and derive negative conclusions as they desire. The thought pattern emphasises that specific targets are beyond the person's reach and get materialised under the influence of determinism, where a person's role turns negligible.

The case of my son's marriage confirms this determinism to some extent. My son was doing an M-Tech in Biotechnology (Integrated, i.e., a five-and-a-half-year course) at Bundelkhand University. However, his entire circle of friends decided to leave the university only after the B-Tech; my son also left M-Tech together. They wanted to do an MBA. My son also cleared the MBA entrance test and appeared in merit but did not join. He said: I have to work as a medical representative. What is to do next will be decided later. After a few ifs and buts, I said okay. It's a matter of your choice; go ahead. I knew he was not going to last long in this field. But I didn't impose my will on him. He went to Mumbai for training. There, he met a girl named Preeti Rajaura. She went on training after doing her D-Pharma. My son completed the training, worked for three to four months, and left. There was no dispute in the house about why he joined the job and left.

In the same way, Preeti Rajaura also left this job. She went to Delhi University to get a B-Pharma degree. My son Mohit went to Dehradun to do MSc (Biochemistry). But the friendship between the two continued. They continued to visit each other's houses. My son later enrolled in PhD after an MSc, and the girl, Preeti, enrolled in M-Pharma at DU. After this, the girl worked in a multinational company in Goa. My son opened an institute and pathology lab named 'The Institute of Molecular Biology and Genomics (IMBG) in Dehradun. After all, there was talk of marriage, and Preeti's parents rejected it. History was repeating itself; i.e., My son was on the same track through which his father passed. There was a separate issue with the father regarding caste. In this case, the caste issue was slightly more complex. The job of the girl's father in the police made it more complicated.

I concealed nothing about my family while dealing with the girl, Preeti. I had left all the avenues open for her to decide. Someday, the girl had to revolt against her family. The story is very long, and my family's struggle was also no less in this matter. Eventually, the girl came to my house, and it was decided that the marriage would occur in court. We got the time fixed with the court. The girl wished that Haldi, Mehandi, Geet, Dance, and all other rituals would be done at our residence as would have been in her family if there had been an adequately arranged marriage. We didn't mind. We knew well how painful it was for a girl to marry, going against her parents' will. We did not want to enhance her suffering. That's why the rituals meant for girls' and boys' marriages took place comfortably at the flat till the first night of the wedding. The whole family was delighted.

But then the girl, Preeti, probably could not abide by the absence of her parents. Suddenly, on the previous night of marriage, the daughter had such a bad dream about her family that she could not even utter a word like a dumb one in the morning. Her hands and feet turned utterly cool. We were afraid that if something untoward happened, my whole family would end up in jail. The working of the girl's father in the police department was a clear indication that there was no hope of sympathy. After a long insistence, she uttered some words that were vague and beyond grasp. Later, we learnt that she said, 'I can't leave my family.' The second thing was that she didn't want to leave us either. Her dilemma was predictable, nothing more.

We apprised her father of the situation, and a meeting in a park near his house was fixed. On meeting, the daughter explained the issue and pleaded for support, but in vain. The walls of caste on the one hand and the police mentality on the other, the result remained negative. Finally, my son and I handed him up to his daughter and returned with the view of a complete breakup. This issue pertains to January 1, 2019. My daughter and son-in-law were at our residence for the ceremony, which now appeared cancelled. The whole atmosphere was gloomy, and it was decided to forget everything.

Parallel to the relationship, another request for a girl's relationship was pending from Shaadi.com. She was a scientist in Pusa. She believed that she would get her transfer at Dehradoon and there would be no issue of living with the family jointly. My daughter Pooja and the girls under consideration for marriage were regularly in touch through phone calls. The final decision was awaited from our side. We had to finalise the girl working in Pusa as a scientist, thinking whatever happened was for the good. One door was closed, and the other was ready to open to better heal the wound.

While the discussion was on, the doorbell rang. The girl, Preeti, was standing at the door severely shattered, and in a way, she was out of sense. Entering the gate, she said loudly: I have left my house entirely. I only want to marry Mohit (my son). I want to live in this house. The whole family was shocked to see her miserable condition. Her cries left no space for others but to calm her down. After much ideological upheaval, it was decided: let us forget the past. It is important to mention again that this issue was very long. A short novel can be written on the topic. But here, only a brief outline of the episode is shared.

It was now about eleven o'clock in the morning. Suddenly, we thought: Why should the cancelled visit not be rearranged? One of my brothers-in-law, Mr Bhanwar Singh, who practised in the court in Tees Hazari, was again taken into the discussion to reschedule the process. He fixed the exact date, but the time was delayed by a few hours. Finally, we were asked to reach the court before two o'clock. We arranged everything again and reached the stipulated time with the lawyer at Tees Hazari court. We completed the court procedure, and later, the rest of the marriage ceremony was also completed in Arya Samaj Mandir Civil Lines, and the marriage certificate was collected. It was January 1 2019, the first date of the new year. Then, on the birthday of the son, i.e. January 12, the reception took place with great pomp.

As I mentioned earlier, I did not want to add to the misery of the absence of my daughter-in-law's family. I did not wish my daughter-in-law to be under any tension regarding her parents. That's why we told her she could invite her family to the reception to avoid unnecessary stress. We, too, requested them to attend the reception. It would be a pleasant moment for all of us to make this day memorable. It is appreciable that they participated in the reception with some of their close relatives and brought some gifts. They danced and enjoyed the ceremony as if everything was normal and pre-planned. They returned back with a broad smile on their faces. Since then, the relationship between both families has been quite normal, like in the case of an arranged marriage.

When I analysed this episode, I found that my son was at Bundelkhand University, Jhansi, and now my daughter-in-law was at DU. Sudden meeting. Both did the job of Medical Representative, and both left it. They went to study different courses and went to other places. An excellent relationship with shaadi.com was pending to get materialised. A day before the wedding, all the ruckus and ultimately cancelled the marriage. The condition of deleting even each other's phone numbers. Despite this, in three hours, all the plans for the marriage were made anew, and the marriage reached its glorious goal. If I do not call it determinism, what should I call it? It was another experience quite different from the coincidence of other experiences for me. Coincidences were full of coincidences, one after the other. Because of such developments, I find the whole universe in my favour.

The few examples I have cited here, but the number is much larger. My belief in the laws of nature is my strength in making my spirits go high. It prevents the entry of frustration and despair into my life. Such activities keep me drenched with positivity and encourage me to move forward. It is not that I have never known hopelessness and sadness. I get frustrated and even disappointed on many occasions. But I never allow them to ride on me for a long time.

However, some time ago, I wrote a post about 'Samay Sangyan' on Facebook and denied any role other than my authorship. But just a few days back, the editorial board of 'Samay Sangyan' entrusted me with a big responsibility by making me the editor. I did not have any such desire, nor did I make any effort in this direction. But I wonder why circumstances have opened a different door for me. I aim to work and always do so with full commitment to myself. I hope to live up to the test of the editorial board. Together, we will do something that will help enrich the legacy of Hope. This may be a new example of Kainaat, the universe being with me.

---000---

CHAPTER THIRTEEN

Literature: The Last Resort

There can be no better companion than literature or books. They need nothing in return, likely a worldly bargain system. They require no maintenance other than a bit of cleanliness and gentle handling. This is a one-time investment and a lifelong gain. Once invested, they serve with no expiry. They do not know about any breakups as we see in human relationships. Since there are no breakups, there is no risk of compensation and revenge. They always have unconditional support and zeal at your adoption.

The same is true of writing or authorship. You need sincere commitment with no bargain. You can enjoy its company anytime and to any extent without tantrums like a beloved. It keeps you alive in readers' minds in different moods while you stay busy elsewhere. It is a treasure and investment that remains unrobbed and unexhausted to enrich. I am enthusiastic about being a humble and unexplored specimen of the global community of books and writings.

Chapter Six introduces me and the circumstances of my entry into the literary world. Under the chapter's current title, I want to share information on each book's journey and publication. I started writing in 1999, and my first book, 'Haar Nahi Manoonga', 'I will not give up' (poetry collection), was published by Atish Prakashan in Delhi in 2000. It has limitations regarding maturity in selecting words, thoughts, treatment, and aesthetics. At the end of the book, there are some Ashaars, I mean Urdu couplets, but nothing but rubbish in the name of Shero-Shayari. I am sorry for saying it that way.

Till the arrival of my first book, I got acquainted with the names Mohandas Naimishray, Kanwal Bharti, Om Prakash Valmiki, Suraj Pal Chauhan, Sudesh Tanwar, Balbir Singh Madhopuri, Karmsheel Bharti, Dr Kusum Viyogi, Prof. Shatrughan Kumar, Dr Sohan Lal Sumanakshar, Vimal Thorat, Professor Tulsi Ram, Shivnath Sheelbodhi, T.P. Singh' Tej' Suraj Badtya and some Marathi writers other than Dr Jai Prakash Kardam who was just like a mentor to me. Some names must have been missed, and I am sorry about that. I had personally met some of these writers. Suraj Badtya was the first to write an excellent review of my book in the newspaper. I am sincerely thankful to Suraj Bhai for the job. There was another category of great writers like Kamleshwar, Rajendra Yadav, Maheep Singh, Ramnika Gupta, Professor Chaman Lal, Roop Singh Chandel, etc.; my literary journey took its course by listening to their stories of achievements and multiple traits of their personalities.

Even though Dr Tej Singh worked as a Research Scientist at the University of Delhi, he had just come to Dalit literature from Marxism. He did not know much about Dalit litterateurs. They looked upon his arrival with suspicion of a Marxist conspiracy. Most Dalit literature advocates were not directly associated with academics. Perhaps they feared Dr Singh's academic flair and the long experience made them insecure.

Dr Tej Singh often had to face controversies in disguise. None dared to face him directly because of his rigid attitude and use of harsh words about the shortcomings of literature. Many would refrain from adding ifs and buts to his viewpoints and criticism in plain words. But his absence was often literally an issue of his criticism and blame game. I am not doubting the abilities of these frustrated fellows. I am not in favour of denying their contribution to giving a foothold to Dalit literature. They have been the warriors who faced every attack of the advocates of traditional literature. The struggle has been long enough, but they did not surrender and ultimately won the battle of Dalit literature's recognition. It is evident that the other battles often appear with no substantial points and never end. It is because it makes the authentic horoscope of so-called civilised society and literature, whether academic or religious. History is not far from their reach.

Like Dr Tej Singh, I was also new to Dalit literature. Yes, because of my association with Dr Kardam, I got the label of Dr Kardam's camp. It is a different matter, as I have never been a camp member. I had the solid trait of my personality to say bluntly what I believed or thought of on any of the issues. I still carry it on faithfully. My poetry collection, 'Har Nahi Manoonga', comforted Dr Tej Singh as I had opted for a different view from existing Dalit literature. It was close to him; he did not articulate it directly but through other gestures. We were almost on the same boat of novelty and unique identities to be part of Dalit literature.

Here, the Marxist identity and Dr Tej Singh's experience could have been more helpful. This was his negative merit in the eyes of the advocates of Dalit literature. I was nowhere in terms of such qualifications. Maybe not even today. It is a different matter that I read and write a little bit, nothing more. It was shared that most Dalit writers viewed Brahmanism and Marxism as enemies to attack. Even today, the situation has not changed much. They weigh both on the same scale and make bizarre remarks.

The idea of publishing a magazine struck Dr Tej Singh's mind. He asked me to join him as we were ideologically close. It was like hitting two birds with a single stone. I agreed with no ifs and buts. Though Dr Tej Singh did not disclose it, he had a long-term strategy to enhance the canvas of Dalit literature to a universal approach. It was not possible without having his platform to work independently. Neither he nor I had any identity to settle the issue. Hence, we extended our hands to seek the support of skilled and established artisans like Dr Kardam. Dr Kardam and I were neighbours then. We approached his residence with a proposal. We proposed to write the first editorial, Dr Tej Singh would write the second, and alternately, the editorials would continue.

Dr Kardam turned down the offer politely. He argued that he was already publishing the Dalit Varshiki', Dalit literature (annual). Secondly, he said that his office hours were also too long. That's why he won't be able to spare time for our journal. His logic was genuine; there was no room to insist on him. As far as I can understand today's development, he could have spared the time. But Dr Kardam is very calculated, and one ought to be; he might have realised that it was unprofitable. That's why he refused to join the magazine. Another side of the coin is that he was an independent and privileged editor of his magazine, and there was no need to compromise his status by joining any other magazine like ours. There was another risk of comparison of the editorials of both. What was needed to invite a bull to hit on?

This situation could have prepared the ground for a comparative analysis of both literary acumen. Dr Kardam considers it best to avoid such comparisons as a ruckus. Dr Tej Singh was trying to play the safe game by giving Dr Kardam the responsibility of two editorials in a year. Our undeclared intention was to take advantage of his popularity in Dalit literature, but this did not emerge. I can confidently say that even today, whatever happened was for the best.

Despite the inappropriate response from Dr Kardam, we published the magazine. The fact is that initially, we had planned to publish the magazine on our own. The idea of the inclusion of Dr Kardam was a later development. I must determine when and how Dr Tej Singh conversed with Jai Prakash Lilwan. He told me that Jai Prakash Lilwan is also with the magazine. Jai Prakash Lilwan was an aggressive Marxist. We must state with great sadness that Mr Lilwan and Dr Tej Singh are no longer among us. Perhaps due to his aggressive nature, he was transferred to Lucknow. The transfer cycle from one place to another did not change, and he could never return to Delhi. However, he gave one thousand rupees monthly as financial support for two to three months. All three of us paid this amount to meet the expenses of publication. Nine thousand rupees were collected in three months, enough to publish an issue of the magazine. Dr Ashwini and Dr Sunil Mandiwal were active in the magazine. The magazine's first issue emerged in October-December 2002, attracting the literary world's attention.

The caravan of the journal 'Apeksha' took off. I spoke of the journey of 'Apeksha' because I was working as a sub-editor for the magazine. My work in the magazine was like multitasking. To assist in the selection of the material that we received for publication. The selected material had to be delivered to the composer, Awadhesh. It was about a kilometre away from my house. Sometimes, I needed to provide or bring back a tiny amount of content from the composer Avdhesh, but I accomplished it faithfully. The first two proofs were read by other colleagues to whom Dr Tej Singh would entrust me. Sunil Mandiwal, Ashwani Kumar, Rajni Disodia, Rajni Anuragi, Mukesh Manas, Anita Bharti, etc., used to read proofs. After some time, TP Singh' Tej' also joined as a sub-editor and was involved in all kinds of work.

After we had read two proofs, Dr Tej Singh read the last proof. In addition, it was my job to bring the magazines from the publisher's place to my residence and wrap them in packets. My wife, too, often helped me make it easy. Dr Tej Singh, too, never shrank from the work whenever it was needed. The address of the magazine's recipient was written on the packet, and the magazine had to be stamped with its address.

Along with this, the stamp of the book post and the printed matter had to be affixed. Postal tickets also had to be pasted. This work was often done at my residence, and other colleagues cooperated. Initially, there was no postal registration for the magazine. That's why while going to school, I dropped three packets in the letter boxes that fell on the way to my school, Timarpur, and the same work had to be done while coming. There was a problem putting too many packets at once. Additionally, answering letters and keeping all records up to date were additional responsibilities of mine. But whatever the work was, it had become a natural part of life's routine and priority.

Even the idea of any benefit regarding joining 'Apeksha' had never had any space in my mind. In other words, I needed to learn the benefits of joining a magazine. The first advantage I got was reading various materials and better understanding the literature. As a sub-editor, one of my articles or any other material continued to be published. I would take four prints of my articles from the composer instead of three on personal grounds. The size of my articles would increase by twenty-five to thirty per cent. The magazine came into existence in October-December 2002, and by 2006, I had the material ready to publish two books.

Since I had learned to type in Hindi also, so, I saved the articles and book review content separately on my computer and saved it on a CD, too. In the meantime, an advertisement came from Hindi Academy Delhi that manuscripts were invited for publication collaboration to encourage new writers. I also sent two copies of the book containing my articles, and the Hindi Academy accepted this book for publication support. Now, a publisher was needed. Mr TP Singh' Tej' had an acquaintance with Kitab Ghar. He had got one of his books published there. By that time, the Kitab Ghar Prakashan had not been a separate identity. Getting two books published was a remarkable achievement for me.

TP Singh asked Dr Tej Singh and me about the book's publication. He also said that we have not one but two books for publication. This is where my tendency for extra awareness was blessed. I had taken the CD of my other book, not just the one. It has been a pattern in my life that I take extra precautions in every matter. If I look at my writings, a different image emerges. Whatever I write in a single sitting, I put it in my email. After each sitting, I keep putting every part of the content in the email and delete the previous ones before posting the next. Following such preventive measures, I have kept soft copies of all my books at different destinations to leave no chance for any loss or deletion.

I learnt this lesson from my friends, who often say that so much of their content was blown away or the whole book got deleted and could not be recovered. Even in my office, if I were asked to submit the work/report in three days, I would furnish it in a day or two without waiting for the deadline. I follow the same approach regarding reaching the railway station, airport, or any meeting or program. It is said that trains arrive on time or late, but never before. My priority has always been to be early or on time but never to be late. My promptness about my articles in 'Apeksha' helped me get my second book, ' Ambedkarwadi Sahitya Vimarsh', published. It contains essays written on all critical and contemporary topics. It was a matter of pride for me to get my book published by a reputed publication like Kitab Ghar.

As a result of awareness, the journal Apeksha put the second book in my account as a bonus. This is a compilation of reviews of various books. It is interesting that, like the first book, the name of this book was also given by Dr Tej Singh. This book, 'Ambedkarwadi Sahitya Ke Pratimaan' (Criticism), was published by Kitab Ghar. TP Singh and I could not discuss the CD of my second book with Dr Tej Singh. Yes, TP Singh certainly knew. He was the one who advised me to take it with me. This came as a surprise to Dr Tej Singh. That's why Dr Tej Singh commented on this episode – 'Gangania Ke To Maje Aa Gaye, on the way back from Darya Ganj. He just won the lottery. He got two books published instead of one, and the publication is also very brilliant and prestigious.' It was a strange coincidence that Dr Tej Singh, in a way, was the master of the magazine, but he got no opportunity to publish his book with the help of Apeksha. He was not even prepared for it because he was not computer literate.

Although I left Apeksha Patrika in 2008. But my third book 'Ambedkarwadi Sahitya Aur Bhartiya Samaj', was registered in my authorship account only because of Apeksha Patrika. It is a collection of essays on literary criticism and contemporary issues. It was published in 2010 by Anubhav Prakashan. This book came a little late. The publisher may need a little longer to publish. The story of separation from Apeksha Patrika is complicated. Despite being no issue, the issue turned so big that I quit Apeksha, my literary lifeline. It was an issue between Dr Tej Singh and me. I have shared it with none and find it unfair to share it as Dr Tej Singh is not alive among us to share his point of view. If he had been alive, I could have thought of it as a sharing issue, as it is not our issue but an issue of a literary movement. Significantly, there has never been any change in our interpersonal relationship, even after our separation. So, we never thought of making it public.

It is not like I was isolated or left idle after separation from Apeksha magazine. By then, I was addicted to literary writing. It had increased so much that I could not afford to live without it. After break up from Apeksha Patrika, TP Singh, Shivnath Sheelbodhi, and I brought out a bilingual (Hindi-English) monthly magazine, 'Aajivak Vision', in 2008. The word 'Aajivak' may sound unfamiliar here. This word was unfamiliar to me even before I met Dr Dharamveer. I thank Dr Dharamveer for familiarising me with the word 'Aajivak'. I also express my gratitude to popular Punjabi writer Prof. Sewa Singh.

'Aajivak' is integral to my life, symbolising my unique and glorious identity. A person can have multiple identities associated with the individual. However, identity in the present context means social identity, which creates a wall of stratification between individuals and communities. This wall leaves a large section of society worse than the animal. Man is compelled to carry it from one generation to the other and the infinite. This burden makes a person's heart and mind crippled. The pain of becoming crippled continues to haunt the person for life. Ultimately, a precious life comes to a tragic end. The whole battle of my writing is for liberation from the handicap and meaningless end of man. This fight is an integral part of my life. I have no choice but to be a soldier in this struggle.

While I was working with Apeksha as a sub-editor, Dr Dharamveer probably knew my attitude and skills through my writings in Apeksha. Dr Dharmaveer was an IAS officer of the Kerala cadre. Later, he was also the principal secretary of the CM of Kerala. Besides his administrative achievement, being Dr Dharamveer means having a library of rare books, a great passion for reading and writing, and a highly skilled thinker and critic. I met him during a program at ISI, Lodhi Colony, Delhi. He was at the pinnacle of literature then, and I was learning to walk on my knees in literature. He asked me to work on Aajivak. He also suggested reading AL Basham's book.

I accepted his advice and made the Identity movement a life mission. Working at Apeksha Patrika, I acquired enough skills to publish a fresh journal. A few months after separation from Apeksha, TP Singh, Sheelbodhi, and I introduced Aajivak Vision (monthly) magazine in June 2008. We had no means of funds. So, both TP Singh and I would manage the funds together. Sheelbodhi gave his technical support to the magazine independently. We would do the rest of the work collectively. Suresh Salil, an editor, published a detailed and brilliant review of the issue in his column in Rashtriya Sahara, a national newspaper. It was an excellent reward for our hardship.

It was the fifth monthly issue; Mr Sheelbodhi said: my children are young enough. They need my support in their studies. I will have to find a way to provide time for the magazine. The separation of one of our active companions was an irreparable loss. TP Singh was already in bad health and unable to rush. I was left alone to stop the publication as a magazine publication needs a collective undertaking. It is painful to recall how I was forced to stop the publication. Certain things are beyond our reach, and we prefer to leave such things to happen in their course with no remorse.

As I have claimed earlier, I am not a man to give up. I focused on my studies on Identity and Aajivak independently. As a result, the book 'Asmita Andolan Mein Dalit Samaj' (Aajivak: Itihas Ke Jharokhe Se) came into existence. Its publication is Academic Pratibha. The canvas of this book was huge. The role Mr TP Singh Tej' played in bringing this book into existence is unmatched. He was serving as an officer in the State Bank of India. Half his Saturdays were spent at the bank, and then till 11-12 PM, Mr TP Singh devoted to proofreading and discussing the book's contents. I need to account for how many Sundays he gave to my work. There was a strange craze in the writing of this book. One day, while working, it was five o'clock in the morning. When I went to sleep, the wife woke up suddenly and said - 'Where are you going now? The morning is far away yet.' I told her - 'I am not getting up for the morning; I am coming to sleep.' Whenever the episode comes into being, I smile to recall the moment.

More was needed to get a magazine named Aajivak, and bringing it to the market was enough. Some more efforts were required to introduce it. In the meantime, we met the three companions of Aajivak magazine and went to Ranchi (Jharkhand) to participate in a Diversity Mission program organised by Mr HL Dusadh. Ambedkar Jayanti, which falls on April 14 every year, was drawing nearer. While travelling on the train, I shared with TP Singh and Sheelbodhi that for the promotion of Aajivak, we will get key rings made and distribute them to friends at the grand gathering to be held on April 14, Parliament Street. As another option, TP Singh proposed a booklet. Sheelbodhi himself took responsibility for drafting, composing, and making it publishable.

We had two weeks. I started writing it, but it turned out to be forty pages instead of sixteen. When I went to the publisher, he said - 'Bring it to page ninety-six, and I will print it in paperback'. I had only one week left. The book was written and published by the Global Books Organization and is titled 'Aajivak' (kal, Aaj Aur Kal). This book was invaluable for building a basic understanding of Aajivak. I have some copies of the book now, and the books are distributed free of cost to friends.

After this, in 2011, my second collection of poetry, 'Ek Waqt Ki Roti', was published by Samkaleen Prakashan with the help of OP. Mishra. This poetry collection differs entirely from my earlier poetry collection in terms of word selection. There is also a lot of variety in the themes of the poems. This poetry collection was my seventh book. Anna's movement came to light after the publication of this book. The perception seemed suspicious and fabricated to me. However, I had no evidence of suspicion, but it was based on my intuition.

As the movement progressed, my intuition gained firm ground. In those days, a new newspaper, Nai Duniya, had emerged. Probably, its editor was Alok Mehta. It was as if he had given special coverage of this movement. This newspaper provided me substantial material for writing this book. It exposed most of the characters related to this movement. My ability to analyse information has led me to conclude that the name of this book should be 'Anna Andolan: Bhartiya Loktantra Ko Chunauti, i.e., Anna Movement: A Challenge to Indian Democracy'.

Ajay Mishra, the proprietor of Swaraj Prakashan, took responsibility for publishing and accomplishing this book, which was published in 2012. I dedicated it to Irom Sharmila. It is worth mentioning that this book has an article, 'Ambedkarwadi Aaine Mein Bhrashtachar', which gives a glimpse of the past, present, and future of corruption in India. I wrote this article in 2011, which was included in this book with a special purpose.

Mukesh Manas, one of my friends, was like a younger brother and was very impressed by this article. He was an associate professor at Satyavati College. He expressed his desire to publish it in the form of a booklet. Sadly, he is no longer with us today. I accepted it, and it was published as a booklet in 2011. Also, he published another article of mine, 'Swadhinta Sangram and Dr Ambedkar', with the same brochure from his publication 'Aarohi' in 2011. Both of these booklets were available to me for free distribution. There are still a few copies left today.

In 2011, I joined Adhikar Darpan. It was the mouthpiece of DIFFER, i.e. 'Dalit Intellectual Forum for Human Rights'. Adhikar Darpan was a small magazine. Earlier, Mr Paramjit Singh would publish it like a letterhead in English. He was an officer of the commissioner rank in a central government office and was the chairman of Adhikar Darpan Patrika. Now he is retired. TP Singh was the editor, and I was the sub-editor. Dr Jai Prakash Kardam and Urmila Harit were associated in their ways. We used to bear the cost of publication collectively. It was our responsibility to publish it. TP Singh and I used to do all the work at home except printing. This magazine came into existence in April-June 2011 and lost its publication in January-March 2015. I do not feel right to talk about those responsible for the loss.

I learnt a lot from working in Adhikar Darpan. Some articles published in it became part of my book 'Ambedkarvad: Ek Samsamyik Vimarsh', which is divided into sections. Section one contains contemporary articles I have occasionally written, and section two includes the articles published in Adhikar Darpan. Thus, Adhikar Darpan made a splendid presence in both of my books.

Just as the articles of Adhikar Darpan became a part of my two books, similarly the editorials of Aajivak Vision became a part of my other book 'Ikkisavin Sadi Mein Asmita Sangharsh' Struggle in the Twenty-First Century' under section two. Section One in this book is also a set of my contemporary articles, though I hadn't thought of using them from this point of view earlier. Doubtlessly, it enhanced my experience, and I got three books published in 2018. While mentioning it here, I have a sigh of relief from my selfless work becoming a source of comfort and peace.

I don't remember 2018 for my three books alone but for the fourth. The fourth book is my story collection 'Intuition'. It is soothing that these four books have filled the gap of my non-publishing of any book from 2012 to 2018. The story of my story collection, 'Intuition', coming into existence, is worth mentioning. I had four stories in all. They were published in different magazines at different intervals. These stories were short, each limited to three or four magazine pages. Before starting my new writing job, I had to finish the old one entirely.

I knew well that four stories do not make a complete book or collection of stories. The first thing I did was rewrite my stories. It increased the size of each by two to three times. I wrote two more stories and sent them to Roop Singh Chandel, an eminent story writer and novelist. He appreciated my stories and asked me to write one or two more to make them a complete collection. I started writing, and the story lasted so long that the book was extended to twenty-four pages. Thus, I prepared a collection of seven stories. It was published by publisher Parag Kaushik, along with three other books. Therefore, these four books have made me the author of twelve books that have been published.

From 2012 to 2018, I could not publish any of my literary work because I was the vice principal, and most of my time was spent extending my office duties. Even at home, I was not free from office assignments. I have no regrets because it made me a successful teacher, school manager, and administrator. This can be a matter of pride for anybody else.

By 2018, the atmosphere of the country and society had become very strange and relatively disturbing. Some fringe elements became very active. Newspapers and TV news were littered with their multiple exploits. There was an atmosphere of peculiar insecurity in society. Wherever you look, mob lynchings, beatings, and wicked statements such as these have become an essential part of everyday life. Today, this environment has gone beyond that. Those who question the regime and the wrongdoers or have a different opinion on any subject are being threatened in stupid ways, that they should go to Pakistan. The period of screaming and shouting on TV made the atmosphere very controversial.

My poetic content is not limited only to love and affection. Nor is it part of my life to bask in the glorification of the past. The sycophant culture has never been a part of my personality and the literature. Literature is a mirror in which the picture of every societal event is presented impeccably. The truth must outshine whatever high the heap of lies may be for burial. I have always objected to literature as nourishing opportunism and hatred. Because of this, society, country, humanity, and the whole environment are the subject matter of literature, clearly in black and white.

Therefore, I chose poetry to express my point of view about the chaotic conditions of society; as a result, in 2019, my poetry collection, 'Kaun Jayega Pakistan', was published. The credit for its publication also goes to Parag Kaushik, which means Parag Books and Anubhav Publications. It was time for the election, and anything ugly could take place to win. To illustrate the ugliness, one of Rahat Indori's couplets is often repeated to correlate the tension on borders with the elections. On the same pattern, the US was also indicating that there could be a terrorist attack or something else in India, as if any untoward incident was related to the election.

Finally, the worst fears came true. There was a terrorist attack, and about fifty army personnel were martyred. In response to this, a surgical strike took place. Probably, this day was Valentine's Day. Although I was planning to write my first novel, suddenly I got the idea to write my own story on this subject, and I named my book 'Surgical Strike'. I tried to connect the outcomes of the current adverse events from history to the present. I started writing this novel on the day of the Surgical Strike and finished it in the second week of May before announcing the results of the Parliamentary elections. One is the lack of experience writing a novel, and the other is writing a book in just two and a half to three months; such coincidences do not ensue together. But I feel blessed to have these two coincidences happen to me simultaneously.

Writing any first novel has its weaknesses. Experience, too, has its limits. There are many types of craft hazards. I admit with an open heart that I have been subjected to many criticisms of the novel. But my purpose has been accomplished, and I am happy about that. I got this novel published by Notion Press. This publication is well-versed in publishing English books but needs to improve in publishing Hindi. Whatever happened has a history, but that novel gave me a new experience. My novel is my fourteenth work, published in the middle of 2019. It is available on all commercial sites.

As a bonus, I got a call from Kuku FM Radio. Their office called to permit an audio recording of it. There was an agreement, and its audio recordings became available in the market and are still available. I also got an audio recording of my story collection, 'Intuition,' available on Kuku FM. I received both gifts because of my novel, 'Surgical Strike.'

Having come in contact with Notion Press, I realised that if books were written or translated into English, the canvas of publicity would become international. I am keen on taking risks. With this, the spirit of not giving up has practically stuck with me from my first poetry collection, 'Haar Nahi Manoonga'. The existence of these two forces with me meant that it was sure to feed them something or the other. After all, the novel 'Surgical Strike' was decided to be translated into English.

Once the decision was made, the work started on a war-like efficiency. The first task was to translate from Hindi to English using Google. Each chapter of Google's rough draft had to be edited first as it was not standard. The editing needed words, and sentences had to be rewritten many times according to the spirit of the Hindi sentence. It was not enough for a publication. I also had to take a Prime membership of Grammarly to sort out the issue. After this, the second draft was put into Grammarly's program. Many suggestions were received from there as well. These suggestions were about the appropriate words and the structure of the sentences. There were also concerns about the length of the sentence. These suggestions were also about punctuation and grammatical correctness. Following Grammarly checks, I finalised the novel Surgical Strike.

Now, the issue of its publication has come up, so I published it under the express publishing scheme. This publication work is very technical. For this, first of all, a lot of information regarding the online book has to be filled out one after the other in the prescribed format. Then, the whole text is copied and pasted into another format following a different process. The cover page should be self-generated. It is combined into a specified number of pixels in the cover page format. Notion Press takes two days to decide whether to publish or not. If the text is worthy of publication, it is published on the third day. While going through this process, I also got my novel 'Surgical Strike' published in 2019 in English.

This translation process continues. On the same lines, I also translated my story collection 'Intuition' into English.

During the translation into English, the titles of almost all the stories were changed as the Hindi titles did not meet the demand of the English story. The title of these stories translated into English became 'Synthetic Eggs' instead of 'Intuition'. The main reason for the title change was that a new story, 'Synthetic Eggs', was added. It was based on a contemporary theme. There are eight stories in this English story collection instead of seven. I also got this book published under the Express Publishing scheme. This translation was also published in 2019. This year, 2019, I got four books published, increasing my number of publications to sixteen.

The year 2020 also brought me two books. During this time, I also tried my hand in the field of ghazals, and a Ghazal collection titled 'Gardo-Gubar' joined my account. I prioritised thought rather than word counting and other technicalities of ghazals. For its publication, I chose the publication 'Book Reverse' as there was no separate format for Ghazals in the format of Notion Press. But here, too, I had to face one problem after the other. The issue of setting up my book came up for a novice. He spoiled everything. Eventually, the publisher had to republish this book with the help of another experienced employee. This caused trouble for me, but it proved to cause additional financial trouble for the publisher.

Writing a book is easier for me than publishing it. But I have never been in the habit of going to anyone for the publication of the book. I am not even such a prominent writer for the publishers to contact me. Therefore, the book's publication has always been an excellent problem for me. I am sorry I found no publisher to meet my mutual coordination and transparency expectations. I do not deny the possibility of my flaws, which the publishers need to understand. It is better to surrender to the 'Benefit of the Doubt' on both levels.

In the same year, 2020, my fifth poetry collection, 'Zinda Rahna Hai Agar', was completed along with my Ghazal collection, Gardo-Gubar. I wanted it published in the River Press publication with Gazal Sangrah, but my experience with this publisher stopped me. That's why I decided to get this new collection of poems published by Notion Press. I fulfilled all the formalities of the Express Publishing Scheme, and my book became available on the commercial site on the third day. It is worth mentioning that I did not write the Ghazal collection and this poetry collection under any plan. Whatever poetry or ghazal I wrote, I kept posting it on Facebook. Readers' responses kept pouring in, and this material was so ready-made that it became the content of two books.

When I translated my novels and short stories into English, I considered translating my poems into English. I accepted this challenge as well. I followed the same process during my novel and story collection. However, the case of the poem was quite typical and complicated. Here, there was the question of rhymes in poems. I tried to fulfil that. However, I need to share some poems I wrote directly in English and tried to translate some from Hindi into English. But the translation was of no use. The real issue is that I had to rewrite almost all the poems. I also liked it and thought, why not do all the further work directly in English.

The main reason for arriving at this conclusion was that my so-called friends in Hindi kept a distance from me because of my different points of view on the issues. They probably didn't like talking about me. Giving any review or feedback on my work was either against their pride, or they needed to be more comfortable sharing their input on my subjects. Both situations were a matter of pain for me in the beginning, but now I have learned to love my isolation. I, too, have learned how to make optimum use of it for literary work and stay relaxed about today's needs.

I sent this book to a foreign publisher. A month and a half later, I got an email of rejection. Then, I sent it to another foreign publisher, but the situation did not change in my favour. My problem is that I need an English partner to discuss things with and share my drafts. Apart from speaking English, I do not have any Hindi colleagues who can discuss my work seriously. After all, I have only one companion like the stick of the blind: Tej Pal Singh' Tej'. Due to his declining age and serious health issues, he has by no means retained 'his sharpness'. Far from being sharp or fast, his world has been reduced to his bed and toilet. This is a harsh issue for me. But the situation is such that nothing substantial can be done.

After all, I had to get my sixth poetry collection, 'Bard's Beloved', published by Notion Press. 'Bard's Beloved' is also my published work of 2021. This poetry collection has been published, but I am seeking more. Still, I don't want to stop; I must keep going, get going. In this ongoing process, my two poetry collections 'Bhagat Singh's Desh Mein' and Hitler Ke Prayay Hain Jo', were also published in 2021, and it has added three poetry collections to my authorship account to enrich it with eight poetry collections.

Significantly, most of my poems have been published on Facebook. But before reaching the publisher, I reviewed them three to four times. The year 2022 welcomed two poetry collections, 'Ishtihar' and 'Barson Purani Nafasat', my twenty-sixth work. In my Hindi autobiography, Mein Aur Mera Girebaan,' where 'I' is a person who includes both my good and evil traits. 'My Girebaan' is to reveal my faults and weaknesses. If a person claims his life as being innocent, I find that person a 'hypocrite'.

As stated, I worked for 'Samay 'Sangyan', a quarterly journal of literary criticism based on Ambedkarite philosophy, for two years. I couldn't do much concrete work besides publishing the magazine as an editor. I composed two poetry collections, 'Khud Hi Tay Karen' and 'Bejuban,' under publication with Rashmi Prakashan, Lucknow, UP. Meanwhile, I had eight editorials published in Samay Sangyan and two unpublished, with five other comprehensively written articles on different occasions. I compiled them into a book titled 'Samay Se Samvad: Ambedkarvad'. It is in the process of being published. The English edition of my autobiography, the thirtieth book, is ready for publication with the title 'Smiling Sores'.

The kind of popularity that some writers get in their early stages, no such popularity is associated with me. My writing could be better. The second reason is that I need to be more knowledgeable in publicity for my books. I find it too shallow to speak about myself; it is a stupid job. I report my work, nothing more. I request that no one write forwards to my books. It has nothing to do with arrogance but is a simple belief to avoid undue buttering. I favour pursuing my work and nothing else.

I have so much to say about my books that if someone likes my works or encourages someone to think the way I do, it consoles me and makes me feel it is a reward for my writing. I don't believe in hypocrisy nor even dream of any recognition. I have to work on worrying about no success, but for a meaningful existence. I am optimistic about my work. It energises and keeps me enthusiastic about continuing. I believe in myself, and this trust is my precious asset. I cannot imagine my life without it.

Often, some of my favourite readers call me for the names of my books and their publisher information. I found it challenging; hence, I typed all the information about my books to share. I wish to share it for my readers' comfort. It is as follows:

1. **Har Nahin Manoonga** (Poetry collection), Year 2000, Atish Prakashan, 9 B, Pocket F-I, G-8 Area, Hari Nagar, Delhi-110064

2. **Ambedkarvadi Sahitya Ke Pratiman**, (Lit. Criticism), Year 2006, Publisher: Kitab Ghar, 24/4855, Ansari Road, Darya Ganj, New Delhi-110002

3. **Ambedkarvadi Sahitya Vimarsh**, (Lit. Criticism) Year 2006, Publisher: Kitab Ghar, 24/4855, Ansari Road, Darya Ganj, New Delhi-110002

4. **Aajivak: Kal, Aaj Aur Kal**, (Lit. Criticism) Year 2009, Global Books Organisation, Current Changed Address: U-9, Saraswati House, Solanki Road, Near Subhash Park, Uttam Nagar, Delhi-110059

5. **Asmitaon Ke Sangharsh Mein Dalit Samaj** (Aajivak: Itihas Ke Jharokhe Se), year 2009, (Lit. Criticism), Publisher: Akadmik Pratibha, Current Changed Address: U-9, Saraswati House, Solanki Road, Near Subhash Park, Uttam Nagar, Delhi-110059

6. **Ambedkarvadi Sahitya Andolan Aur Bhartiya Samaj**, (Lit. Criticism), Year 2010, Anubhav Prakashan: E-28, Lajpat Nagar, Sahibabad, Ghaziabad-05, Phone: 9911179368, 9811279368

7. **Ek Waqt Ki Roti**, (Poetry collection), Year 2011, Samkalin Prakashan: L-13, Aruna Nagar, Magazine Road, Civil Lines, Delhi--110054, 09811801273

8. **Ambedkarvadi Aaine Mein Bhrashtachar**, (Lit. Criticism), Year 2011, (For free distribution) Aarohi

Prakashan, A-2/128, Sector 11, Rohini, New Delhi-110085 (The publisher is not alive now)

9. **Swadhinta Sangram Aur Ambedkar**, (Lit. Criticism), Year 2011, (For free distribution) Aarohi Prakashan, A-2/128, Sector 11, Rohini, New Delhi-110085 (The publisher is not alive now)

10. **Anna Andolan: Bhartiya Loktantra Ko Chunauti** (Lit. Criticism), Year 2012, Swaraj Prakashan-4648/1,21, Ansari Road, Darya Ganj, Nai Delhi-110002

11. **Ambedkarvad Ek Samsamyik Vimarsh**, (Lit. Criticism), Year 2018, Anubhav Prakashan: E-28, Lajpat Nagar, Sahibabad, Ghaziabad-05, Phone: 9911179368, 9811279368

12. **Intuition** (Collection of Hindi Stories) Year 2018, Prag Books, Anubhav Prakashan: E-28, Lajpat Nagar, Sahibabad, Ghaziabad-05, Phone: 9911179368, 9811279368

13. **Ekkisveen Sadi Mein Asmita Sangharsh**, (Lit. Criticism), Year 2018, Anubhav Prakashan: E-28, Lajpat Nagar, Sahibabad, Ghaziabad-05, Phone: 9911179368, 9811279368

14. **Mukhyadhara Ke Aaine Mein Ambedkarvadi Sahitya**, (Lit. Criticism), Year 2018, Anubhav Prakashan: E-28, Lajpat Nagar, Sahibabad, Ghaziabad-05, Phone: 9911179368, 9811279368

15. **Kaun Jaega Pakistan** (Poetry Collection) Year 2019, Prag Books, Anubhav Prakashan: E-28, Lajpat Nagar, Sahibabad, Ghaziabad-05, Phone: 9911179368, 9811279368

16. **Surgical Strike** (Hindi Novel) Edition 2019, Notion Press, Old No.38, New No. 6, McNichols Road, Chetpet, Chennai-600031, (Currently, it is Republished by Prabhat Paperbacks in 2023, An Imprint of Prabhat

Prakashan, 4/19, Asaf Ali Road, New Delhi-110002)

17. **Surgical Strike** (Novel, translated in English) Edition 2019, Notion Press, Old No.38, New No. 6, McNichols Road, Chetpet, Chennai-600031 (Currently, it is Republished by Prabhat Paperbacks in 2022, An Imprint of Prabhat Prakashan, 4/19, Asaf Ali Road, New Delhi-110002)

18. **Synthetic Eggs** (Collection of Stories) Edition 2019, Notion Press, Old No.38, New No. 6, McNichols Road, Chetpet, Chennai-600031 (Currently it is published with the title **Intuition** by Academic Publication, B-578, Gali No. 08, Near Shanti Palace, Pahala Pusta, Sonia Vihar, Delhi-110098, Mob. 9811966475, 9811966603)

19. **Gardo Gubar** (Gazal Collection) Year 2020, Prakashak: River Press, Publish@bookriver.com

20. **Jinda Rahana Hai Agar** (Poetry collection) 2020, Notion Press, Old No.38, New No. 6, McNichols Road, Chetpet, Chennai-600031(Currently it is published by Academic Publication, B-578, Gali No. 08, Near Shanti Palace, Pahala Pusta, Sonia Vihar, Delhi-110098, Mob. 9811966475, 9811966603)

21. **Bard's Beloved** (English Poetry) Edition 2021, Notion Press, Old No.38, New No. 6, McNichols Road, Chetpet, Chennai-600031 (Currently it is published by Academic Publication, B-578, Gali No. 08, Near Shanti Palace, Pahala Pusta, Sonia Vihar, Delhi-110098, Mob. 9811966475, 9811966603)

22. **Bhagat Singh Ke Desh Mein**, (Poetry Collection) Year 2021, Prag Books, Anubhav Prakashan: E-28, Lajpat Nagar, Sahibabad, Ghaziabad-05, Phone: 9911179368, 9811279368

23. **Hitlar Ke Prayay Hain Jo** (Poetry Collection) Year 2021, Prag Books, Anubhav Prakashan: E-28, Lajpat

Nagar, Sahibabad, Ghaziabad-05, Phone: 9911179368, 9811279368

24. **Ishtihar** (Poetry Collection), Year 2022, Academic Publication, B-578, Gali No. 08, Near Shanti Palace, Pahala Pusta, Sonia Vihar, Delhi-110098, Mob. 9811966475, 9811966603

25. **Main Aur Mera Gireban** (Autobiography in Hindi), Year 2022, Academic Publication, B-578, Gali No. 08, Near Shanti Palace, Pahala Pusta, Sonia Vihar, Delhi-110098, Mob. 9811966475, 9811966603

26. **Barson Purani Nafasat** (Poetry Collection) Year 2022, Academic Publication, B-578, Gali No. 08, Near Shanti Palace, Pahala Pusta, Sonia Vihar, Delhi-110098, Mob. 9811966475, 9811966603

27. **Khud Hi Tay Karen**, (Poetry Collection) Year 2025 Maharajapuram, Near Kesrikheda Railway Crossing, Krishana Nagar, Lucknow-226011, Mob.08756219902

28. **Bezuban**, (Poetry Collection), Year 2025 Maharajapuram, Near Kesrikheda Railway Crossing, Krishana Nagar, Lucknow-226011, Mob.08756219902

29. **Samay Se Samvad: Ambedkarvad**, Year 2025 (Lit. Criticism), Year 2012, Swaraj Prakashan-4648/1,21, Ansari Road, Darya Ganj, Nai Delhi-110002

30. **Smiling Sores** (Autobiography) Edition 2025, Notion Press, Old No.38, New No. 6, McNichols Road, Chetpet, Chennai-600031

---000---

CHAPTER FOURTEEN

The World of Doubts and Dilemmas

When I joined the literary fraternity, I didn't know why a shadow of a strange vendetta was chasing me. But coining the above terms is like feasting on trouble. I am in a great dilemma about how to deal with this issue. Ignoring it will cause resentment within me and put my honesty and dignity at stake. If I discuss it freely, a visible threat will surely come from my literary brethren. To escape the dilemma, whatever I discuss here may be taken as unrealistic and a product of my wrong notion.

When I entered the literary world, I was a lecturer in English at Timarpur. I knew Dr Jai Prakash Kardam, one of the eminent Dalit litterateurs. We knew each other because our wives were teachers in the same school. Dr Kardam had once visited my house at Balram Nagar, but I was not a litterateur. Later, I was. Whenever I visited Dr Kardam's house, there would be talk about literature. He often spoke of many Dalit and non-Dalit writers. He would talk about the writers and Dalit journals.

He would discuss writers of diverse genres, their writing patterns, uniqueness, and drawbacks. He often had long discussions about Rajendra Yadav and Kamleshwar.

Being a litterateur, he visited different states frequently and shared the details. Whatever he talked about was no less than a workshop for me. Without meeting people face to face, I had a significant image in mind.

I had no choice but to listen. I asked questions but had nothing to add as I was a novice in the field. It was not so while having discussions on ideological issues. I had a different mindset, so the themes of my poems and titles differed from the traditional Dalit literature paradigm. Today, I am entirely different, and the canvas of my thoughts cannot fit under any umbrella or ism. It is nothing to influence the readers but to familiarise them with the state of affairs to reach appropriate conclusions.

Dalit literature nourishes the word 'Dalit' to fight against caste prejudice and atrocities. My first collection of poems, 'Har Nahi Manoonga', was not free from this trend as it was composed under Dr Kardam's supervision. Hence, the frequent use of the word 'Dalit' diluted the intensity of the content. I was no less influenced by the word 'Dalit' than a newly converted Muslim reciting the word Allah! But that was not the case with Dr Kardam. He could have suggested ways to escape, but in vain. Due to my ignorance, the last three to four pages had the title Ghazal, which is nothing like Gazal.

Dr Kardam could have saved me from committing such a blunder as I was holding his finger in the arena of literature. Nobody is to blame here or finding faults in others. It is my blunder; perhaps I was in a hurry to be an author by publishing my book soon. If not, I should have waited or tried to take guidance from someone else. I should have read multiple authors to gain proper wisdom. I know that to err is human, but learning not to get trapped is divine. But I took lessons from my mistakes not to be a victim of such silly mistakes. Still, the flaws in my first book give me a strange prick even today.

One of the speakers during the launch of my book was Jai Prakash Lilwan. Like others, Dr Kardam also allowed him to be a speaker. He was an officer in Indian Oil, was educated at JNU and had a strong interest in literary criticism. During his critical remarks on my book, he became as aggressive as a wolf starving for several days to attack an innocent prey. There is no account of the aggressive attitude adopted by Mr Lilwan in the form of criticism. He provocatively cited the number of the words 'Dalit' used in the book. At the same time, the other speakers spoke very genuinely and guided me gently.

I do not understand whether it was all the product of Lilwan's mind or some other force that provoked him for such unusual conduct. Even in the work of any great writer, something can be traced to challenge the intellect and the writer's maturity comfortably. My poetry collection was my first chance to enter literature. I was unaware of the process and character of the book launch. None is to blame but myself. A similar incident happened during my second book 'Ambedkarwadi Sahitya Vimarsh'. Prof. Gopeshwar Singh represented Mr Lilwan during the release. He found some lines in my book that matched the history of Hindi literature. These were about four or five lines. It can be under the criterion of plagiarism.

I agree that what it was was wrong on my part. This should not have happened. However, the write-off of the entire book based on one mistake cannot be justified, but Prof. Gopeshwar could, as he was a professor at Delhi University. Prof. Shyam Lal presided over the launch program. He had been Vice-Chancellor twice. Prof. Prem Singh from Delhi University was also another speaker. He found a lot in my book and discussed it sincerely, but Prof. Gopeshwar couldn't.

Prof. Gopeshwar was Dr Tej Singh's choice. It is also worth mentioning that all the articles published in the book had already been published in Apeksha (Quarterly Journal of Literary Criticism) under the supervision of Dr Tej Singh, and all received good support. Such critical work of a schoolmaster like me could not please Prof. Gopeshwar. Well, this book launch, too, gave me an excellent experience.

It would be creditable to talk about another launch when the round of launches is going on. In 2018, four of my books were published simultaneously. Three of them were books of literary criticism. There was a book, 'Ambedkarism—A Samsamyik Vimarsh,' and Prof. Vivek from JNU took the entire responsibility when I discussed its launch. The responsibility of releasing the remaining three books was unplanned.

For this, the 'Dalit Dastak' platform was chosen. The venue was Institutional Area Lodhi Colony. I was under the illusion that Prof. Vivek and 'Dalit Dastak' were both big names. They will compensate for the gathering in their way. I invited a small number of my friends to attend it. Some were my family members. But when we reached there, we found the gathering negligible. Although the payment for the auditorium, refreshments, and a well-known TV anchor and thinker, Urmilesh, everything was at Prof. Vivek's expense. Despite repeated requests, he disclosed nothing for me to pay for.

I respect Prof. Vivek's generosity deeply. I also thank Ashok Das, the proprietor of 'Dalit Dastak', but whenever I remember the gathering scene, I feel cheated. Such a poor audience presence raises upheavals in my mind to question.

I tried to find a positive response but was in vain. It hits me a lot like a nightmare. The launching has become a synonym for uninvited pain and suffering. Launching books is merely to learn more lessons at an individual level, but they have nothing to teach as a desired goal we expect. The first benefit of this learning was that I stopped releasing my other three books.

I go back to the same period I was learning to crawl on my knees to enter the literary world. Meanwhile, Dr Kardam informed me about Dalit Sahitya Academy's annual program. I also expressed my desire to go there. However, Dr Kardam made me aware of the problems involved in participating. Later, he paved the way for my joining this program, and I learned about its ugly show. I am sorry if I call the show ugly. I have no other options to explore. It was the year 2000. I saw a line of applicants waiting for their turn. Later, I learned that the fellowship cost was Rs 500. I need to find out how much it costs these days.

Earlier, this event was probably held at Talkatora Indoor Stadium. Later, it started happening in a field in Burari. Its bright side was that many people attended it from all over India. They considered Ambedkar's fellowship awarded by this organisation an outstanding achievement and even submitted a copy to their departments. Even today, people can be seen sharing it on Facebook as their significant achievement. Dr Kardam had said that you, too, get these fellowships. I had refused to be a part of this spectacle from the beginning. I also got a chance to meet some of the writers. It was because of Dr Kardam to thank him.

A great feature of Dr Kardam is that he portrays the mountain of problems regarding any issue. Ultimately, he wins over all the obstacles, such as Superman. Another instance is that he said we are bringing out a collective poetry collection. I said include me, too. He said it could not be because the poems would be included by those who have at least one poetry collection published. I wonder whether he found a way out for me; I do not remember. But those poems have also been included, whose poetry collections are awaited yet.

Similarly, Kanwal Bharti also brought out a collective poetry collection. During this time, my poetry collection had been published. I had also presented it to Mr Kanwal Bharti. I was not a novice now as I was a sub-editor in a quarterly journal, Apeksha. It isn't right to claim any seniority. However, I need help finding a place in his shared poetry collection. My poems cannot become a part of this collective poetry collection. There is no doubt that Kanwal Bharti is a studious, profound thinker and a great critic. I sent him many books, but I still await his response. I am sorry that I failed to get his response.

It does not mean we do not have any communication; we do have. Kanwal Bharti and I communicated. Often, we talked in a cordial and constructive environment. When I countered Dr Dharamveer's stand in support of Buddha and Dr Ambedkar through my article published in Hans magazine, he greatly appreciated me on the phone, commenting that no one else could respond so brilliantly. It was a big compliment for me. Prof. Chauthi Ram Yadav also shared a similar reaction. Suraj Badtya probably informed me about this. But Chauthi Ram Yadav has yet to utter a word about my books written about Aajivak, even though I have presented both my books to him in a program.

Kanwal Bharti also congratulated me on my novel 'Surgical Strike'. But simultaneously, he reacted that he had no interest in reading books. But I do not believe Kanwal Bharti reads or has read novels. But two queries struck my mind regarding his reaction. Firstly, I should send my book to him with a request to read and comment. But I couldn't. It does not mean I am arrogant or a victim of a superiority complex. I do make such requests only when I find it a healthy practice not to be a prey to opportunism or literary politics. I have never made such a request to Mukesh Manas, who was dear to me. He would talk to write about a different matter in my books, but he hasn't done it to date. Sorry to share, but he is not among us now. My stand in connection with Kanwal Bhari may be taken as my mistake. Secondly, another side of the coin is that Mr Kanwal Bharti could have asked me to send him the novel to read. He has the right to exercise; I could have followed it with pride. It could have gone better with his high stature. However, it does not match his personality, which widens the ditch of everyday discourse or relations. Despite it all, I have deep respect for his great stature.

Regarding my novel 'Surgical Strike', mentioning two characters, Harpal 'Arush' and Roop Singh' Chandel', becomes relevant. Let's talk about Arush first. Arush probably had cancer; he shared a post on Facebook saying that he had read all the books he had. There was no new book, so he was rereading the old books. He had desired to read my story collection, 'Intuition,' earlier. Its forward was written by Roop Singh Chandel and shared on Facebook. I am deeply grateful to Mr Chandel. Indeed, the work is worth it.

Let's return to Mr Arush, about whom I wanted to share my experience. I was sorry for not being able to send the story collection he asked for. To cover it up, I sent my novel to him. On the one hand, he was upset due to the lack of books. While I sent him my novel, he reacted awkwardly. I do not know in what context he made a strangely negative and arrogant remark on Facebook to the senders of the books. I know it wasn't for me directly. It might be for anybody else; it ought not be like that. It disturbed me greatly, and I regretted sending my novel to him. Whatever happened, the comments he made on Facebook about my book put a big question mark on the integrity of his authorship. I am not doing this unnecessarily. The issue is that Mukesh Manas posted a critical comment on this novel on his Facebook wall after some time. It was very positive and encouraging.

In response to this comment, Arush took a U-turn and started supporting it with the same enthusiasm as Mr Mukesh had vented his heart. I had questioned Arush's honesty based on his duality and literary hypocrisy. However, I did not oppose Arush's freedom of thought on Facebook. It's not that I couldn't do it, but I didn't. My problem is that I avoid such situations where I find authorship doubtful. It is a permanent part of my personality, and I never compromise it, whatever its pros and cons.

Mr. Chandel is very soft-spoken. He is a good storyteller and a popular novelist. I have had good relations with him because of Dr Tej Singh. I also sent him my novel. He also made a brief but nice comment on Facebook. I had to talk to him enough to learn about novel writing through his reaction to the book. He sweetly said: Gangania ji, I will call; you do not. I said- 'Okay'. I received his phone call, and he discussed several issues based on my novel. I agreed more with what he said and shared some of my drawbacks.

I wanted to discuss some more points rather than doubts about the novel. Mr Chandel concluded his discussion and said, 'Gangania ji, we will talk again on this subject someday.' Here, he was saying, 'I will call'; in a way, he refused me to call. It wasn't that we didn't talk earlier; sometimes, we spoke at length. He sometimes fixed the time according to his convenience.

I wanted clarity on some more points to avoid further mistakes in my future work. But after turning back, Mr Chandel did not call again as promised. He might have forgotten due to his busy schedule. Contrarily, it was against my ethics to make him a call, as Mr Chandel had talked of. The bitter truth is that while he told me not to make a call, he would, and it struck my self-esteem that day. But I didn't express it out of courtesy. Later, I also received a couple of messages regarding some other issues. He called to get some of his work done through me. I spoke to him to the point and did whatever little help he needed but did not remind him of talking about the novel he had committed. It was a question of my self-respect, which knew no compromise.

This episode of my novel forced me to see Mr Chandel free from the lens of trust. The reverse gear of his episodes came into taking different shapes. I reviewed his book, Natasar, which we published in our journal, Apeksha. In the sequence, he reviewed two of my books together. He sent it to his friend Kamar Mewari, as he had told. But I don't know what happened to the review. He has published his writing in multiple magazines, but I could not find one for my book review. It remained unpublished. Contrarily, he said I should get the draft to get published elsewhere.

Mr. Chandel edited and published two books of stories each. My story, 'Intuition,' could find a place in either of the two, but in vain. It is relevant to talk here as he had praised the treatment and craft of the story so enthusiastically that he did not forget to comment: had I written the story, I could not have written it so brilliantly. His enthusiasm about my story was so high that he shared it with some of his close friends known for their literary brilliance. He spoke generously about the rest of the stories in my story collection. Commonly, some consoling comments are made by fellow friends to the writer's high spirits. I don't find an exception to the practice regarding my job. My story didn't deserve to be part of Mr Chandel's book of story collection, which he edited. But it raises a big question mark on the dignity of an author who is supposed to be free from worldly wickedness.

Undoubtedly, it was Mr Chandel's prerogative to decide whom to publish. There should be no room for accusation. But when I observe Dr Tej Singh and Mr Chandel's relationship, I know why certain doubts put me in a dilemma and inconvenience. Let's leave the world of questions; they are meant to question. They may cause trouble; while the questions are mine, why put others in trouble but me alone. I, too, am not free to spoil myself by digging in the garbage to find filth alone. I have a wonderful world to make it worth enjoying as my paradise.

Mohan Das Naimish Rai is also one of the famous figures of Dalit literature. He has written dozens of books on the history of Dalit literature. My early books have also been with him. Today, more than two dozen of my books are available in the literary world. Despite all this, I have yet to find a place in his book, History of Dalit Literature. Even though I was the sub-editor of Apeksha Patrika for eight years, editor of my magazine 'Aajivak Vision', sub-editor of Adhikar Darpan, and actively associated with the Golden Age of Dalit Writers' Association for four years, I still could not become a part of Dalit litterateurs. Even though the reason for this is beyond my comprehension, I still accept my incompetence.

Dr Kardam's frequent presence in my discussion is not sudden but because of memories from around 2000. Every year, on April 14, there is a massive gathering on Parliament Street. There is a festive atmosphere. There are stalls for books and other materials. There are also many pandals for food and drink. It is an excellent opportunity to meet old friends and relatives. One gets to see the whole of India there. I didn't know anything about it before I met Dr Kardam.

Dr Kardam made me familiar with the day's attractions at Parliament Street. I needed someone's help to go there. Dr Kardam also took out a solution to this problem. Even though I am older than him, he made me sit with his three children in the back seat and his wife in the front of his car. I am also grateful to Dr Kardam for this favour. Regarding the crucial cover page of my first book, 'Haar Nahi Manoonga', I have to say nothing as I have discussed Dr Kardam's generosity on the phone with ample detail.

Since I became a sub-editor for Apeksha, a quarterly journal of literary criticism, I wrote at least one article for each issue. Apart from this, I also wrote critically in outside magazines. During this, I gave feedback on writers' content from different states. My reactions have generally been acrimonious. Due to this sharpness, Prof. Shyam Lal jokingly gave me the name 'Kalam Kasai'- a pen butcher. I also liked it and shared it with my friends in many contexts. Even today, Prof Lal calls me the carrier of Kabir's tradition because of my firm and fearless reactions.

It is a standard feature that people have been fond of hearing praise. Social media platforms like Facebook made it an ugly show where reality lost its gleam entirely. Under such circumstances, my factual criticism in the literary arena made me a villain to be ignored and criticised under an unannounced oath. I am proud of my literary friends, who have not broken their oath to date. Despite all this, I gift my books to my friends, who honour their oath and remain silent.

TP Singh' Tej', Sheelbodhi and Mukesh Manas have been verbally discussing my work seriously. Sheelbodhi and TP Singh have certain limits. But Mukesh Manas repeatedly told me what he had noted about my writings. Manas assured me he would discuss it when free from his busy schedule. The circumstances of Mukesh Manas were so complicated that he was not serious about solving them. The traps of busyness had no end; finally, he lost the battle of life to say goodbye to the world. In a way, he said goodbye to the promise of writing about me in detail.

In the current context, sharing some detailed excerpts from Mukesh's verbal response is relevant. This is also a way to refresh his memories. He often commented: you will be known for English titles in Hindi literature. Your writing is different from the typical literature that is being written now. When Arun, who was associated with the Ambedkarite writer's forum, interviewed many people on Facebook, he said this was the easiest way of interviewing, without even reading or knowing about a writer. Continuing his statement, he commented about me- 'If I have to interview you, I will have to study for at least a month.

He had discussed in detail many times about writing my autobiography. I told him that it would be of a different type. It would be different from reporting the facts of life or glorifying oneself. It would also have a novel-like glimpse. He firmly remarked that your autobiography must be different, I know. Together, we would read and finalise it. He would write his diary almost regularly and register everything substantial daily as the raw material of his autobiography. He also used to share its glimpses with me. He also told me that his story collection was like an autobiography of a short period of his life. Now, call it a brief or detailed comment of Mukesh Manas; this is only a heritage, a memory, the essence of which I am sharing here.

Once, he shared a post of my novel, Surgical Strike, on Facebook. There were also very adverse reactions to it from self-victimised friends. It was simple and nothing surprising. But a fellow professor called and asked why he had written a post about Gangania. You shouldn't talk about him. He didn't say why he shouldn't be talking about it. Mukesh also told me the gentleman's name, but I do not find it necessary to mention such a person. It is better to stop talking about Dr Manas; it is like waking up the sleeping giant of pain in the grave again. Who can keep buried whatever we have as a reservoir in us?

Well, I don't care what anyone says about me. I am accustomed to living in a world of isolation, and my comfort is in a constructive zone. I realise the world I live in has a negative side. Some of my relatives are not happy with it. They miss no chance to remind me how careless I am about my kin. Presently, two reasons have made things worse. One is Corona, and the other one is my addiction to literature. The Corona was a temporary one, but my addiction to literature and to writing on social issues is my priority.

To move forward in this episode, it is becoming necessary to remember Sudesh Tanwar. He was present in literature before me. He had one of his books published. This incident is from around the year 2002-03. There was a campaign to collect some funds for the Dalit Writers' Association. I was its treasurer. Tanwar invited us to his village, where he held a poetry session. About ten to twelve people from Delhi were involved in this. Dr Tej Singh and Dr Kardam were in a leading capacity. I also recited my poetry in a poetry session. Everyone's name appeared in the newspaper, but my name needed to be added. When I asked him why, he tried to cover it up with baseless arguments, but in vain. I understood what motivated him, but I stayed calm. Even today, I can see the diverse examples of common weaknesses in my colleagues like him. After all, human beings are balm of other humans. That is why I take such incidents as gifts from myself to console my friends.

The latest incident I encountered was from the journal's editor, Gaon Ke Log. It was when my friend Dr Mukesh Manas passed away. The editor and the owner of this magazine, Ramji Yadav, asked me for the cover pages of Mukesh Manas' books, photos, poems, and some information about him. I provided the report, and it was published on his portal. I found that he had collected some information directly from Facebook. Surprisingly, their names were available in the report, but my name needed to be added outright. It is a different matter that Vidya Bhushan Rawat interviewed me online. It was lengthy and aired on the 'Gaon Ke Log' portal in three instalments. I give credit to Mr Rawat and the team Gaon Ke Log wholeheartedly. But sometimes I think that newspapers, magazines, etc., have some allergy to my name; perhaps only then do they prevent me away. It isn't beneficial to mention all the instances. My sole duty is to save my friends from all the allergies which cause significant pain.

The Dalit special issue of the monthly magazine' Gaon Ke Log' was also brought out some time back. Its editor was Dr N Singh, and the editing collaboration was probably

Arun Kumar. He runs the Ambedkarite Writers' Forum. When I was asked for material for this issue, I sent three chapters of my novel with the consent of Ramji Yadav. But I don't know anything about what happened to the content I sent for publication. There could be an allergy issue there, too. Nowadays, I do not send my poetry, article, story, etc., anywhere. But sometimes, the urge is such that I cannot stop myself. But this allergy creates panic everywhere. I can easily see this panic in my friends' reactions.

Sometime back, Dr Ajay Navaria asked me for a story for the popular Hindi magazine 'Hans'. He was editing the Dalit special issue. I sent my story, 'Synthetic Eggs'. Several days later, when I asked for his opinion about the story, he said he was reading a popular story translated from a foreign language. He said that initially, I was afraid that reading my story with that story would do injustice to my story. But Navaria replied that I had no problem reading your story after reading the foreign story. The story is good. I was convinced of its publication. But when the first part of Hans magazine came out, it did not contain my story. When the second part came, my story was not there either.

I felt terrible about it. So, I wanted to know the reason for this. Navaria told me that the ingredients were enough. The problem before us was whose story to print or not. He told me the process followed to be eligible to publish the story. He said many stories of storywriters of the 'A' caste were printed. So, many stories of story writers of the 'B' caste were published, and so many stories of the 'C' caste got a place in this special issue of Hans. He also said that the stories of 'A' and 'B' were printed because they were women. Story 'C' and 'D' are printed to represent another state. He also gave some logic about the translated story; I do not care. Due to the seniority of some story writers, they could find their place in 'Hans'. Some stories became a part of this unique 'Hans' magazine issue to cultivate their relationships.

No room was left for my story in 'Hans' because I needed to fit more criteria. My story was not printed, and now I do not regret it. However, the formula adopted to publish the story is undoubtedly patentable. If someone stole it and adopted it in any literature, it would be a loss-making deal to this formula's creator, Mr Navaria. I shouldn't have shared it here, as someone can steal it from here, too. I have complete faith in Bhai Navaria's ability to invent new and unique formulas even further in a pinch. To underestimate him in any way would be a big mistake.

Navaria's maths and formulas were terrific. How could I have interfered with his formula? This was not the first time that I had been treated like this. Earlier, when Rajendra Yadav was alive. Even then, 'Hans magazine published a voluminous Dalit special issue. Today's Professor, Sheoraj Singh Baichain, was the editor. Another interesting incident happened during that time. I wrote an article about the media for the Dalit special issue of Hans. During that time, 'Hans magazine followed the procedure that the unique material to be published in the next issue was announced in the previous issue. I am still determining what the pattern is today.

During that time, on the fourth page of the cover of 'Hans', the title of my article was published with a few other selected writers. My name was also mentioned in the article. But when the issue was released, my article needed to be included. When I asked Ajay Navaria why, he refused to provide any information. I didn't ask anyone else about it. To this day, I am still looking for the formula adopted for publication on that issue. Bhai Baichain may not have been a professor then, but his qualifications in such matters were 'beyond doubt'. In terms of merit, he has been much sharper than Mr Navaria and is still bigger today. Something bigger can be expected of him, but I am sure he would meet every criterion, as gold maintains its 24-karat.

Here, I am presenting only a few examples. Otherwise, there are many examples available indicating an allergy. It should be a matter of researching what kind of allergies there are to magazines with my name and the publication of my work. It should also be known that apart from the publication of my name and work, what other safety measures have been adopted to prevent the allergy? In this series of allergies, I share one more thing. I wrote a book 'Asmitaaon Ke Sangharsh Mein Dalit Samaj, Aajivak: Itihas Ke Jharokhe Se' to solve the question of identity. I couriered this book to about fifty established authors from Delhi and authors in other states.

I also mentioned in the preface of this book that the issue of identity demands a comprehensive study. It is not the work of an individual. If scholars related to the subject joined hands with the mission, it would be an excellent foundation for bringing a profound philosophy to light. With this, the solution to the problem of casteism, both high and low, will be accessible. A lofty building of identity can be erected on the land. A great flag can be hoisted as a vehicle of self-respect. I did not request anyone to read my book, praise, or embroider my pride. This issue was of public interest. It was a matter of interest not only for a particular community but also for humanity.

In this context, it is also worth mentioning that whenever I present my book to someone, I often say there is no need to tell what is good in it. Just tell me your points of disagreement in my book and why? I intend to learn something from these disagreements. But it is a matter of regret that none of my colleagues have felt the need to discuss it so far. This book may not be worthy of their consideration. In this case, the needle of blame turns towards me. I was ready to face this needle prick yesterday and even today.

When I got my book published on Aajivak first, Kanwal Bharati said on the phone that you were hasty in publishing the book. But did not react to the content as a critic. One reason is that he was trying to enrol himself as the author of the first book on Aajivak. If so, I regret that I have unintentionally blocked his path. That is why he talked about my book's early publication and did not find the content worthy of his comment. Dr Dharamveer also reacted once. But his issue was a little different. I wrote an article about Ajivika for the Hindi magazine' Anabhai Sancha'. Dr Dharamveer responded: you are working under a well-thought-out strategy. You are creating obstacles in my way. After this reaction, he stopped communicating with me forever. On the contrary, while I was working on Aajavik's philosophy, he used to talk to me for hours from Kerala. He was in the habit of lengthy talks to whoever he spoke to. Mukesh Manas was also the carrier of this tradition.

At this point, I cannot understand what conclusions I should derive from the remarks of the great stalwarts of these pieces of literature. Dr Dharamveer didn't see any need to talk about the content. Both these great writers have also written one book each after me on Aajivak. This situation reminds me of a court decision where the defendant was not told of his fault nor allowed to argue the case and passed a one-sided judgment. I would have said if these gentlemen disagreed with me at any point. I didn't mind, even if they could reject my conclusions. But they didn't do any such thing. Had I been reactions from these two scholars, I would have learnt something out of it. I could not understand whether there was a danger of any allergy or disease, like magazines, or something else?

What is this 'something else'? This is a highly complex puzzle. Talking about this would be like making unnecessary speculations. It would be better to put it in my escapism account. But in this context, I never dictate to anyone. I write only what gives me satisfaction. No matter how big a calibre person is in front. It is not my nature to be anybody's mouthpiece. Such actions are another major drawback of mine. I don't want to be a fanatic. On the contrary, wherever I see logical and forward-looking material or any tendency that leads to further betterment, I accept it with no ifs and buts. I embrace it and make it a part of my personality. I am in favour of updating myself.

Although I am not interested in following Ramayana and other mythological texts, if I find something worth accepting, I never miss it. In one place in Ramayana, it is said through Rama, 'To be cheated is not a crime, but cheating is a crime'. This line plays a vital role in my life. It saves me from doubting the intentions of others. It also doesn't mean that I have stopped questioning; I do. The incidents I have discussed in this chapter earlier are clear-cut examples of the same.

It is about the Dalit Writers' Association. Its second session was probably in Triveni Auditorium, Mandi House, Delhi. The second term of Dr Tej Singh was coming to an end. During that period, it was the only Dalit Writers' Association. All writers associated with Dalit literature were part of this platform. But there was an atmosphere of protest inside it. Suraj Pal Chauhan was responsible for reading the introductory speech during this program. A draft was prepared by consensus and was to be read. But Suraj Pal Chauhan read an extra page on which there was no discussion. Nor was it part of this introductory speech. Everyone was shocked, but interrupting him would have made the program a failure. Prima facie, it was Mr Chauhan's mischief. But later, when the truth dug into the whole conspiracy, it unmasked the rest behind the secret conspiracy.

A new body of the Dalit Writers Association was to be elected after the program was over. There was a strange unrest among some of its members. They proposed Dr Vimal Thorat's name for the post of President. Suraj Pal Chauhan, Sudesh Tanwar, Brij Pal Bharti, Karmsheel Bharti, Arun Gautam, Suraj Badtya, and Mr Navaria were also present as discontented. Apart from these, many other companions looked more aggressive. Perhaps this resistance was against Dr Tej Singh's style of functioning or prevented him from becoming the President of DALES (Dalit Lekhak Sangh) for the third time. Mr Brijpal Bharti was probably nominated treasurer in the newly elected body. Regarding the fact that Brijpal Bharti was not even a writer, Sudesh Tanwar reacted: we would get two to four poems published in any journal. The problem is settled, and it is not a big deal.

It was a good thing to have an election. Dr Tej Singh had been the President for two terms. Replacing him or electing a new president was not an insignificant act—however, the attitude and process adopted for this change needed to be corrected. I can only express my regret for demolishing a democratic and civilised pattern of an organisation and nothing else. Dr Tej Singh took it so seriously that he did not back the organisation. Suraj Pal Chauhan called me a virtuous disciple of Dr Tej Singh. At the same time, I continued to attend Dalit Lekhak Sangh's (DALES') programs regularly or occasionally, despite Dr Tej Singh's dissent. But the desolate DALES of that time could only get its lost land today. Today, there is a flood of writers' associations, but the output is worrying.

I agree that undue or impractical aspirations bring disaster. One of the main reasons for this was to take over the magazine 'Apeksha' by removing Dr Tej Singh from DALES—the 'Apeksha' began with the first issue in October-December 2002. Since Dr Tej Singh became the President of DALES, it was thought that the magazine and the organisation must go hand in hand for their boost. That is why the second issue of Apeksha was declared as Dalit Lekhak Sangh's Mukh Patra. Overall, it ran from January to March 2004, which means up to the fifth issue of Apeksha. Dr Tej Singh withdrew the declaration when he was no longer DALES President.

It is also worth noting that DALES did not have any role in publishing five issues of Apeksha. Nor did any of its officials participate in it. DALES also had nothing to do with its publication, fund arrangement, proofreading, maintenance and distribution, etc. It is worth mentioning that I have been a part of DALES and Apeksha. Still, some people accused us of being Dr Tej Singh and Gangania who captured the magazine. In one sentence, it can be said that it was Apeksha's gleam that the poor DALES became a victim of politics and a scapegoat, and today, people across the country look at this scapegoat with great contempt.

When the issue of Apeksha is debated, despite its popularity, it often seems synonymous with controversies. Apeksha symbolises the saying: Any popularity carries a world of controversies. I have been associated with it as a sub-editor for almost eight years, up to 22 issues of Apeksha. Then, I snapped my deal away. The speculations of my separation from Apeksha have no ending. Some people know the whole reality, and the rest are hypotheses.

Before we parted ways, Dr Tej Singh, Sunil Mandiwal, Ashwani Kumar, TP Singh, Tej, and I met at Ashwani's house when he lived in his Loni Road flat. They know what happened, and no one else does. I'd like to know if Dr Tej Singh has shared anything with anyone at any level. Today, Dr Tej Singh is not with us. So, nothing is going to come out of him, and nothing will come out from this side, either.

TP Singh, too, got separated automatically from Apeksha due to my separation. Both were sub-editors, and Dr Tej Singh was left alone as the editor. We published the 'Aajivak Vision' monthly magazine. I mentioned earlier that TP Singh' Tej' was editor-in-chief, Sheelbodhi and Urmila Harit were sub-editors, and I worked as an editor. Exceptional support from Raj Valmiki and Dr Puran Singh continued. But here, Sheelbodhi withdrew from participating, citing his children's education. Eventually, the magazine left us with the 'stigma of closure'.

Even today, Sheelbodhi and I are neighbours. Get to know each other's families very well. I believe the children's education was a flimsy excuse for leaving the magazine, and the fact is far from reach. I never insisted on him, but jokingly, I did not hesitate to accuse him of the magazine's closure. He laughs and nothing else. The relationship between Sheelbodhi and me is such that he often crosses all limits in his passion but, eventually, has no peace without TP Singh and me.

Nowadays, he is fond of blaming TP Singh and me by saying we conspired against him by dragging him to ancient history and philosophy away from his writing plays, poems and articles. He claims we have left nothing with him but our company, not even his identity. All his time goes to reading but nothing to write. We smile and comment: It is your choice to stay with us and return to your world. His humour ends in saying I will stay with you, and lentil on your chest means to keep you troubled.

All my literary friends I know have a wonderful personality. They have learnt the gimmicks of politics and getting hands-on. Hence, literature's soil of morality, justice, and fairness is losing fertility. It's crop became like some malnourished child. However, some selfless-minded people like TP Singh are always ready for reasonable support and charity. Due to the waist problem, he is often tight-belted and has little liberty to move. Both of us regret why we got united so late. Had we met earlier, the picture of our work would have been different.

Now, I have crossed sixty-eight years of age. Once again, Apeksha, in Samay Sangyan's new costume, is reaching out smiling and needs to learn to signal. It is calling me. However, Apeksha was lost after Dr Tej Singh left us. Now, Apeksha has a changed identity, 'Samay Sangyan'. The team and the circumstances have changed. My role, too, has changed from sub-editor to the editor. I wrote a poem titled 'Zameen Pathrili Hai' to express the hardship of affairs. Now, we have to make a way out of this rocky land. Let's see, how jealousy, we follow Dashrath Majhi. Time is the best judge to answer.

Apart from those I mentioned earlier in one form or another, I can share much more about Rajendra Yadav, Ramnika Gupta, and Mata Prasad. Some other companions have not been mentioned before, nor will they come. I have had strange experiences with them, but I don't know why;

it is credible to end my talk here. I have felt that there is no fault in my eyesight, and I look at my loved ones differently.

Lastly, it is necessary to share again that every person is a set of good and evil. I am also no exception; I mean without blemishes. I, too, have so many demerits to underline. But everybody has a different vision of how to judge a person and his personality. The affairs, too, have a decisive role to play. This is a point to be considered. The person who respects the glasses and is free from bias can judge the person with better clarity. Anyway, one should be seen in the mirror of totality. Only then can we do justice to ourselves, others, and the circumstances.

The title of this chapter, 'The World of Doubts and Dilemmas,'refers to how I saw a particular person or event under reliable circumstances. It is necessary to repeat that as I have seen my loved ones, it is their reflection through my glasses. If I see something away from reality or under the wrong perception, it may be my fault and my glasses' fault. If my glasses have presented a bad image in front of me, I will try my best to change the number of my glasses. Indeed, the goal of my life is to see the proper reflection. Based on this image, I share my experience and participate in the dream of a better world.

---000---

CHAPTER FIFTEEN

My Lifestyle: A World of Euphoria

It may feel utopian, but my daily activities and the environment give me an enchanting peace and wings to fly on. This flight gives me what is beyond monetary reach. This does not mean that the hoaxes of politics and the unprotected communal hysteria in society do not bother me. Of course, they do, and I resist them to whatever extent my circumstances are destined to. It is a natural outburst of my actions, that doesn't require any preplanned substantial effort. It works like the driver who does not bother when to press the clutch or accelerator and when to apply the brakes.

It functions naturally as a common practice. I share it on social media and publish it in multiple genres of literature, which is essential to satisfying my inner urge as a phenomenon of nature. It comforts me, not just because I desire it. I don't understand how it has become my way of living and a natural reservoir of relief. As a result, when I look into my inner self, turning my attention away from the outside world, I find unearthly joy and contentment.

It did not happen suddenly, but I found the journey a little long to reach the current destination. Each person's life journey has its manifestations. I intend to share specific points of my trip that nourish the peace in my life. Some of these may be common in others' comfort and peace.

I don't know precisely when peace became my soul mate. But by adding the thread of life's pattern one after the other, I may visualise it. I am sharing the beam because it may pave the way for others. Let's come out of this world of speculation to face the reality. I often encounter my authentic self as a simple guy. Let's begin with early life, a teacher to pave the way for a rural boy to a euphoric future. The boy is the one who does not hesitate to carry bundles of grass on his head from one corner to the other of the village to his house. He has no hesitation in carrying a sack of wheat on his head or shoulder to the flour mill for grinding.

This 'He' wore whatever got to cover the body. It never prevented him from sweeping the street outside. This 'he' never stopped him from cleaning or digging with his students. He went to a relative's place in Parel (Bhoiwada), Mumbai with his family and stayed for a week. He also did not hesitate to live in the hut. He compromised comfortably without frowning when visiting the public toilet or behind the bushes with a bin for defecation and cleaning. He had no beard issue; It had the liberty to grow anyway with no care of trimming or shaving. Those days, he had no French beard, no matter if it was left uncared for a week or more. He had his life pattern as the proverb says: when in Rome, do as Romans do. Even today, He doesn't have any complaints about it.

This 'He' was an introvert and avoided expressing himself to others. He believes an individual's work should speak louder than the person himself. He is not the one who is averse to talking about himself. He also speaks about himself when needed. But his nature is like that of a turtle, which keeps his mouth, hands and feet lurking in its outer shell. He also takes them out when needed and uses them brilliantly. He believes the work must represent one's identity, not the tongue that slips frequently as it doesn't have bones.

On the contrary, tongue and hypocrisy dominate, and work stays isolated these days. Caste and surname have dominated for centuries. A man worth nothing but his hypocritical caste and superiority of surname ignores the brilliance of have-nots. They often attack and exploit the masses in the name of religion. They treat genuine men as their enemies and turn into devils against humanity and commit genocide. Sometimes, the post or position of an individual becomes everything to crush the work and hardships under its toes. It is the duplicity that enables dictators like Hitler to eliminate innocent masses. Such specimens are hampering the social harmony to impose social and mental slavery.

Let's leave the arena of nonsense to return to the point of focus. The person in the centre should now appear in human form as Ish Kumar Gangania. It will facilitate further understanding of the matter.

Firstly, I want to discuss 'Sorry, Please, and Thank you'. These words are essential to my colloquial language and play a tremendous role in my dealings. They help me to remain fair, clean and ethical. For instance, if I were a little late to take my students' class, I would first say sorry, followed by my explanation. Similarly, the word 'Please' in my dealings makes it soothing. My granddaughter Anaisha is just one and a half years old. She can't speak. I am still determining exactly how much she understands our words, but 'Sorry,' 'Please,' and 'Thank you' dominate our dealings.

I have no account of it with the grown-ups.

Similarly, 'Dear' is a vital part of my vocabulary. Whenever I post a comment on Facebook, I often use it as 'Dear' for younger people and 'Dear Sir' for elders. I find my reaction hollow, dry, and incomplete in its absence. In the case of women, I use their names alone. If she is much younger, I use 'daughter'.

I habitually restrict my language and carefully select words in my dealings. In the same way, I always stay conscious of the selection of words while writing. I want to credit it to Apeksha magazine and Dr Tej Singh. He was very strict about the choice of words. Had I not joined Apeksha as a sub-editor, I could not have attained such meticulousness. I constantly use the language most suited to the content's spirit and intensity of the thought. An individual's language plays a significant role in determining his personality. Still, I, too, have certain limitations and flaws regarding the genuineness of the language. At times, my wife also uses selective words that I use in my dealings with her. It is companionship and the environment that matters.

While scolding children, whether from family or school, I never cross the boundaries of words like unworthy, Badtameej, Jungli, or shameless when needed. Possibly, I had inherited the words from my father. None in my family abuses anybody's mother or sister. Even if I could never repeat the abuse that is common in several areas in our country, it worries me when I find kids abusing like older people, crossing the limits of ugliness. It annoys me, but I dare not check them.

I often encounter incidents with me in traffic, too, where a wild-type man or youth abuses freely. I never feel the need to answer them in their tone. It may help satisfy their egos and save me from further attacks on my mental peace. I know I can never go to the level of these strangers; it is in no way constructive. But it forces me to think about why the value system is deteriorating to leave the simple guys helpless.

I accept my mistakes without arguments or ifs and buts in situations where I am at fault. My family, including my wife and children, follows this to a significant extent. I never change my stand even though a family member insists not to say sorry. Words like sorry, please, and thank are spontaneous and a part of my personality, as if they were the natural demands of the situation. I love it as it consoles me a lot.

I often encounter inappropriate and baseless arguments from my own. In such a situation, I react keeping in view the person's state of mind, family background, and environment one belongs to. It is because they are the deciding factors of an individual's mindset. The upbringing of an individual, too, matters a lot.

When I am genuinely right, I need not compromise with any wrong. It keeps me confident and free from fear. Once, while I was working as a lecturer (Eng.) in Timarpur and sitting in the staff room having no class engagement, our Principal, Mr Bhatnagar, asked me, 'Ish Kumar ji, is this your vacant period?' My words were harsh when I responded: Please don't ask me such a question while sitting free like this.

A similar issue came up during one of our school inspections. The team came from the headquarters. There was some panic among the teachers. The inspection team passed twice from where I was sitting in my room. I didn't have any classes, so I relaxed. It was not usual for a DDE, the deputy director of education and his team; she asked me to go to the office with my teacher's diary. I followed her directions in a relaxed mood. She checked my diary and found nothing to show her attitude and authoritarian gesture. Our self-confidence stays soothing if we are conscious and sincerely committed to our work, no matter the odd situation.

On the contrary, many of our friends are victims of court matters for not following a reasonable thought pattern. When we analyse the situation, we find that the dispute could have been avoided, but the ego did not let the dispute settle. Litigation has been going on for years, a waste of money and time, engulfing my mental peace. The family is troubled in its way. The energy that could have been devoted to the betterment and upliftment of the individual and the family is unnecessarily wasted in unproductive work.

Such cases often come to the fore in mutual dealings with the in-laws of the daughter or son. There is a dispute among themselves over some small matter. The matter reaches the divorce. In such situations, the era of accusation and counter-accusation goes to the extent of enmity. The lives of both families are ruined. The daughter of a friend of mine is a professor in the college. The matter of her marriage went to the court for divorce. The issue is stuck on the return of the dowry amount. It has been five years since the daughter was at her parents' home, and she is over forty. As a result, the issue of the younger daughter's marriage is at stake. She has come of the age of over thirty.

My friend has a surplus of money and property. He has no son, and his age is beyond sixty-five. He has no chance of getting the son he desires. He is the only male in the family, and his health is declining considerably. Due to a lack of maturity in decision-making and false ego, the whole family is trapped in the court's controversy, and there is no chance of getting out soon. The purpose of my discussion is to tell that I calculate the pros and cons before making any decision. There is nothing wrong with taking a step back when needed. Otherwise, we have seen people bear the terrible loss and agony from one generation to the other, primarily due to ego. The way out of such a trauma is the middle path of Buddha, which is the right vision and decision. It can be termed 'Educated' in the eyes of Dr Ambedkar's philosophy. Despite this, such accidents can happen; we need not be victims of such ego-boosted actions.

Freedom of expression is the common feature we enjoy in the family as our inheritance. My father often made decisions based on consensus in the family. This opinion-seeking process is followed even in day-to-day common issues of food and drinks. At that time, when our financial condition was terrible, and we had to deal with odd situations at each step, even then, collective decision-making worked as our lifeline. Our family exited that wretched phase following solidarity and collective decisions.

My wife has been almost an equal earner; although our bank accounts were separate, nothing was there as hers or mine. Priority of the issues helps us decide how to manage the funds. Whether it was the construction or marriage of any of my brothers or sisters, all the expenses were met with no ifs and buts. We followed the same pattern when we purchased our independent flat and began to live as a nuclear family. Some social responsibilities that the previous norms of joint family demands are still fulfilled on mutual consent with the same zeal. There is nothing to avoid in the future.

The special care during the declining phase of my parents comforts me a lot. I would massage them on Sundays in winter, making them sit in the sun and helping them bathe. It was for my pleasure, and sometimes they needed it. I would spare time to refresh memories of the past. The present was not to let them even feel unworthy of any decision or discussion. When my father was paralysed and had a problem with defecation, I did not hesitate to stand by him, even to take the stool out of his rectum with my own hands. By the way, my father did not leave much scope for me to serve him more. Whatever we did was the source of a unique ease. The blessings of my parents always gave wings to take us to the world of ecstasy. It made me selfish to be worthy of more, never to end.

My mother was relatively healthy. But I got a chance to serve her a little more. Her hip bone had to be amputated, so the one leg had become a little short. One and a half bricks were hanging by, putting a nail in one of her knees. It was winter, and my mother was in Balram Nagar. She could not live with us in our fourth-floor flat. Hence, I would go to Balaram daily to bring her out in the sun for two hours. I massaged her there, gossiped, and picked her up in the house again around noon as it needed some muscle power to accomplish the job. It was my daily routine, and then I would attend school in the evening hours.

Ultimately, my mother recovered after a few months from the imbalance in her legs to live an everyday life. My mother was a pensioner, but I had told her to utilise that money as she liked. Hence, she used to give her pension to my elder sister to support her financial condition. I had taken responsibility for her expenses or treatment as needed. Serving my parents comforted and even energised me a lot. I can see the comfort visible in the attitude of our children for us. Here, the saying 'As you sow, so shall you reap' symbolises a precise meaning.

I wrote a poem, 'Motherhood Evolved In A Son,' on my mother's declining life. That is enough to learn the kinship between us. It is as follows:

Motherhood Evolved In A Son
A mother is a
Wonderful character
Who is blessed with
Is a genuine victor
She has lovely dreams
To nourish her child
Never bothers whether
Her journey is smooth or wild
*

I know a great mom
I greet her nobility
I love her dedication
And her nonstop mobility
She gave birth to
Several children
All were unique
With a diverse tantrum
*

Her passion for love
Began to rise
Her children's growth
Come up with a surprise
All survived
She faced no demise
She felt blessed
But always in disguise
*

Mother's dreams
Changed into
Pearls of beauty
The children's love
Come to a rare reality
They got married
And got
The family multiplied
*
The mother got
New names in the relationship
It was a change
In her, a broader kinship
Her age gave her
A new threat and irate
Support of a stick
Turned out to be a regular trait
*
She has a family of
Many a loving one
But their thought
Were utterly undone
They made
Their deity and God
The mother was left
Into a worthless mode
*
The affairs turned her.
Into a junk dealer's product
Uncared and as if
An outdated conduct
She began to lose
Of her worthy identity

None cared for
Her love and solemnity
*

One of her sons
Loved her as if a God
He made his house
Her permanent abode
Put her bed
Close to his own
Served her faithfully
Whether night or dawn
*

Mother's Day and Night
Became his own
Mother's happiness
Became his dream brown
He woke
To make the mother sleep
As in childhood
Mother used to keep
*

The son gave her mother.
A motherly wash to clean
His motherhood
Evolved into fair green
He did everything
What did the mother do for him
The son became a mother
When Mother had her eyes dim
*

The son was happy
To be her mother's son
He was worried for

The parents who had none
Shame on those who
Send parents to old homes
They are living dead
To breathe in stone tombs.
---000---

The legacy of individual freedom and family solidarity extends to my children's education and careers. The issues of their marriage illustrate it beautifully. Once a family decides, consensus or majority becomes the family's decision. The failure or success of the decision is welcomed collectively. There is no question of pointing fingers at anybody else.

Transparency and openness are regular features of my functioning to comfort. While teaching in school, if I had any doubts about the spelling of a word, I would tell my students to confirm it. Even at home, if I have made an expenditure and find it wrong, I do not conceal it. Even the love affairs of my youth are well known to my family.

It was common for my children to share their lives and their love affairs. We always knew who my children had boyfriends or girlfriends. Since my children have been in the science and bio-stream, there has been no hesitation in openly talking about sex within the family. We enjoyed a sense of mutual understanding and transparency within the family. It is essential to strengthen mutual trust and maintain the warmth of mutual relations. Transparency and trust are the foundation of human relationships. In its absence, the natural flow of the river of relations dries up. I endeavour to keep this river free from pollution and not let it dry up.

Everyone has his own beliefs about God. In the same way, people define their feelings and faith regarding worship. I do not believe in any form of God or any divinity. I believe in the philosophy that work is worship, and all actions of my life are destined with the utmost sincerity and dedication. I enjoy the pattern of life, which is a boon to lead my life smoothly. I primarily follow the laws of nature and its justice, as nature is the most prominent teacher in my life. There should be nothing to define, small or big, regarding a teacher, nor should there be any sense of comparison, but still, I am bound to do so here.

Significantly, a teacher is the one who can give a flavour to any belief. Teachers with traditional instead of fundamentalist approaches are often responsible for a more significant extent of anti-scientific temperament in society. I have been involved in teaching for forty years. But I never imposed my opinion and my faith on my students. Yes, I have openly discussed those points that do not meet the scientific criteria and beliefs. I put my point forward with the logic I believe in, but never betrayed the liberty of my students to reach their conclusions. I never derived my judgments about any right or wrong. This issue has not been limited to me and my students. I have always been in the habit of leaving everything open-ended for others to decide fair or foul of their own. It gives me a unique comfort and solace.

My family and my environment have been a workshop for experiments. I observe changes in their beliefs and thought patterns in my family. During my dialogue, I share what I believe and why? The thought that does not go with my criterion of scientism, I discuss that, too, liberally. But I insist no one follows my pattern or beliefs as I do. I never claim the house is mine and the product of my hard-earned money, and everything must be done accordingly. Doing so would violate the personal liberty of other family members and cause dissatisfaction and, ultimately, division in the family. I do not prefer such chaos, and I wholeheartedly welcome all the family members to live under the same roof and with their diverse beliefs.

The literary world is also an integral part of my broader world. I often feel that I don't fit in with my literary friends. They frequently disagree with my views. I differ from most of my literary friends. This fuss is about their style of working and thinking. This clash separates me from them, like two railroad tracks. I do not claim that they are wrong, and I am right. I favour emphasising my arguments in the lead than me. I have no right to decide who is right or wrong. However, I stand by my beliefs and opt for any change based on logical grounds.

I am not in a hurry to react to someone's point of view and say something right or wrong, as it is risky and, to some extent, immature. Sometimes, our eyes, ears and other senses fail to lay open the facts. Hence, it is worthless to react impulsively. I stay a constant observer to reach the facts. I wait for at least three or four points before pointing a finger at a person in question. The point is that I may be wrong in assessment at one place or the other, but not at all the places. That's why I often don't feel sorry for myself for pointing fingers at someone. Despite being proved wrong by others, I do not usually get aggressive but accept it humbly. The thought pattern often supports me as a true friend; it brings me relief.

There is another way of making others realise their mistakes. Whether it is my student, a family member, or someone in my friend circle, I put some of the plus points issues of their personality first, then let them know where they lagged or failed. In such a situation, no one moves on, justifying himself right and accepting to repair the wrongs.

It has a far-reaching advantage in avoiding such mistakes in the future. It, too, keeps the atmosphere cordial.

This strategy not only rectifies mistakes but also helps get some extra work done. When I was the head of the school, I had a staff of over a hundred and three thousand students. I knew my teachers were overburdened; I was no exception. I appreciated my teachers' hardships but politely asked them for their favour to get extra work done. I always had something positive about them; hence, feedback was soothing. Whatever additional work was done, they did it with great zeal. Had I shown my power or threatened them, the work could not have been done so smoothly and with devotion.

I have also encountered people who are in the habit of boasting without limits. Knowing the reality of their false paradise, I often do not counter them. But whenever the matter goes beyond the limit, my patience pays off. So, I patiently remove the curtain from their rhetoric and return to my silent mode. Consequently, the person in front faces little trouble. It saves me from listening to worthless gossip.

Many friends also believe in long, serious discussions but balance their talk. In such a situation, I endeavour not to interfere in anyone's comfort zone. But when the debate crosses the limits of seriousness and genuineness, I am forced to blacksmith's blow to subdue the hundreds of goldsmith's blows. It helps me put my point of view, and the person in front understands what I mean to convey. I also have my freedom and domain protected.

In some situations, listening and continuing to listen are necessary; in others, terming wrong as correct or fact becomes obligatory. I stand by it. Once, one of my friends fell into depression. I often talked to him for a long time. I talked about what he liked, and it comforted him. I would focus on his positive side instead of questioning his evil things. I would send him videos or messages to enhance enthusiasm in his life and let him come out of his state of depression. I am of the firm belief that we should take even mental illness like that of cough, fever, cold, etc. It is a different matter that the mental ailment takes longer to heal. But our little patience can work as an effective medicine.

Nowadays, there is a strange trend of identifying a person by our casteist glasses. It has become common to blame or exonerate someone based on caste. The identity of man became caste, not the qualities and wisdom of the person. Religion has also become a means of identifying a person as a friend or foe. It has never been the nature of my life that I should locate a person by keeping his religion or caste as a middleman. I do not see any end to this war. The day we get used to seeing a man through the eyes of a human being, more than half of the problems of society and the country will automatically end.

Allah and God have become a product of propaganda for the opportunists today. They are almighty, omnipresent, omniscient, and nothing is hidden from their eyes. There is no break in this propaganda machinery as it is serving the regime and the religion as a faithful servant. Presently, wealth is the most prominent God in practice. By the grace of the Lord of wealth, the power of God and Allah is maintained. If the role of the God of wealth is removed, the whole business of God and religion will collapse like a pack of cards. In this regard, wealth has become the most incredible God. It has swallowed morality and wisdom, and the man left no better than a beast.

It is a matter of my comfort that I am not in the race for wealth. The role of wealth in my life is to meet my basic survival needs and nothing else. It is not merely to preach but is the reality of my life. Sometimes, the wife inspires me, saying that Mr X has bought a plot there and Mr Y has bought a flat. One has earned that profit, and the other has benefited the other way. But my singular reply does not change: I do not want to disturb my peace of mind. Whatever I have and will have after retirement would be more than enough. Please let me live in my comfort zone.

It does not mean that I do not race for my life; of course, it is. It's just a race to study and write whatever satisfies me. It is the race to discuss whatever a global citizen is expected to do. It is an addiction to life rather than a race to win where nothing is certain. This addiction is causing some adverse effects on my health. I often have sleepless nights and a terrible loss of memory. My doctor has allowed me not to stay engaged for more than four hours in mental activities daily. Sitting is allowed, but not for long in a single stretch.

A few days back, there was a regular seating of ten to twelve hours. One day, the blood pressure shot up at three o'clock in the morning. I was scared, and the doctor advised me to get an ECG and an echo done the next day. Thankfully, it turned out to be expected. The children often ask questions, saying: Papa, you are not following the doctor's instructions; keep sitting for long regularly. I listen to them and try to be careful when taking remedial measures. Even if I try to maintain distance from reading and writing, it causes mental restlessness. I have nothing more to say but wait for the affairs destined.

I don't even race for fame. There is no such temptation that people recognise me and praise me. It does not lure me into asking someone to write about my books. I would appreciate it if someone wrote something about my work.

It does not mean I get upset if people do not write and talk about me praiseworthy. There is no thought of any gimmick or running for any award. I believe in working nonstop without much expectation. It may sound unrealistic, but the fact is, I have never had any illusion of getting recognition or popularity. My job is to work without bothering for any appropriate result or success. It keeps me calm and relaxed.

I have 'today' to live in and work with all my might as if there is no tomorrow. That is why I don't want to sacrifice my today for tomorrow, as today is the foundation of all tomorrows. I know the past is to analyse and learn lessons to live in the present in a whole spirit. If today's ground is tilled appropriately, the best seeds are sown, and the rest of the things are taken care of zealously, no matter how the crop would enrich the future. There is no need to go to any astrologer as I am the best astrologer. Hence, I am farming on today's soil by thoroughly analysing the climatic conditions. I am satisfied with the job I am engaged in.

It may seem impractical, but I still abstain from lying. Contemporary circumstances that are full of falsehood do not witness such a claim. Still, I don't need any certification, as it is my commitment. I don't care how other people take it. No one else needs to believe it.

Indeed, my truth is my most significant source of comfort. It saves me from being dishonest, deceitful, or a traitor. As a shield, it protects me from the blows of shallow people. My honesty and commitment encouraged me to share my drawbacks in the previous chapters without fear or pressure. It is worth soothing to share my evils. Revealing the dark side of my life makes me internally bold not to be a victim of those evils again. As a human being, I still have specific weaknesses to overcome. Looking back at this age, I find myself full of flaws as a trait of youth and immaturity, but filtering flaws will end with the last breath.

It would be far from the truth if a great man or a saint claimed to be free from faults. These flaws can take various forms, but none is free. The person himself is the best witness. It is a distinct issue whether someone dares to reveal or not. To what extent he allows others to look into his personal life is an individual's prerogative. About five per cent of my life is optional to share. I am not even doing it; it is my prerogative.

Another point of my comfort is the person I once called good; I do not call him evil. If I find someone going against the image of goodness, I will stop calling him good or talking about him, but there is no way to call him evil. I have many people who helped me. I called them genuinely good but did not make them beyond doubt. When I found something suspicious, I needed to correct a mistake when evaluating it. If I saw my doubts of no essence, I withdrew and apologised. Such acts relieve me without pain and embarrassment.

These traits determine my personality and confirm my comfort and calm. Following the beaten track does not necessarily ensure one's comfort zone and solace. It suggests ways to introspect, experiment, and draw conclusions. Hence, every individual must have their trail to uninterrupted peace and pleasure.

---oOo---